the

Spirited Kitchen

the

Spirited Kitchen

Recipes and Rituals
for the Wheel of the Year

EVERYDAY ANIMISM
FOLK MAGIC ✦ WITCHCRAFT

Carmen Spagnola

Countryman Press

An Imprint of W. W. Norton & Company
Independent Publishers Since 1923

For information about permission to reproduce selections from this book, write to
Permissions, Countryman Press, 500 Fifth Avenue, New York, NY 10110

For information about special discounts for bulk purchases, please contact
W. W. Norton Special Sales at specialsales@wwnorton.com or 800-233-4830

Manufacturing by Toppan Leefung Pte. Ltd.
Book design by Allison Chi
Production manager: Devon Zahn

Countryman Press
www.countrymanpress.com

An imprint of W. W. Norton & Company, Inc.
500 Fifth Avenue, New York, NY 10110
www.wwnorton.com

978-1-68268-667-6

10 9 8 7 6 5 4 3 2 1

To all the
brave initiates.

Bless, O Chief of generous chiefs,
Myself and everything anear me,
Bless me in all my actions,
Make Thou me safe forever,
Make Thou me safe forever.

From every brownie and banshee,
From every evil wish and sorrow,
From every nymph and water-wraith,
From every fairy-mouse and grass-mouse,
From every fairy-mouse and grass-mouse.

From every troll among the hills,
From every siren hard pressing me,
From every ghoul within the glens,
Oh! Save me till the end of my day.
Oh! Save me till the end of my day.
—Carmina Gadelica

Contents

Introduction

I didn't grow up in a spiritual household. Nobody in my family ever uttered the word "spirit."

In my early childhood I lived with my great-grandmother, Granny, and my grandmother, Isobell, my mother, and her three younger sisters. We lived in a 3-bedroom, 1-bathroom house, with a scary, dusty food cellar, and Isobell's Beauty Salon in the converted garage. When I was about 8 years old, Granny helped me draw our family tree. She told me about my Scottish great-great-grandmother, Bella Mackenzie Graham, who had the "second sight" and saw ghosts walk the stony halls of the old estate she'd worked in as a young seamstress near her village of Delny. She told me about my great-great-grandfather, John Graham, and his uncanny way with his Highland ponies—that he was what we'd now describe as a horse whisperer. She said he knew what they were thinking and that he could speak with them like friends.

And that's it. That's all I've got for passed-down family lore and traditions. Sure, there are other stories, but they're the not-fully-articulated ones. The deep sighs and slow headshakes, eyes quickly wiped, bodies turning to tasking after a few low words about the drought times, the young ones who died early, the death of beloved horses. Almost everything about my ancestral inheritance I've had to intuit, patch together with research, and genetically decode. Nonetheless, my ability to track down clues about my heritage is a privilege and one I feel a responsibility to explore.

Even if you haven't heard family lore of the supernatural, many of us have heard stories about relatives who had a certain kind of inexplicable luck. There might be a story about this auntie who grew giant vegetables, or that grandfather who was an unlikely survivor in wartime. Perhaps they had a healing way with touch. Very often, these people also have a large inner world, though they may keep it mostly to themselves.

As someone who was always described as an "imaginative" child, I know this feeling. From a young age, I had a sense of the holographic nature of the universe—that there was another world that paralleled and often supported ours. I masked this sense pretty well in my teen years. I knew that talking to animals, listening to trees, and petitioning stars for help was not what the cool kids did. My ability to attune to the messages and magic of life became more subterranean and covert as I grew up.

As soon as I stepped out on my own, I did what many people who don't know they're witches do: I visited my local bookstore and bought all the books on tarot, crystals, and shamanism. I took loads of courses and workshops. But something always seemed a bit graspy, a bit shallow. I was constantly seeking, never feeling settled. And then, as is foretold by pretty much every mythic journey tale there is, I had my Long Dark Night of the Soul. It led me to the lifeline that would guide me out of the existential dark: a scrawny roadside vegetable garden.

During the Great Recession of 2008, I was a small business owner with a retail shop. As the economy gasped for air, so did I. I went through bankruptcy, and I woke up one morning a newly incomeless single mother of a toddler, with no savings or food in my fridge. I kept my shame hidden from friends and family. Each day, it was all I could do to get my child to and from prekindergarten. From 9 AM to 3 PM, I lay in bed crying, enveloped in a dark fog of fear and worry. I had no money. I couldn't find a job. If it hadn't been for my 5-year-old, I probably would have let myself disappear into the void, but I had enough wherewithal to realize I needed to do whatever was needed to feed my little family.

There was a strip of vegetable patch on the side of the road not far from my house. It was a "guerrilla gardening" effort that now languished, overgrown and unwatered. A chef by training, I recognized some spindly kale, a few herbs. I could see the shoulders of some yellow potatoes pushing through the surface of the soil. Some other frondy things I didn't recognize were also there. The house across the street let me use their hose once a week. I placed a want ad seeking free gardening tools. I posted pictures on Facebook asking for help identifying the frondy things (parsnips!). After some study, I learned that the kale and parsnips could self-seed, and the potatoes, if some were left in the ground, could perpetuate themselves for who knew how long. In other words, an ongoing supply of free food.

As recently as the early 20th century, kale was so singularly prolific in the rough, unyielding land of my ancestors, the Scottish Highlands, that one referred to the vegetable garden as the kale yard. The common term for a savory water-based meal was not "soup" but rather "kale broth." Coming in for lunch was called "taking your kale." Brassicas being one of the few vegetables hardy enough to grow in the punishing landscape of the Gaels, it would surely surprise and amuse my Granny Graham to know that by 2008, kale had become an iconic vegetable of the wealthy modern world.

Kale with potatoes and parsnips became as crucially life sustaining for me and my kiddo as it had for Granny Graham and her Highlander people. In my lowest time of destitution, it was almost like I had some kind of deep cellular remembrance. I came into a timely inheritance, not of money, but an ancestral memory of much-needed endurance, will, and work ethic. I got my hands dirty with earth and remembered how to survive.

There's a concept in psychology called post-traumatic growth. It means exactly what it sounds like: Coming through a traumatic period develops within us a whole slew of new skills not possessed before the trauma occurred. The post-traumatic growth I experienced was a heightened awareness of the precarity of the world—the Western world, in particular. It's like I developed X-ray vision and overnight could see past the shiny veneer of our sleek society and instead perceive the shadows, gaps, cracks, holes, and fault lines.

As I became more attuned to individual and collective patterns of collapse, I also noticed patterns of growth, regeneration, and resilience. I recognized resourcefulness in the plants I tended and the (actually quite delicious) meals I was able to make from them. I grew to love the plants and the soil like friends—friends I genuinely relied on. As I tended that tenacious kale yard, I recognized resilience in myself, too. I came to understand that this was my spiritual practice, this kinship with the natural world, and that this animistic way of perceiving the world was my form of witchcraft.

Put simply, all witches are animists, but not every animist is a witch. The essence of animism, for me, comes down to two things: the ensoulment of the world and nature as our family of origin. Ensoulment means that everything has a soul and awareness, though it may be very different from human consciousness. This implies that as

much as I am aware of the soil, or my dog, or my child, so are they aware of me. If we regard nature as our family of origin, then this tree, the watershed, the mice, and the wind, these are all our ancestors. We share an ancient organic lineage.

To practice witchcraft is to court alliance, nurture friendship, and engage in mutual aid with these ancestors. Many animists do not call themselves witches. But if you call yourself a witch—whether hedgewitch, green witch, kitchen witch, word witch, faerie, Gardnerian, Norse, Thelemic, Wiccan, or folk like me—there is at least a through line of animism in your craft.

In that hard year of recovery, I recalled how, as a child, I would disappear into the forest beside our house and pretend to make pies out of mud decorated with little rock berries. I remembered how to let myself be soothed by a tree and companioned by the clouds. As I turned these basic ingredients into soul-nourishing

meals, wonder and magic began to coexist with despair and overwhelm. As I allowed myself to be enfolded into the awe of the ordinary, I was renewed and refilled with love. As my mentor, Desiree Adaway, says, this is the kind of soul care required for ourselves in order to stay in deeper community, to be in right relationship with each other and with the world.

Here's another through line that I've found offers possibility and relief: People dealing with traumatic experiences (like, let's say, surviving a pandemic during late-stage racialized capitalism) tend to have very sensitive nervous systems. People with sensitive nervous systems are often highly intuitive. People who are highly intuitive are *immeasurably* renewed and strengthened through attunement—careful noticing and coming into resonance—to the hopefulness inherent in seasonal cycles. They provide a container in which to manage the chaos. The seasons show us again and again that re-emergence and growth never stop. You don't need to have a garden to remember this. The same liberatory Love of Life that we see in caterpillars becoming butterflies is in our hands every time we bring reverence to our meals and ritual to our partaking.

Now, I'm not saying that starting a victory garden or learning to forage will cure your depression or help you triumph in the apocalypse (though I'm also not *not* saying that). What I *am* saying is that honing your intuition as you work with seasons in a deeply connected and animistic way makes life magical, meaningful, and more grounded. It's a pathway to personal healing and revolutionary communal care. I'm also saying that the capacity for attunement that comes from devotion to seasonal cycles is the very essence of witchcraft and animism. Whether you're a witch ready to play with your powers in the kitchen, or an adventurous home cook wanting to infuse more spiritual sustenance into mealtimes, this book is a calendar of connections, taking you step by step through a year of eating magically.

Blending Traditions through the Wheel of the Year

As my folklore friend, Sophie Macklin, says, "There is no pristine prior tradition." With this book, we're not reconstructing a tradition, nor can anyone after several centuries of Western cultural imperialism claim to have intact traditions. I know many folk who feel that despite the miracle of internet connectivity, we are living in an age of cultural loss, disconnection, and spiritual bereftness, piecing together new traditions mostly through research rather than lived experience. Even Indigenous nations who experienced later colonial contact, today must fill in gaps of lost language and customs destroyed by oppression,

and create new links to the old ways. One such nation is the people of Kwakwaka'wakw territory, just a few hours north of where I live, who have maintained a robust cultural lineage and potlatch tradition.

It raises the question: What do we even mean by "intact" in a time when all of us are the result of multiple generations of cultural exchange woven together like an elaborate braid through time? Even if humans hadn't been displaced from belonging, land, and lifeways, traditions today would still be different because they'd have evolved to suit the needs of the moment. What can guide us today in our patchwork effort is the human impulse to mark the passage of time and stages of growth, change, decline, and rebirth, together in community. This is where attunement, observation, feasting, and cultivating new seasonal traditions come in. Establishing a seasonal calendar of observances reflecting inner and outer evolution helps us maintain connection with time, place, ourself, and each other.

This book is based on a syncretic approach—a blend of animism, Gaelic polytheism, neo-Druidism, ancestral veneration, Wicca, and even some vaguely Christian mysticism. But mainly these are Western European folk customs since that is my heritage, and they come largely from the 18th through 20th centuries. Though scholars of Indo-European culture have tried to locate a common cradle of "European" tradition, there is nothing conclusive pointing to any "original European" people. What seems most plausible is that repeated generations of wider and wider diffusion carried snippets of tradition from region to region by wandering craftspeople, magicians, and bards, traveling in search of a patron. The result is multitudes of localized "origin" stories with individual histories, characters, and deities that often sound similar.

Alexander Carmichael was a 19th-century collector of folklore (not without controversy) from the Scottish Highlands who wrote, "Customs assume the complexion of their surroundings, as fishes, birds, and beasts assume the colours of their habitats." To some extent, the custom of collectors of folklore is to adapt it somewhat to their own perspective. I don't mind standing with Carmichael and other unfashionable, "inaccurate" storytellers in this lineage, as I aim to inspire the creation of new rites based on relationship to the land you currently live on rather than make faithful reproductions of old traditions. I personally believe that if you picked up this book, your ancestors are trying to get your attention. The traditions of your own lineages, whether intact or lost, are wanting to come alive and be blended together through you now, adapted to the needs and capacities of this moment.

To be clear, that's not to say that we can therefore cherry-pick attractive traditions from *any* culture, nor that we shouldn't fight to protect vulnerable living traditions. But it is to say that there's no place for purist supremacy in our practice. If you're wondering whether you should undertake a spiritual practice from a living culture, a good starting place is to ask yourself, *Would I know about this practice if Wikipedia hadn't told me?* In other words, do you have a genuine relationship with a person or teacher of that culture who has taught you this way? If not, it is probably best for you to appreciate from afar, or at the very least undertake your study humbly, privately, and with genuine effort to cultivate authentic relationships with wisdom-keepers so you are not being extractive or appropriative.

In every aspect of life, spiritual or otherwise, it's wise to be aware of our power and how it impacts the world. The more we study and track the power lines through our lives, the more apparent our privilege becomes to us. Recognize that we all make mistakes along the way. Aim to become more at ease with repair without shame. In the past, I've used plants in my spiritual practice that are sacred specifically to Indigenous people in what's known as North America. These plants are currently exploited to near extinction to cater to the growing numbers of people, mostly white women, inspired by witchcraft. Because I was insulated from the voices of Indigenous peoples talking about how painful it is to see white people appropriating their spiritual practices, I unknowingly contributed to that pain. But in the words of Maya Angelou, "When you know better, you do better."

With that said, it still feels important to me to situate myself as the voice speaking to you. As a white settler recently ascended from lower working class to middle class, I can't talk about food without talking about systemic oppression, and I can't talk about spirituality without naming collective ancestral grief and trauma. These things are nuanced and complex, and often beyond the scope of this book, but these are the times we live in, and this is the context our rituals must account for. My magic and my cooking serve an underlying commitment to truth, justice, spirit, and healing. If you're up for that, this book is a talisman that will empower those same forces through you.

This book is one of ideas and prompts; every recipe, ritual, and craft can be modified for use at *any* time of the year. It all depends on what makes meaningful sense to you given where you are and what's happening outside. Because the climate where I live is so similar to that of my Highland ancestors, I share what intuitively feels right for me, which happens to map pretty closely onto Gaelic lifeways. You should feel free—empowered, even—to adapt the concepts and ingredients to your own bioregion, ancestry, local influences, and intuitive impulse. That means you might cook recipes from the "Harvest Home" chapter during your Beltane season, or perform a ritual from Yuletide at Midsummer. This is not only perfectly acceptable, it's wonderful—ritual born of need and creative instinct is the best kind.

Not only do I encourage you to play with timing and ingredients as you ritually cook your way through the seasons, I encourage you to come up with new rituals. Yet this is where I also wish to introduce another layer of care and thoughtfulness when it comes to invoking deities and supernatural allies. From an animistic perspective, every ritual you do is in some way a form of ancestral veneration, whether you're calling on a god, a plant, an animal, or a deceased relative. When performing your magic, consider a framework I once heard in a workshop, namely that we can think about being in relationship to allies as three currents: Blood Lines, Milk Lines, and Story Lines.

There are ancestors by blood: you share their DNA, though most of their names and even knowledge of their lifeways are lost to time. This lineage extends to your way-, way-, wayback people—even your microbe people such as fungi, protozoa, and bacteria. Your Milk Lines include all the human and nonhuman beings who actively support you, with whom you share some special affinity. These lineages of nurturance can include not only beloved teachers and coaches but also the family dog, the Douglas fir in the forest, the foxgloves on the side of the road, the library, or the lake. Finally, Story Lines are the ancestors who come to us through books, movies, music, oral tradition, art, and myth. For some people that includes Jesus; for others, it's Hekate; and for some people it's both of them. For me, it includes Bruce Springsteen. I know folks with strong spiritual connections to Freddie Mercury, Octavia Butler, Sophie Scholl, Boudica, Mary Magdalene, and Lilith. You, too, probably have been claimed by a kind of chosen family whose life or work has shaped your character. They've gotten you through tough times. You feel like if they knew you in real life, you'd be friends. They're the ones who led you to this book, and the ones who will cheerlead you along this path of rediscovery of your own seasonal rhythm.

When planning your seasonal rituals, your ancestors from your Blood, Milk, and Story Lines can, and should, be invoked in your observances. They are not just metaphors; they are the true power behind all of your ritual craft.

The four Gaelic festivals featured in this book are Samhain (November), Imbolc (February), Beltane (May), and Lughnasadh (August). My personal observance of these festivals is inspired by the incomparable work of Scottish folk historian F. Marian McNeill. The first three festivals are concerned with the breeding and husbandry of animals, and the last one is concerned with agricultural harvest. These are known as the quarter days. There are also four other festivals, which occur in the halfway points between the quarter days and line up with the solstices and equinoxes.

The Wheel of the Year in this book is not a Wiccan calendar of sabbats. In these pages, you'll see some overlap with that tradition and also divergence. I titled the chapters by the terms that I personally use as someone with mixed European ancestry, and also as someone with a lifelong fascination with folklore and fables, and Greek and Roman mythology. For instance, I use the term *Harvest Home,* as shared by McNeill, to capture the essence of the myriad fall season festivals that occurred throughout the Old World in late September near the autumnal equinox. I also use the term *Vestalia,* which refers to a summer solstice festival that reaches back to Roman times. I must rely on you to do your research when it comes to your own lineages and interests in order to adapt this book appropriately. My aim is to provide enough instruction on the principles and intention of the rituals that you can use them as a jumping-off point.

The recipes I include are mostly neither traditional nor customary to the festivals. This is a prime example of turning what you already know, love, and do *into* a ritual. Some of the recipes I

Wheel of the Year

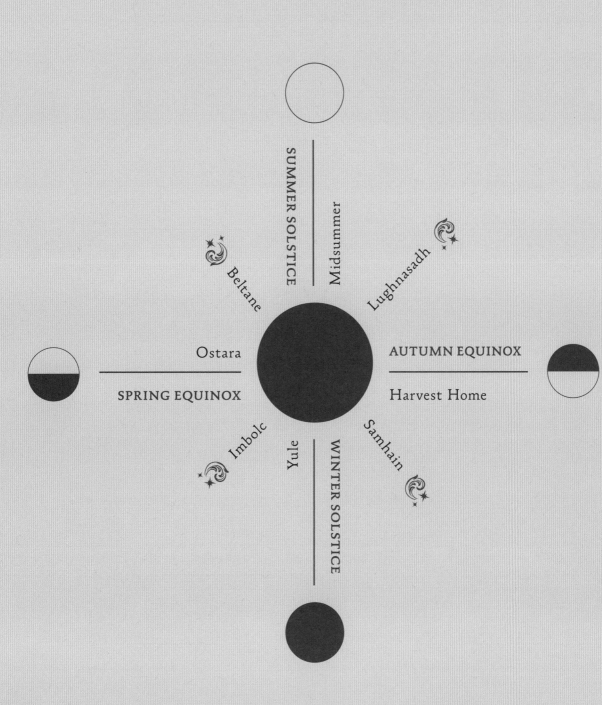

SUMMER SOLSTICE

Midsummer

Beltane

Lughnasadh

Ostara

AUTUMN EQUINOX

SPRING EQUINOX

Harvest Home

Imbolc

Yule

Samhain

WINTER SOLSTICE

A WORD ON
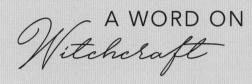

Although I'd been privately practicing witchcraft for a number of years, it wasn't until 2014 when I read Silvia Federici's indomitable book, *Caliban and the Witch: Women, the Body and Primitive Accumulation*, that I finally admitted publicly I'm a witch. I had studied the history of heresy and the Burning Times, and I read biographies of figures and cultures that were victims of the Holy Inquisition such as Joan of Arc and the Cathars. But it was Federici's work that transformed my life and my worldview as it pertains to witchcraft. Federici details how women's history has not been a linear progression from having fewer to more rights, as we've been taught. Rather, we've experienced a fairly recent and rapid *loss* of rights and station along with the naturalization of oppressive gender and class hierarchies that did not always exist.

Through the privatization of the commons; the enslavement and genocide of Black and Indigenous peoples; the vilification of queer folk, Jews, Romani, and other resisters; and the subjugation of women and their bodies, society was transitioned from collectivism to feudalism to capitalism, in just a few hundred years. One method of control over the masses was the terror campaign of the Holy Inquisition, the witch hunt that killed an estimated 50 million people, mostly women, in Europe. The subjugation of women was key to this economic transition because the means of subsistence, production of food, and transmission of intergenerational knowledge and cooperation—in other words, most forms of social power—were fundamentally in their hands.

As the noted bore and patriarchy hype-man, Francis Bacon, once said, "Magic kills industry." The notion of "witchcraft" was an invention of the 15th century as a negative rebrand of millennia-old folk practice, which served to protect powerful rich white people, mostly men, from the outrage of the people they enslaved and stole from. Eventually in the 19th century, to create a more disciplined workforce and diffuse social protest, Federici writes, "All forms of collective sociality and sexuality including sports, games, dances, ale-wakes, festivals and other group-rituals that had been a source of bonding and solidarity among workers" were banned. All that to say: If resisting oppression, reclaiming my body as my own, praying to my ancestor tree, fighting for collective liberation, and organizing around a culture of care and dignity for all makes me a witch . . . my friend, I am *that*. Whether you identify that way or not, publicly or not, is your own business. I say, let's just be in practice together. Let us create sanctuary together. And let's not allow anyone to shame us, our identities, our bodies, or our cultures, ever again.

selected are based on what's happening in my garden at that time of year. My tomato harvest is prolific at Lughnasadh (which my Highlander ancestors definitely didn't experience), hence the two tomato-heavy salads. Others are perennial favorites from my time at cooking school in Paris in the 1990s. Still others I've chosen because they conjure a particular magic with their ingredients that is appropriate to the themes of the specific festival.

In the recipe notes, I highlight the magical essences carried by the ingredients so that you can develop a sense of what to aim for when making substitutions. My main goal when teaching magic is to demystify the process. I hope to do the same for cooking, especially with recipes that are notoriously difficult or look intimidating. I'm one thousand percent confident that you can make a wonderful macaron, and I *know* you can pull off a Paris-Brest if you give yourself enough time. Making an offering to Hestia can't hurt your chances, either. In the same way that cakes with candles carry the magic of wishes better than cakes that don't, I'm sure you have beloved family recipes or even tried-and-true weekday meals that can be included in your seasonal observances in a fashion that delivers more blessing. Consult the "Magical Correspondences" section on page 235 for ways you can sprinkle more magic on your meals.

The "Magical Correspondences" section is there to help you create your own rituals and use your ingredients with deeper intention. In a way, this cookbook is a bit like a grimoire—a book of spells. The qualities noted for each "ingredient" in the "Magical Correspondences" section have come to me by way of decades of study and experimentation, and are quite personal. You may have very different, sometimes even opposite, correspondences. I believe them both to be true. My aim is to ensure this book is practical and handy, not comprehensive or definitive. The interaction of

your physical-spiritual makeup with the physical-spiritual essence of yarrow or chicken or salt is going to be highly unique to you. In other words, your mileage will vary. Once again, attunement—careful noticing and coming into resonance—will guide you to the ingredients that are best suited for you and your intentions.

Kitchen Magic as Spiritual Practice

To understand the multidimensional nature of our kitchen magic, it can be useful to think of life as occurring on four levels, from material to pure potential. For this, I'll paraphrase John Michael Greer, former Archdruid of the Ancient Order of Druids in America, expert on ceremonial magic, and someone from whom I've learned a tremendous amount. Consider a simple ingredient like a hazelnut. On the physical level, the hazelnut is small and firm in your fingers. Toasted, it has a mellow, almost sweet nutty flavor and leaves a mildly oily residue that pleasantly lingers in your mouth. But the hazelnut also exists on an etheric level—a complex of forces that hold the hazelnut together and even emanate from it. I'm not talking about fats and proteins here; I'm talking about life force energies.

Western cultures don't speak much of etheric energies. The sad irony is that our best understanding of etheric energies comes to us through a blockbuster movie slash mega merch franchise. "May the Force be with you" is a bit like a culturally appropriated counterpart to the Chinese concept of chi and the Indian concept of prana. Each of these concepts are pointing at a similar thing: the idea that everything is permeated with a vital principle, a life force, an etheric energy.

In magic, the hazelnut also exists on the astral level. The astral level is related to resonances set in motion by the sun, moon, and planets of our solar system. In natural magic, hazelnuts flow on a metaphorical energy current with Mercury, specifically in Virgo, which is a particularly exalted combination. This astrological "recipe" means that hazelnuts are resonant with super effective communication. And then there is the mental level of hazelnuts, which is more about the abstract concept of them—this would include all the myth and lore about hazelnuts as food from a tree of wisdom, all the divination done with hazelnuts over the centuries, and everything you know about them and associate with them. So when we speak about the "spirit" of hazelnut, we're grasping all of these levels at once. Spirit is the maximum potential, encompassing all of these dimensions simultaneously.

Long after the physical dimension of the hazelnut is no longer perceptible, after it has moved through and out of your body, the nutrients it has provided you remain in the glow of your skin, the strength of your nails, and the luster of your hair. The memories of it are carried forward and added to hazelnut lore. The resonances still exist and can be revived as soon as you catch the scent of hazelnut syrup in a coffee shop. The aroma ignites a cellular memory that inspires mindfulness and a moment of spiritual resonance.

This modern druidic explanation of the resonances between all things is helpful to keep in mind as you use this book. Though sometimes I use the word *symbol* as a convenient term, what I actually believe is that everything carries a multidimensional resonance through which the magic flows. When we maintain awareness of the multidimensional nature of our ingredients, and the significance of how and when we employ them, then each recipe we make is actually a ritual in itself. We are blending energies, conjuring something new and specific, taking that into our body and integrating it into our being. We become the talisman. We are the magic.

The Kitchen Witch Pantry

I actually don't usually cook from recipes. When I attended Le Cordon Bleu in Paris, they didn't provide recipes, either. Instead, they taught us principles and techniques. They described a technique in detail then we practiced it at length until we could see, hear, smell, feel, and taste what was and wasn't working with our creation. That's why I love antique cookbooks. Often there are no measurements, just a paragraph describing ingredients and how to handle them, and what to look for to determine doneness. Once you understand the principles and techniques of cooking, you can create any recipe you wish. So it is with magic and witchcraft, too. Once you understand the inherent properties of ingredients, there is no difference between crafting a recipe and crafting a ritual. You're just mixing components together in a particular way to achieve a desired result, and paying close attention to outcomes.

Pantry Staples

BUTTER: All of my recipes call for salted butter. I don't understand unsalted butter. I mean, technically I do, but philosophically, that's a full body No for me.

SALT AND PEPPER: Salt is always kosher in my recipes unless otherwise indicated. If substituting table salt, use half the amount. (See Salt Spells on page 31 for details on the magical properties of different types of salt.) I recommend freshly ground Tellicherry pepper.

STOCK: I always use bouillon paste reconstituted with boiling water for stock. Chicken, beef, and vegetable bouillon are in my fridge door at all times.

HERBS: If you're able to grow herbs in a garden or windowsill, fresh herbs are the best—except in the very special cases of oregano and dill where a high-quality dried product is actually much richer and more complex than fresh. Must-have herbs for cooking are thyme, rosemary, flat-leaf parsley, chives, basil, dill, oregano, fennel, cilantro, and sage. For teas, I grow nettle, orange mint (which smells like Earl Grey tea), spearmint, peppermint, lemon balm, tulsi (also called holy basil), stevia, violet leaf, chamomile, rose, lavender, calendula, and bachelor's button. I forage pineapple weed and fireweed.

EDIBLE FLOWERS: For salads, syrups, and garnish these must be pesticide-free from the garden or bought at the farmers' market. These include roses, violas, calendula, marigolds, bergamot, borage, bachelor's button, hollyhock, lavender, nasturtium, runner bean blossoms, pea blossoms (the vegetable kind, not ornamental sweet peas), Japanese chrysanthemums, and all herb blossoms. Left to go to seed, the most prolific self-sowers will be borage, calendula, and violas.

NUTS AND SEEDS: If stored at room temperature, once opened, most nuts and seeds go rancid within a few months. Pistachios and pine nuts last only about 1 to 3 months beyond their printed date so buy them shortly before use. Buy high quality pine nuts and only ever eat them toasted. Why? Because "pine mouth" is a real thing, my friends! It's a condition that develops about 24 to 48 hours after eating poor-quality raw pine nuts that makes your mouth taste like you've been sucking on dirty pennies, a condition that can last for up to 2 weeks! It only happens to a small percentage of the population. Ask me how I know.

WHOLE SPICES: Using whole nutmeg and allspice grated with a microplane rasp, and cloves and cardamom crushed with a mortar and pestle, will majorly up-level your baking. Like, *majorly.*

OIL AND VINEGAR: I cook with extra virgin olive oil and keep a small bottle of grapeseed or

sunflower oil on hand for salad dressings and salve making. I always keep sherry, red wine, balsamic, and apple cider vinegar in stock and a gallon or more of plain white vinegar at the ready for cleaning and space clearing.

SUGAR AND FLOUR: I use raw cane sugar for baking, which is free-flowing and pale golden in color, unless otherwise noted. Substituting white sugar is fine. When demerara is called for, use a dark, moist brown sugar. For flour, I always use white organic all-purpose.

Ritual

"Ritual is poetry in the realm of acts."
—Ross Nichols

The seasonal rituals in this book add a layer of the sacred to everyday life. Ritual is a life-affirming and soothing act where we bring awareness and intention to what we treasure, offer our devotion, and tend to what we love. In this book, I deal mostly with folk magic, meaning magic that is woven into ordinary life by ordinary people, as opposed to high magic done by people initiated into a magical order. Folk magic is pagan practice: of the Earth, dreamed through us, and often flowing quite spontaneously as instinct.

A spell is a form of ritual that is usually less elaborate. You might call it a microritual, even, like an embellished prayer. Think of the difference between doing your dishes and a big spring clean. With ritual, there's some additional energy brought to bear.

If I were to simplify ritual to a basic structure, I'd say the most important parts are intention, invocation, and demonstration. For more involved rituals, you'd probably add steps to cleanse yourself, to open and close sacred space. You might add participatory parts for a community ritual.

Your intention is a very clear sense of purpose. Ask yourself, *What do I want to be different?* Try to distill your desire into one word, a verb. Your action word will determine the form of your ritual. It could be something like: to honor, appreciate, celebrate, cleanse, banish, transform, bring, bind, fix, help, lift, make, manifest, support, protect, shield, or attract. During Samhain, for instance, you might want to prepare a ritual if a seasonal depression often grips you during winter. So the action could be to *release* the urge to be productive, *receive* care more easily, or *balance* grief with gratitude and beauty.

Your invocation is a way to channel the most appropriate cosmic energies for your intention. It increases the resonance, power, and attractiveness of your ritual by inviting nonhuman forces to participate. This is where your Blood Lines, Milk Lines, and Story Lines come in. You might invite deities, icons, ancestors, plant and earth medicine, stone and crystal powers, mythological creatures and fictional characters—anyone or anything that resonates with your intention. Of course, calling on support from the other-than-human entities is just like connecting with human people. You wouldn't just tap a stranger on the shoulder and say, *Hey, can you support me to release the stress I'm experiencing as I transition between jobs?* You would ask someone you know and trust.

COURTING THE Divine

It's a good idea to dedicate some time getting to know a few allies that intrigue you *before* you're in crisis rather than wait till emergency strikes. You know, *make friends*. For instance, if you're trying to woo a deity to be your guardian—let's say you want to court Persephone, Goddess of the Underworld—you might start with having an altar to her. Bring her flowers once in a while. Leave food offerings during moon phases that are special to her, and so on. That way, if you become stuck in a vortex of grief, despair, or darkness, you've already got a solid relationship with the Goddess of the Underworld to comfort and maybe even rescue you.

Then do your demonstration. Act out what you'd like to have happen. This is what American comparative mythologist Joseph Campbell would call "keeping up our end of the conversation with spirit." Spirit speaks in metaphor, so when you use metaphor and symbol to speak your desire, it's like you're using Spirit's "love language." You're demonstrating to Spirit what you'd like to have happen as though it's connect-the-dots or paint-by-numbers. This is what's called sympathetic magic—you perform the act in micro that you'd like to see in macro.

Bearing your intention in mind, design your ritual with specific symbols that match the demonstration to the energy of your action word. Consider which elements, animals, plants, colors, or other items best symbolize your action word. I've provided a basic guide here. Consult the "Magical Correspondences" section on page 235 to go deeper into symbolism for your demonstration.

ELEMENTS: Each element carries energy in a very particular way. If you're trying to support, grow, heal, or compost into something new, work with the Earth element. To call in strength like a mountain, or the endurance of stone, use rocks or a picture of a landscape to invoke that energy. Air offers purification and clarity, can expel or usher in with the winds of change. Fire can help transmute, ignite, soothe, bring protection and safety; it can also banish and destroy. Water helps emotions flow more freely. It cleanses, harmonizes, and helps us find balance.

ANIMALS: It should be recognized that animals are their own people and their spiritual meaning is highly contextual and relational. As an animist, I'll warn against "animal spirit interpretation" guides, as these can be appropriated ideas about the animism of Indigenous peoples. Learn about the animals you're interested in and make your interpretation of them with their agency in mind, as well as your own experience. The best animal spirit interpretation guide is a naturalist handbook.

PLANTS: Work with what grows where you are. Consider that a dandelion pushing through the concrete outside your door has vastly more potent energy than a poor white sage bundle that has been trafficked thousands of miles from its homeland. Some of us, particularly white folk (myself included), have much work to do to divest from the desire to have, to own, to use, to consume. If you really feel a strong affinity for a plant that is uncommon in your area, buy seeds. Put a pot on your windowsill. Cultivate a relationship. See whether this attraction is mutual. Research the plants of your own ancestral lineages and the native plants of your own neighborhood—all of them are sacred in their own way.

FOOD AND DRINK: The culinary traditions of your heritage and life context can be powerful symbols. If you come from bread people, or live in a "bread basket" territory, you may find affinity with certain grains. The same goes if you come from rice people, potato people, camas people, moose people, salmon people, or any other ancestral foodway.

TOOLS: Tools are excellent to use in ritual because they symbolize action. Chalices, cauldrons, and bowls can contain, combine, and alchemize. Knives, swords, rasps, and blades release, reveal, and distribute. Wands, spoons, and ladles convey energy from one place to another. They combine. They focus attention. A standing mixer is a miracle of alchemy! Use brooms, besoms, and cleaning tools to banish, transport, cleanse, and reset. Knitting needles, looms, and distaffs have archetypical associations with enshrouding and carrying, particularly carrying stories, as well as manifesting. Baskets symbolize portals, offerings, nurturance, and sustenance. Plates and open vessels gather energies in a generous and nourishing way, whereas lidded vessels help us contain energy in a protective, sometimes even secretive way.

OTHER SYMBOLS: Tarot decks, oracle cards, candles, colors, sacred geometry, sigils, tinctures, balms, jewelry, tattoo, and adornment—the list of possible symbols is endless. You can also create your own ritual object, something we'll do a lot through the Wheel of the Year with our sun wheels, spells jars, corn dollies, and so on.

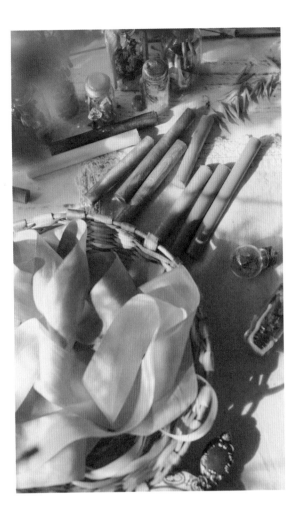

DELINEATING

Sacred Space

Once you've assembled your symbols, you might be wondering, *Now what?*

You may want to begin by delineating sacred space. Depending on your lineage and how elaborate your ritual is, you may have a familiar process, like calling the cardinal directions or casting a circle. In many Irish and Scottish traditions, there is acknowledgment of Land, Sea, and Sky. An Indigenous elder and friend of mine, Norman Retasket of the Secwepemc Nation, has a cloth he lays down on the ground and steps onto as he opens ceremony. He says it's not traditional among his people; he just likes it. I think that example is a really lovely and accessible way to think about sacred space. I highly recommend it as a way to begin if you don't know much about your own cultural heritage: delineate the space where you will do this ritual, focus your energies, then step into it.

American journalist Krista Tippett wrote, "Rituals are sophisticated ancient intelligence about the body." And within your body, in your heart, in your belly and bones, there are rituals already pressing on you. Take a year to experiment, play, practice, and observe. Trust yourself and trust the cycle; let yourself be enfolded into the mystery of this ancient intelligence.

Let's begin.

CHAPTER ONE

Samhain

"The universe is full of magical things patiently waiting for our wits to grow sharper."
—Eden Phillpotts

In old Scotland, nightfall was considered the beginning of a new day and the darkening time of the year was considered the beginning of a new annual cycle. So we begin our Wheel of the Year in the fall at Hallowe'en, the modern Witches' New Year. In the Scottish calendar it's known as Samhain (pronounced SOW-in), sometimes spelled Samhuinn.

Autumnal days are getting shorter and the earth is sapped of color. We need to look with softer eyes to appreciate the jewel-like tones of drunken blackberries still on the vine and pumpkins giving way to decay under giant silvering leaves. It's harvest season for apples, which feature prominently in divination practice at this time. When sliced in half, the apple reveals the five pointed star, the pentagram, symbolizing the five elements. Of the five elements that form the foundation of Western neo-pagan witchcraft—Fire, Air, Earth, Water, and Spirit—it is Spirit that is most ever-present in Samhain festivities. Samhain is a shrouded and misty time when the veil is thin between this world and the world of the Spirit. Looking ahead to a long dark winter can be a bit scary, but Spirit can be our womb of protection, keeping us centered and safe when all seems dark.

The word *spirit* speaks to the essence of a thing and means much more than simply "apparition." Over the centuries and across cultures, the word has been associated with notions of breath, soul, nature, character, ghost, and divine substance. At this time of year, the untended souls of the forgotten dead may appear as ghosts, whereas the well cared for ancestors can appear to us as guides and helpmates on our spiritual journey. In order to maintain the cosmic order, we honor the friendly spirits by making offerings and inviting them to join us in festivities.

We protect ourselves from the restless spirits through spells and ritual.

Our modern custom of dressing up for Hallowe'en is an example of an ancient protection ritual. Known as guising, dressing up is meant to trick demonic spirits into believing you're one of them so they pass you by, and so generally Hallowe'en costumes were much scarier in the past than they are today. Costumes are about transformation and liminality. This is why we see masks and costumes crop up at Samhain, winter solstice, Yuletide, and New Year's Eve, times of the year when the cosmic balance is tipped precariously in favor of darkness. Costumes enable shapeshifting, help us mirror the changing form of the season, and escape detection by malefic forces.

Yet we can do more than hide to protect ourselves from spiritual harm. Charms, runes, spells—these are all terms to describe prayerful utterances that invoke greater forces to bless or curse. Charms are one way we can secure our psychic sphere, and for that reason in this chapter you'll find Medea's Hymn to Hekate (page 28) to go along with Salt Spells (page 31) for protection. Beyond charms and spells, we can petition powerful deities to watch over us. A deity I work with a lot, especially near Samhain, is the Greek goddess Hekate. She is the Gatekeeper to the Underworld, the land of the dead. Hekate is the one who helps us see into our own personal shadow. She teaches us to see in the dark, uncover the truth, face our fears, and find our path to freedom and re-emergence. You'll find ritual crafts in this chapter dedicated to her, from altar suggestions (see The Altar on page 26) to Hekate's Torch (page 33). Known by hundreds of names, Hekate is now popularly referred to as the Queen of Witches so it's quite appropriate to begin the year acknowledging her first.

The Altar

A shrine is a devotional space dedicated to an ancestor or deity. If we work other magic there, then it's commonly called an altar. Leaving offerings at the altar ensures we're in a relationship of mutual exchange with the greater-than-human elements. Think of a friend who always calls for help but never checks on how you're doing. Eventually that relationship feels extractive and exhausting, right? The altar ritual is a way we can engage in reciprocity with The More Than, another term we can use to name the Greater Forces, the Other Than Human, the gods, or spirits.

For every Wheel of the Year event I host, I create an altar and invite guests to bring an item to add. This charges their item with the empowering energies of a community in celebration, not to mention the overlighting power of the deities invoked, in this case, Hekate. Guests might bring pictures of their Beloved Dead, or a piece of their jewelry or a special memento. Other altar items include power objects or talismans, which become infused with Hekatean energy when placed there.

I often tend several altars in and around my home at once—one in the bedroom for harmonious marriage, another near my desk for career fulfilment and success, a shrine to my ancestors, a devotional space dedicated to Spirits of Place at an ash tree in the yard, and a seasonal altar that is often a central feature in our living room. If I showed you every altar at every season, this would be an entire book of altars.

I usually delineate sacred space with fabric of a symbolic color, then anchor my altar with a focus object and items representing one or all of

MAKING

Offerings

What makes for a good offering? Let's say I want to acknowledge the full moon for providing upliftment during a hard time. I'll ask myself, "How could I *delight* the moon? How can I woo them to be my friend?" I might offer the most beautiful rose from my garden, or a sip of my best wine, or a piece of chocolate. Of course, the spirit realm doesn't place the same value on things as the capitalist human realm. A pretty rock, a found feather, or a strand of your hair are all worthy offerings. After some time, the inherent energy of your offering may fade. If it's something reusable, you can recharge it under the full moon or sun and save it for another use. If it's edible or compostable, it's perfectly appropriate to return it to the earth and the cycle of life.

the elements. Many lineages have more elemental categories than just four or five. They might include ether, metal, wood, time, soul, space, and beyond. You may want to add a central feature such as a statue, a picture of an ancestor, a symbolic ornament, or an offerings plate. The pentagram, a classic symbol of the witch, is a portal to the Otherworld through which Hekate or any other deity you invoke can find their

MEDEA'S HYMN TO

Hekate

Medea is a powerful sorceress of Greek mythology. From Ovid's *Metamorphoses,* here is her prayer to petition Hekate, which you could adopt or adapt for your own ritual.

"O night, faithful friend of mysteries; and you, golden stars and moon, who follow the fiery star of day; and you, Hekate, goddess with threefold head, you know my designs and come to strengthen my spells and magic arts; and you, Earth, who offer your potent herbs to magi; and airs, winds, mountains, streams, and lakes, and all you woodland gods, and all you gods of the night: Be present now."

three heads: human, dog, and horse. Sometimes she appears with (or as) her three-headed dog, Cerberus.

Hekate is known as The World Soul—the creative, dynamic life force energy from which the cosmos emerges and by which it is sustained. She mediates between the realms of gods and mortals. My mentor, renowned scholar of Hekatean witchcraft, Dr. Cyndi Brannen, distills three of Hekate's main aspects as Lightbearer, Guide, and Gatekeeper.

Hekate the Lightbearer is our Guardian in the Underworld, the one whose torches and moonlight protect us from night terrors. She helps us see and honor our shadows and find strength when hope seems lost. She protects our true self, deepest emotions, and keeps us on a path of integrity. In this aspect, she is associated with dogs and torches, and the colors white and gold.

Hekate of the Crossroads is our Guide in the Middle World, helping us find our way when we feel lost or confused in a world of chaos and uncertainty. She helps us locate ourselves, remember our center, and find courage to take the next step. This is her compassionate, maternal aspect that connects us with the land, our ancestors and groundedness. Her Guide aspect is especially associated with horses and her special sigil, the Strophalos, as well as the colors green and brown.

As Keeper of the Keys, Hekate the Gatekeeper holds the keys to death and life and carries the wisdom of the Great Crone. She reveals secrets, but also helps us uncover our own intuitive gifts. She is known as the Bringer of Beginnings and Mistress of Corpses, but at Samhain she is most often honored as the Mother of Witchcraft. In this aspect, she appears with snakes and keys, the color black, and darker shades of blue and purple.

way to you. A pentagram is therefore a centering and grounding symbol that often takes pride of place on the altar.

As for symbols on your altar to Hekate, you have nearly endless options. Hekate is a threefold goddess, so her symbols are often repeated in threes. She's frequently depicted as having

Other Hekatean Symbols

Owl, crow, bee, bull, goat, dragon, lion, pig, polecat/ferret, waning moon, dark moon, bay, belladonna, datura, garlic, lavender, mandrake, mugwort, oak, rose, sage, verbena, wormwood, clear quartz, black obsidian, red jasper, hematite, and iron.

Salt Spells

As we enter the dark season of the year, when the veil is thin and the restless dead are more active, we are wise to have protective tools such as quick and easy salt spells at the ready.

A Witch Bottle made with salt will absorb curses, negative energy, or jealousy directed toward you. In this case, your protection salt becomes a stand-in or decoy. To protect from negative energies, you might also put sharp-edged items in the salt jar that will break up curses and dissipate their power. Likewise, you can make a Witch Bottle that absorbs positive magic and attracts beneficial energies to you. Make sure you include something of yourself in your bottle. This could be a single hair, an eyelash, or a small scroll with your name on it.

Consult the "Magical Correspondences" section on page 235 to determine which ingredients are the best match for your intention.

TO CLEANSE A HOME

Mix together some kosher salt with herbs and flowers you love. Sprinkle this mixture all over the floor of a room and let it sit for a few minutes while you picture the salt absorbing memories and energetic signatures from past events. Meanwhile, allow the herbs and flowers to offer their essence to the space. After a few minutes, sweep it all up. When you're finished, discard the used salt blend in the garbage or rinse it down the drain.

TO ATTRACT HARMONY AND LOVE

Find a small decorative bottle, enough pink salt to fill it, and some flower petals and stones representing harmony and love. On a small piece of paper, write down the qualities you'd like to anchor into your love life. Fill the bottom third of your vessel with pink salt as you focus on your intention. Insert your paper, flowers, and stones. Top with remaining salt. You can permanently seal the jar to keep on your altar, or leave it unsealed to use

Magical PROPERTIES OF SALTS

EPSOM SALT: Purification, detoxification, and ritual baths.

COARSE OR KOSHER SALT: Grief work (as tears offered to water in a chalice, for example), space clearing, protection.

PINK SALT: Attracts love, romance, friendship, and contentment. Absorbs, anchors, and retains blessings. Leave little dishes of it out wherever you'd like to attract more goodness into your life.

SEL GRIS: Cleansing, blessing, balance, stability. Combine with herbs to bless a home or a meal.

BLACK SALT: Any salt mixed with charcoal, especially from a sacred fire, is a conduit for good luck. It absorbs and dispels negativity, sadness, emotional toxins, and spiritual burdens.

the salts for a ritual bath in the future (which could be handy after an argument). To cleanse a room of conflict, move the bottle into the space for a day and then move it into the moonlight to dispel the old energy.

TO EXTRACT CURSES AND RELIEVE BURDENS

How do you know if you've been cursed? Well, if you've had harsh words with someone recently, they're probably not sending good thoughts your way. You may want to have a cleansing salt bath to pull out the icky stuff. Mix a cup of Epsom salts with soothing plant allies such as rose, oat florets, and calendula. Place the mixture in a small sachet or in a square of cotton tied with twine and place in the bath. As you soak, imagine everything that is not yours to hold being extracted from your body by the salt. When you're done, empty the tub and rinse with fresh water right away. Dispose of the contents of your sachet in the compost so there are no lingering residues left in your space.

TO ASK FOR PROTECTION

For this spell, you're offering a deity a place to live on your altar, asking them to bless and protect you. Choose ingredients you feel this deity would love. In my spell to invoke Hekate, I include rock salt mixed with black ash from the Samhain fire and gold luster dust, gold leaf, snake skin, and a charm in the shape of a key. Seal your vessel with a charm, ribbon, and wax. Place it on your altar as a homing beacon.

Hekate's Torch

The symbol of Hekate as torchbearer offers reassurance in times of great personal and collective darkness. As we face the most overwhelming prospects of being human— our own mortality and overwhelming perils—the torch reminds us that with her guidance we are safe. We are not alone.

In the 19th-century Highlands, Samhain bonfires were kindled at dusk. It was customary for farmers to make a torch from firwood or a few branches of dried heather tied together and lit from the bonfire. The whole family and farm hands would walk around the property in a sunwise direction. Walking sunwise, east to west, is called deiseil (jay-shil) in Scottish Gaelic, and the opposite is called widdershins.

These torches are made from woolly mullein. Remember this is a dangerous fire-bearing tool. Always have a functioning water hose at hand and a bucket of sand or dirt. In other words, don't go for an evening stroll with your torch! They burn quickly and are only for ritual use in a safe environment.

Mullein can be harvested all summer long, before the flowers bloom, and hung upside down to dry. Small torches with stems of ¼ inch thick will burn their heads off within about a minute.

A medium saucepan

A disposable aluminum pie plate larger than your saucepan that can rest on the rim like a double boiler

½ pound solid beeswax (the amount of beeswax you'll need very much depends on the size of your torches, but this should be plenty)

A parchment-paper-covered work surface or another aluminum pie plate

Mullein stems with heads (the thicker flower end) intact, as many as you want to make

About 2 cups dried herbs and flower petals

A vase to place the finished torches in to dry

Fill the saucepan halfway with water and bring to a simmer. Pinch the pie plate on one side to make a small pour spout for later. Add about a quarter of your beeswax to the pie plate and allow it to slowly melt. A gentle heat is best. If you want to use a meat thermometer to check, it's best somewhere between 140°F–150°F. The flashpoint for beeswax (the point at which it will ignite), is 400°F.

Once the wax is fully melted, place a stem of mullein over the sheet of parchment paper. Use an oven mitt to carefully pick up the hot pie plate. Very slowly pour a thin stream of beeswax onto the mullein head.

Working quickly with your free hand, press some dried flower petals onto the wax before it hardens. Turn your mullein head a quarter turn and repeat. Continue until the flower head is completely covered. Feel free to add a second or third coat of wax if you like. Place in a vase to dry.

When it's time to light your torch, light from the very top so it gradually burns downward.

See the "Magical Correspondences" section on page 235 to create the combination of herbs and flowers you'd like to use.

Used together, mugwort and wormwood can conjure spirits. To invite your Beloved Dead to be with you, light a torch sprinkled with those two herbs to signal them.

✶ continued

Pour from one aluminum vessel into another and reheat the beeswax as often as you need, switching the vessels over the pot of simmering water to keep the beeswax warm and liquefied.

Mise en Place:
A SAFE SET-UP

For this ritual craft, use disposable pie plates. Unless you dedicate a particular pot for beeswax melting evermore, you will never in a million years get off all the beeswax, and definitely not in a way that doesn't clog your plumbing.

And let's talk safety: *never, ever, ever, ever* leave your melting beeswax unattended. If the water boils over and causes your beeswax to spill onto your stovetop, you've got a big problem. Keep a large box of baking soda at hand. If there's an accident, immediately turn off the heat and douse your stovetop with baking soda to stop the fire. (That sounds like a big hassle you want to avoid, right? Never leave your beeswax unattended.)

Walnut Fortunes

This ritual craft comes from my sweet neighbor, Beth Threlfall, a community witch and artist. On Samhain, Beth carries a pouch full of walnut fortunes for trick-or-treaters. They just reach in and pull out their fortune. I'd feel cursed with bad luck if I didn't run around the corner to Beth's house to receive my fortune on Hallowe'en night.

Walnut shells, enough for each guest

White acrylic paint

A black marker or paint pen

Fortune words written on small slips of paper. Some of my favorite are "lightness," "delight," "beginnings," "clarity," "boldness," "strength," and "revolution."

Paint all the walnut shell halves with 2 coats of white acrylic paint. Allow to dry well between coats. Once dried, use a black felt pen to draw a skeleton face on each. Fold your pieces of paper in half and tuck them into the half shell. It can be helpful to affix them in place with a bit of tape so they don't fall out if you're mixing them up in a bag. If you're having a sit-down meal, these can be placed at each place setting as a small party favor.

HEKATE'S FEAST DINNER

In this season, we feast to honor the abundant gifts that Hekate gives us and to nourish our Beloved Dead. When we prepare this meal with sacred intent, we're saying, *I will feed your memory.* This helps bring wholeness to our ancestral lineages. We can honor ancestors who weren't very honorable by feeding our bodies—their legacies—with the nourishment of intentional repair. We're ritually declaring, *I will not feed on your hurt. I will live into something new, something more vibrant, and I will show you how to come home to belonging.* With the recipes that follow, we create an abundant Samhain feast to extend a hearty welcome to all who wish to be in community with us, human and beyond.

The Grazing Table

Food is a form of sympathetic magic. Sympathetic magic is when you enact something in the material world to signal your wishes to the spiritual world. The giddy overflowing variety of a charcuterie board or grazing table is an ideal way to celebrate the Witches' New Year, and to alert the more-than-human world that we hope for a year of prosperity, abundance, and vibrant well-being. Another bonus of a grazing table: "serve yourself" is an easy and convenient way for a host to accommodate a multitude of dietary restrictions.

Charcuterie boards have been a lunchtime staple for my family for years, except we call them a ploughman's lunch.

MAIN: PROTEINS AND CHEESE
Salamis and cured meats, rillettes, pâté, terrine, chicken liver mousse, smoked salmon, and mussels or oysters are lovely choices. For vegan guests, I provide hummus or a cashew-based cheese or dip. For vegetarians, perfectly hard-boiled or pickled eggs are often appreciated.

GRAIN: CRACKERS AND NUTS
Provide something plain and salty with good body, then include secondary options that have more seeds, interesting shapes, and bold flavors. For nuts, I tend to offer one kind jazzed up with sweet spice like caramelized pecans, and one that is raw and salty like Marcona almonds or pistachios.

FRUIT: FRESH, DRIED, OR BOTH
Dried cranberries are a 1990s staple, but you can also serve them fresh with a little preparation (Cranberry Custard Tarts, page 81). I've also candied orange zest this way, which works beautifully with Cambozola and more strongly flavored cheeses.

✳ continued

VEGETABLE: RAW OR BLANCHED

My go-to is haricots verts (small French-style green beans) blanched for 2 minutes in boiling water, then plunged into ice water. Allow them to drain on a towel until very dry before arranging them on the platter. Yes, I'm Type A about placing the finely pointed tips all in the same direction. Slice small tomatoes along their equator and sprinkle with a mix of chopped herbs and sea salt.

PICKLE: ANYTHING BRINED
OR FERMENTED

We always have homemade canned dilly beans, fermented gherkins, and sauerkraut on hand. Olives can be dressed up with strips of orange zest and a sprinkling of crushed, lightly toasted fennel seeds.

SWEET

Chocolate is always appropriate. I'm one of those rare exceptions who doesn't like dark chocolate. I don't care if that makes me unsophisticated or whatever. Mini cookies, Jordan almonds, gummy bears—all are acceptable options. Or opt for the classic elegance of fresh fruit.

When arranging a board, place your mains in the most convenient spots first—large chunks of cheese that everyone will reach for, and pâtés that require space for cutting, should get prime real estate. Line the edge of your board with a containment layer to prevent items from spilling off. This could be thinly sliced meats or frilly kale. To add more dimension, anything that can stand, should. Triangular slices of cheese can stand on their sides in an interlocking pattern. If you cut a wedge from a round of cheese, stack it on top and add a drizzle of honey, dollops of chutney, or quince jelly to create some flowing lines and sensuality. The final touch on all charcuterie boards, no matter how humble, is colorful herbs and a sprinkling of edible flowers.

Corn Chowder

In some homes even today, corn is worshipped as a deity to the extent that if kernels fall on the floor while cooking, they're quickly snatched back up out of respect.

To make your own corncob stock for this recipe, simply cut the corn off the cobs and reserve for later. Place the cobs in a large pot with about 4 quarts of water. Add a whole onion, a carrot, some celery, and a fistful of fresh herbs. Keep on a low boil for about an hour. Season to taste with salt and pepper, strain, and voilà! A little extra time to create this perfect soup base is well worth it for the final product.

SERVES 6

2 tablespoons olive oil

1½ cups finely diced onion

½ cup finely sliced celery

1 cup finely chopped carrots

4 large garlic cloves, minced

3 tablespoons potato starch

8 cups vegetable stock or corncob stock

2 tablespoons honey, plus more if needed

2 cups cubed new potatoes

2 cups corn, frozen, canned, or fresh

½ teaspoon kosher or sea salt

2 eggs

1 cup heavy cream

Parsley or chives, finely chopped for garnish

Heat the olive oil in a pan over low-medium heat. Add the onions and soften them in the olive oil until just beginning to brown. Add the celery and carrots and continue cooking, stirring often until the vegetables are soft and the pot sounds and looks dry and things are starting to look caramel-colored, about 10 minutes.

Add the garlic and stir constantly for 1 minute, then add the potato starch and stir continuously for another minute. While continuing to stir, add the stock and turn up the heat to medium-high. Bring the soup to a boil, frequently stirring and scraping the bottom of the pot as the starch begins to thicken the broth.

Once boiling, add the honey and stir well, then add the potatoes, corn, and salt. Turn down the heat slightly and simmer for 10 minutes more. Taste the broth and see if it has bold enough flavor. Add more honey if you like. Things will mellow out quite a bit once you add the cream so the flavor should be strong. Test the potatoes for doneness. Once the potatoes in the soup are soft, turn off the heat and allow the soup to mellow for about 5 minutes. In a separate bowl, whisk the 2 eggs until they're very light with no visible lumps, then add the cream, whisking until very smooth to create a custard. Very slowly, add the egg custard in a thin, continuous stream to the soup broth while stirring constantly. Do not boil after this stage or the eggs will separate. Serve with a sprinkling of parsley or chives.

Rowan Berry Mule

Rowan is said to be the ultimate protector, making this drink a perfect elixir as the nights grow longer.

SERVES 1

1 sprig rosemary

2 ounces vodka (omit for a non-alcoholic soda)

1 ounce Rowan Berry Ginger
    Syrup (recipe to follow)

½ ounce lime juice

4 ounces soda

Slap the edge of your tall serving glass with the sprig of rosemary—that's right, spank it! This will release the essential oils onto the rim of the glass and add extra complexity and woodsiness to your cocktail. Fill the serving glass with ice.

Add the vodka, syrup, and lime juice to an ice-filled cocktail shaker and shake vigorously for 10 to 15 seconds. Pour over ice in the serving glass and top with soda. Garnish with a tiny sprig of rosemary.

Rowan Berry Ginger Syrup

MAKES ABOUT 1 CUP

1 cup rowan berries, cleaned
    with stems removed

3 cups water

1 tablespoon grated ginger

1 teaspoon lemon zest

1 cup sugar

Preheat the oven to 250°F. Pat dry the berries and place on a baking sheet. Bake until the berries burst and ooze juices, about 10 minutes depending on the size, ripeness, and moisture content of your berries. This will help deepen and intensify the flavor of the fruit.

Add the roasted berries and any of their oozy juices to 2 cups of the water and bring to a simmer.

Continue to cook for 5 more minutes, crushing the fruit slightly if it hasn't already burst open. Take off the heat and blitz with a hand mixer or in a blender to chop the berries to a rough pulp. Strain the pulpy mixture through cheesecloth or a jelly bag. Add the ginger and lemon zest to the berry juice and set aside.

Return the pulp to the pot and add the remaining 1 cup of water. Bring to a boil, then lower and simmer until you get a nice pink color, no more than 7 minutes. Strain again through cheesecloth or a jelly bag.

Clean your pot, add both juices and the sugar. Bring to a boil and reduce by one-third to one-half, tasting as it goes along, until it has just the right sweetness for you. Keep sealed in a jar in the fridge for cocktails or waffles.

RESPECTFUL
Foraging

Rowan berries come from the rowan tree, also known as the mountain ash or round-wood. It has a distinct leaf character: up to 12 inches long with 11 to 17 oblong spear-shaped leaflets in pairs on either side of the stem, with one single leaf at the tip. In the autumn, the rowan tree yields clusters of small, red or orange-red oval-shaped berries of about ⅜ inch in diameter, which linger on through winter after all the foliage has dropped. Naturally, you'll want to use only foraged berries from trees that are unsprayed and away from busy roads.

When foraging, first introduce yourself to the tree. Offering a piece of your hair (your DNA) is a way to say, *Hello! This is me.* Then ask the tree whether it would like to share with you. First notice what a "yes" would feel like in your body. Stand in a neutral posture, feet hip-width apart, close your eyes and ask your body, "Show me yes." Track what sensations arise. Some people feel a slight urge to tip forward. Some people feel a warm, bright, happy feeling. Note what yes feels like to you. Then ask your body, "Show me no," and track the sensations. Maybe it's an opposite sensation to yes, such as tipping backward. Maybe it's a feeling of instability or simply the absence of a yes. Once you have at least a vague sense of what yes and no feel like, ask the tree, *Can I have some of your fruit?* You might find some branches seem neutral or kind of grumpy, but others may seem to wave to you enthusiastically, *Pick me! Pick me!* When you receive a no, *receive the no.* This is nature teaching you about consent and respecting limits.

Mini Pumpkins Stuffed with Barley, Hazelnuts, and Crab Apples

This recipe combines two lucky ingredients, hazelnuts and apples, with a most sacred grain, barley. Here, they're presented together in a tiny pumpkin cauldron to alchemize good fortune. This is robust enough to become a vegetarian main course if you serve it with Shallot Gravy (see page 46) on the side.

SERVES 6

6 very small pumpkins or gourds, about ½ pound each, seeds scooped out

1 cup pearl barley

4 cups chicken or vegetable stock, or water

1 teaspoon sea salt (if using salted stock, reduce to ½ teaspoon)

1 teaspoon potato starch (optional)

1 tablespoon olive oil or butter

1 cup finely chopped onion

1½ cups chopped crab apples, cored and all seeds removed

1 tablespoon finely minced fresh sage

¼ cup white wine (a sweeter wine like Riesling or Gewurztraminer is best) or water

2 cups packed finely shredded Swiss chard leaves

¼ cup finely chopped parsley

¾ cup chopped roasted hazelnuts

Salt and freshly ground black pepper

Fresh herbs

Squeeze of lemon (optional)

Preheat the oven to 400°F. Line a rimmed cookie sheet with parchment paper and place the scraped pumpkins upside down on the sheet. Add about ¼ inch of water to the rimmed sheet. Place in the hot oven and roast for about 15 minutes. The pumpkins should be only partially cooked and still firm enough to hold their shape. The flesh should yield only slightly to a fork inserted in the side. Remove from the oven and pour off the excess water.

Place your barley in a fine mesh strainer and rinse under cold water in the sink. In a large pot, add the barley, stock, and salt and bring to a boil. Reduce the heat to a low simmer and cover the pot with a tight-fitting lid. Simmer for 25 to 30 minutes until tender. Drain the barley through the fine mesh strainer to remove any excess liquid and place back in the pot with the lid on. The potato starch will help bind the barley together nicely so if you're adding it, this is the time to sprinkle it evenly over the top and mix well to combine. Let the pot sit on the hot stovetop with no heat, just to allow the barley to dry out a little more, about 10 minutes.

While the barley is resting, heat the oil over low-medium heat. Add the onions and cook until soft, about 5 minutes. Once the onions are softened, add the crab apples, sage, and wine.

Increase the heat to medium. Stir frequently until the crab apples are slightly soft. At the last minute, add the chard and stir to combine well. Remove from heat and add this mixture to the barley, then stir in the parsley and hazelnuts. Season with salt, pepper, fresh herbs, and lemon juice, if using, to taste.

Preheat the oven to 375°F. Spoon the barley mixture into the mini pumpkins and then roast in the oven until the internal temperature reads 165°F on a food thermometer and the pumpkin flesh can be easily pierced with a fork, about 20 minutes.

Shallot Gravy

Garlic and onions are classic ingredients in protection magic, including protection from vampires. Serve this alongside pork or stuffed pumpkins for added richness.

MAKES ABOUT 1 CUP

1 tablespoon butter

2 tablespoons finely minced shallot or onion

3 finely minced garlic cloves

1 cup vegetable stock

1 teaspoon low sodium tamari or soy sauce

1 teaspoon Dijon mustard

1 tablespoon all-purpose flour

2 teaspoons nutritional yeast

A few sprigs fresh thyme, leaves
    stripped from stems

Salt and freshly ground black pepper

Heat the butter over medium heat and add the shallots and garlic. Sauté for about 3 minutes until softened but not yet browning. Meanwhile, whisk the vegetable stock, tamari, and mustard until thoroughly combined. Sprinkle the flour over the onions and garlic and stir for about a minute, allowing the flour to be absorbed and dried out a little. Then, while stirring continuously, slowly add the stock mixture to the onion mixture. Stir in the nutritional yeast and leaves of thyme, and season with salt and pepper to taste.

Colcannon (Creamy Garlicky Mashed Potatoes with Cabbage and Kale)

In the 1800s, potatoes and kale with milk and butter was the principal dinner of Highland Scots in all but summer months. This recipe is an example of an ancestral food that in this context becomes an offering to nourish the Beloved Dead.

SERVES 4 TO 6

½ cup butter for topping (optional; but is it, really?)

Salt

½ pound kale, washed, chopped

½ pound cabbage, chopped

1 pound russet or yellow waxed potatoes, peeled and cut into 1-inch cubes

1 cup whole milk

2 leeks or green onions, cleaned well and chopped

4 garlic cloves, roughly chopped

½ cup butter

Freshly ground black pepper

Pinch of nutmeg (optional)

Melt ½ cup of butter in a small saucepan over very low heat. Once it is mostly melted, whisk to melt the last of the solids. Turn off the heat and pour into a small carafe, keeping it in a warm place until service. Bring a large pot of heavily salted water to the boil—so salty it tastes like the sea. Add the kale and boil until bright green and tender, which should take no more than about 2 minutes.

Remove using tongs or a slotted spoon to a colander set over a bowl or in the sink. Add the cabbage to the water and boil for a few minutes until softened and nice to eat. Remove from the water and add to the kale to continue draining. Add the potatoes to the salt water and boil until tender. Meanwhile, bring the milk to a simmer in a medium saucepan. Add the leeks and garlic, and cook till soft, about 4 minutes. Drain all the water off the softened potatoes, then add the remaining unmelted ½ cup of butter. Use a potato masher to blend until smooth and fluffy, then season with salt and pepper to taste.

Return the potatoes to the stove over low heat. Add the milk, leek, and garlic mixture along with the kale and cabbage to the mashed potatoes. Stir to blend and adjust seasonings. Remove from heat and serve with the small carafe of warm melted butter, if using. Traditionally, you'd pile the colcannon high on your plate and make a well in the middle. The small carafe of melted butter would be passed around the table for folks to fill their well.

Roast Pork Coppa with Wild Mushrooms and Pomegranate Seeds

Pigs represent the earth and are sacred to Persephone and Demeter, two counterparts to Hekate who complete the maiden, mother, crone triad. It's especially fitting to serve pork with pomegranate seeds, a symbol of the Underworld journey begun in the fall.

This recipe calls for a cut of meat that Italians call the coppa. It's a smaller cut from the neck and shoulder of the pig. In America, it's known as part of the Boston butt cut. It's commonly used in Southern pulled pork and Mexican carnitas. You may need to call your butcher to request this in advance because there are only two of these cuts available per pig. However, its juicy tenderness makes it a foolproof, crowd-pleasing pork roast that is well worth any hassle. Calculate approximately ¼ pound of meat per person. Remember that pork needs to be salted a bit more than beef to really shine.

SERVES 4 TO 6

1 to 1½ pounds pork coppa

2 tablespoons olive oil

Sea salt and freshly ground black pepper

1 tablespoon butter, plus more if needed

1 pound mixed mushrooms (chanterelles, oyster, lobster, porcini, or brown button will do)

2 garlic cloves, minced

2 teaspoons fresh thyme leaves

½ cup dry sherry or dry white wine

⅓ cup pomegranate seeds

Dry the pork with a paper towel and allow it to come to room temperature for 30 minutes. Preheat the oven to 400°F. Heat a sauté pan or cast-iron skillet to medium heat. Rub the roast with 1 tablespoon of the olive oil and season with salt and pepper to taste. Sear each side of the roast until it releases from the pan without sticking, about 2 to 3 minutes per side. Place in the oven

for 15 minutes. Reduce the heat to 375°F and cook for another 45 minutes.

About 20 minutes before you expect your roast to be done, melt the butter with remaining 1 tablespoon of olive oil in a large pan over medium heat. Add the mushrooms and sauté for 5 minutes—try to resist stirring. To sauté means to "jump," so you do want a bit of excitement in your pan. It should sound active and make you a bit nervous about turning your back for too long. Add the garlic and sauté 5 more minutes, this time stirring only occasionally—you want the mushrooms to get some nice dark color on them.

Once they've got a nicely caramelized look and aroma, add the thyme and sherry. Turn down the heat to low-medium and simmer for about 10 more minutes, until the liquid is reduced by about half. Add any meat juices from your resting roast to the mushrooms and simmer 1 more minute to blend flavors.

Check the roast for doneness with a meat thermometer. It needs to reach 145°F at the center of the thickest part of the roast. If it's not done, keep cooking and monitor the temperature every 10 to 15 minutes. Once it has achieved 145°F, remove from the oven and transfer to a cutting board or platter that will catch the juices. Cover with foil and allow to rest for about 10 minutes. Serve in ¼-inch slices.

Lift the mushrooms with a slotted spoon and transfer to a serving platter, sprinkle with most of the pomegranate seeds, top with slices of roast coppa, then drizzle the meat with the mushroom pan juices. (If you want the pan jus to be a bit more velvety and delicious, whisk in another tablespoon of cold butter before drizzling.) Sprinkle with the remaining pomegranate seeds and serve.

Buttered Green Beans with Hazelnuts

Beans are connected to immortality, long life, and resurrection, making them well fitted to herald the beginning of the journey through winter; a good luck charm for a perilous time of year.

SERVES 6

1½ pounds trimmed green beans

⅔ cup hazelnuts, skins removed*
    and coarsely chopped

¼ cup butter

2 teaspoons apple cider vinegar

Salt and freshly ground black pepper

Cook the beans in a large pot of boiling water until tender but still bright green and crisp, about 4 minutes. Drain off the hot water and immediately run very cold water over the beans for a few minutes until they are completely cooled. Drain the beans in a colander. Place the hazelnuts in a small skillet and stir over medium heat until lightly toasted, about 3 minutes. When ready to serve, melt the butter in a wide saucepan over medium-high heat. Add the beans and vinegar; toss to coat and heat through, about 2 minutes. Sprinkle with the hazelnuts then season with salt and pepper.

*To remove the hazelnut skins: Toast the nuts in an even layer on a cookie sheet in a 375°F oven for about 10 minutes. While the nuts are still warm, roll them into a clean towel (that you don't mind getting oil stains on), rubbing them together really well until the skins come off easily. If it's not working, you need to toast them a bit longer.

Carrot Fortune Cake
with Creamsicle Frosting

MAKES THREE 6-INCH CAKES (3 THICK LAYERS) OR TWO 7-INCH CAKES (CUT INTO 4 LAYERS)

CARROT CAKE

1 cup sugar

1 cup vegetable oil

2 large eggs

1¾ cups all-purpose flour

1 tablespoon ground cinnamon

¼ teaspoon ground nutmeg

¼ teaspoon ground allspice

1 teaspoon ground ginger

1 teaspoon baking soda

½ teaspoon baking powder

½ teaspoon salt

1½ cups shredded carrots

¾ cup crushed pineapple with juice

½ cup chopped walnuts

½ cup unsweetened shredded coconut plus 1 cup for decorating

Store-bought charms tied to ribbons, enough for each guest

ORANGE CREAMSICLE FROSTING

1¼ cups very soft room temperature butter

½ cup spreadable cream cheese

¼ cup liquid honey

¼ cup frozen orange juice concentrate (not made into juice—still concentrated)

Zest of 2 oranges

3 cups confectioners' sugar

2 teaspoons vanilla

Food divination often includes special cakes with tokens tucked inside. Whoever finds the ring token is blessed in marriage, the coin in wealth, a wishbone for the heart's desire, and so on. At Samhain, our divination often includes tarot cards or trance journeys to the Otherworld, but guests of all ages are always delighted to find their fortune in this cake.

For this recipe, I highly recommend you use whole nutmeg and allspice if you have them, using a microplane to grate them. The frosting for this cake really benefits from being left overnight in the fridge, not only to blend the flavors but also to firm up for piping. Prepare this cake in stages: I usually bake the cake layers and freeze them a week before the event, make the frosting 2 days prior, and then assemble and decorate the day before the event. This cake is best kept in the fridge until just before serving.

TO MAKE THE CARROT CAKE

Preheat the oven to 350°F. To prepare your cake pans, butter them, dust them with flour, line the bottoms with parchment, and place them in the fridge until you are ready to fill them. In a standing mixer, whisk together the sugar and oil. Add the eggs and whisk until the batter is pale in color and falls slowly from the beaters, about 7 minutes. In a separate bowl, sift together the dry ingredients, including the spices. When the egg mixture is light and fluffy, add the carrots and pineapple with juice and whisk to incorporate. Using a spatula by hand, fold the dry ingredients into the batter. Stir in the walnuts and ½ cup of the coconut. Spoon the batter evenly into the prepared pans. Bake for 30 to 35 minutes, until a toothpick comes

 *continued*

out clean. Cool in the pans for 10 minutes then turn out onto wire racks to cool completely.

TO MAKE THE ORANGE CREAMSICLE FROSTING

In a stand mixer with paddle, beat the butter and cream cheese on high until very pale in color, about 4 minutes. Scrape down the sides every so often. Turn the mixer to medium and add the honey, orange concentrate, and orange zest. Turn to low and slowly add the confectioners' sugar. Mix until very well blended, then slowly add the vanilla. Turn the mixer to high again and allow it to run for 10 minutes until the frosting is fluffy. Place in an airtight container and leave in the fridge overnight.

When you're ready to frost your cake, remove half the frosting to a mixing bowl and stir until smooth. Reseal the rest of the frosting in the airtight container but leave it out on the counter to come to room temperature so it's easier to spread.

Spread one-third of the bowl frosting onto the bottom layer of your cake. I usually flip my cake layers upside down so the crisp edge is on top. Cover with the middle cake layer and spread one-third of the frosting on top, smoothing it evenly to the edges, then top with the final layer. Using a pastry brush, remove as many crumbs as possible from the top and sides of your stacked cake. Begin frosting the sides, then the top of the cake with a thin crumb coat. A crumb coat is just a very, very thin layer of icing that you apply to trap crumbs. Once you've applied this thin layer, not worrying about the fact that it might have tons of crumbs smeared in it, place it in the fridge for at least 15 minutes to firm up.

Remove the chilled cake from the fridge and finish icing the sides and top with the room temperature frosting. Press the remaining shredded coconut onto the side of the cake. Place the remaining frosting in a piping bag to decorate the top if you like. Tie ribbons onto your charms and press them into the top of the cake. Return to the fridge to chill until dessert time.

CHAPTER TWO

Yuletide

"God gave us memory so that we might have roses in December."
—James M. Barrie

Yuletide is more a season than an event, which adapts well to the complexities of modern self-directed spirituality. Yule is the Anglo-Saxon name for a 2-month midwinter season that spans all of December and January. By the time Christianity swept across Europe in the 15th century, "Yuletide" had narrowed to mean more or less "a 12-day feast of the Nativity." In this chapter, I hope to give you enough space to determine what feels spiritually significant for you, whether that means connecting with the holiday spirit for a single night at the winter solstice, for 8 days of Hanukkah, during 12 days of the Nativity, or a 4-week break for winter with a 12-day period of daily ritual observance in the middle, like myself.

Many traditions hold certain celebratory winter days in common:

- The winter solstice
- One night (or more) to honor the ancestors
- One night (or more) to honor kinship, community, and feasting
- One night (or more) to acknowledge supernatural beings
- One night for divination and oath making for the year ahead

In our family, the 12 days of Yuletide are a replay of the year in miniature with a small ritual, special recipe, or sacred craft done each day. So the work of January is replicated on the first night of Yule, celebrated on the solstice, December 21. The energies of February are mirrored on the second night, and so on. To great extent, this gives us permission to interpret and plan our Yuletide observances in a way that reflects the seasonal Wheel of the Year where we live. The 12 days of Yuletide ritual culminate on New Year's Day. The following examples show how we observe the 12 days of Yuletide.

1. Mother's Night

Everything begins with Mother. Tonight, we acknowledge the line of mothers that gave us life. Or you might acknowledge a deity of nurturance, abundance, and homey comforts such as Mother Mary, Brigid, Demeter, Frigg, or a guide like Mother Bear or her constellation, Ursa Major. Rituals for this day include freecycling, finishing up repairs, putting fresh linens on the bed, and making sure the larder is full, ready for a season of hosting. This is a good day to prepare the favorite foods of your matrilineage. Host an outdoor fire for solstice or light the Yule log to represent the tilt of the Wheel toward lightness again.

2. Father's Night

Tonight we honor our patrilineage. In some places they also honor the man who cleared the land upon which the home now stands, who presumably continues to watch over it for us. This is a good time to think about the blessings and also the grief of your relationship to the land you now occupy. Are you on your ancestral lands? What people, animals, mountains, waterways, or others were displaced for you to live here? How can you demonstrate gratitude for the land that now supports you? Today pull out the favorite recipes of your menfolk.

3. The Wild Hunt

The Wild Hunt is a European folklore motif involving a large ghostly hunting party that travels at night on horseback composed of the souls of the dead and deities associated with the Underworld. Celebrations acknowledge the animal familiars involved—horses, wild boar, and deer. Tonight, we remember our ancient dead, the ones whose names are forgotten to time, especially those whose souls may not be at rest. To appease them, we might prepare a traditional dish from the place where our wayback people lived. Tonight, leave gifts outside for wild animals and birds, such as popcorn on a string, birdseed, or raw nuts. Today, I'll add a rabbit figurine to the altar to honor the energy of spring since this day is connected with March.

4. Children's Night

This is the theme that has most strongly survived into the modern era—the night of laying out treats, gifts, stockings, and surprises for kids. On this day, we honor children as living expressions of innocence, acceptance, and love. Tonight, we light our Yule log. In some places, the Yule log burns throughout the night, in others it's a giant log that burns for the entire 12 days! Either way, some wood is often retained as a fire starter for next year's fire. If you have a fireplace, this is a perfect night to have a cozy fire. Make Surprise Balls (page 62) for gifting tomorrow.

5. Return of the Light

In Christian traditions, this day marks the birth of Jesus, often described as bearing a "great Light unto the world." But many non-Christian traditions also mark a time to celebrate the lengthening days and the sun returning to the world, bringing with it hope and healing. The Christmas wreath is a modern interpretation of the sun cross, a Neolithic solar symbol. You could display clove-studded oranges representing the blessings of solar energies. Singing carols that mention "light" is also very appropriate. Hang a himmeli over the dining table to signal peace and gratitude.

6. Gifting to House Elves and Supernatural Allies

Today we give gifts to the gnomes, elves, fairies, brownies, tomte, nisse, kobold, domovoy, or other Little People living in your home. These are tutelary spirits who protect your house and property.

In the Scottish tradition, brownies help out with chores and yard work, watch over livestock, and generally bring good luck throughout the year. Bowls of porridge or rice pudding and tiny glasses of milk, beer, cider, or brandy are common offerings. Little People are not always benevolent, especially if they feel slighted or taken for granted, so this is an important observance to ensure smooth operations in the coming year!

7. Balance

This observance pertains to the balance of equals and binaries such as active/receptive, lightness/darkness, masculine/feminine. Many ancient mythologies feature a sibling pair honored in winter, for instance Freyr and Freyja or Apollo and Artemis. In Irish mythology, the Holly King and the Oak King are brothers who signify the dark and light halves of the year. They come together for a momentary truce at Midsummer and at Yule. If binaries are not your jam, you could honor deities depicted as shape-shifting or nonbinary today such as Loki or Inanna. Decorate gingerbread people to get playful with this observance.

8. Hearth and Home

In the Highlands of the 18th and 19th centuries, no unnecessary work was permitted during Yuletide. Specific time was set aside for catching up, organization, and squaring away last minute preparations for ringing in a new year. Bad luck would befall you if you hadn't wrapped up old business by then. The kitchen must have a thorough cleaning, anything borrowed must be returned, and all debts must be repaid. Hang a sprig of any kind of banishing herb as a simple protection ritual for this day. Many banishing herbs make themselves known by being very spiky, such as milk thistle, cardoon, blackberry vine, or holly.

9. Bounty

Now we give thanks to Land and Community for the abundance that sustains us. Fruit, vegetables, grain, flowers, greenery, and animal figurines are all appropriate on the altar. Some places in Europe still have a tradition of guising, going loudly from house to house asking for hospitality. In Wales, the tradition of the Mari Lwyd involves a horse skeleton on a broomstick held by someone hiding under a white sheet. Accompanied by a rowdy troupe, Mari Lwyd engages neighbors in a sort of rap battle of songs and jokes until they're let inside for a drink and some food. With this night reflecting the month of September, remember with gratitude all you harvested this year.

10. Remembrance

There's usually one somewhat somber night during Yuletide when candles are lit and a place at the table is laid for the visitor who will never materialize; a place for those we loved who died in the past year. This doesn't need to be a sad affair, mind you. It could follow an Irish wake tradition where laughter and song commingle with tears. The food offering can be buried under a tree afterward. Perhaps your ritual is to simply raise a toast to your Beloved Departed. Let them know you're thinking of them and wish them to rest in peace. Say a prayer and light a candle for those who are grieving during the holidays.

11. Gathering

This is the night we gather with loved ones to let them know they've enriched our lives. Yes, it's about fancy dress and sparkly adornment. But it's also about raising a toast to say *Thank you for being in my life*. Rituals for today involve sharing treats and libations, possibly reviving the custom of wassailing. Wassail is a drink made of spiced mulled apple cider. "Wassail" is also a greeting that basically means *To your health!* Wassail is also a verb that describes house-to-house visiting to share music, food, and drink. And at midnight, we usher the old year out and the new year in. We might bang pots and pans to banish the past year from the house. Having a roaring fire is good luck but not if the fire goes out before midnight, so take care to ensure a strong store of wood.

12. Oath Making/Divination

In days of old in Scandinavia, this celebration was known as Oath Night. Words said on this day wield great power, especially when witnessed by the community. The best New Year's resolutions are undertaken with some forethought and are ceremonialized to seal their power. Divination is customary today. While we honor all the gods and goddesses today, those presiding over oracular gifts are featured in particular. These deities include the Völva, the Norns, and the Wyrd in Scandinavia; the Fates, Apollo, Hermes, the Pythia, and of course, Hekate, from ancient Greece. Today is the perfect moment to pull out your tarot deck and perform a reading for the year ahead.

The Yule Log Centerpiece

The Yule log carries a long and complex history, in some places linked to the World Tree, in others to the return of the Light, in others simply a cause to gather round the hearth in community. Light your log on the eve of whatever day is the heart of Yuletide for you as a form of sympathetic magic, beckoning the sun to return.

SELECT THE LOG: Hardwoods such as ash, oak, birch, or cherry are great, but any dry log will do. Either green or dead wood is fine so long as the bark is well attached to the wood. Pine bark splits easily when drilled, though it's only an aesthetic concern.

LEVEL THE BOTTOM: If your log has a flat side and sits stable, you can skip this step. Use a plane, belt sander, or palm sander to create a flat face on the bottom side of your log.

DRILL THE HOLES: Use a drill press or hand drill with a spade bit to make the desired number of holes. If you make your holes too big, you can fold a ring of tinfoil and place it in the hole to wedge the candles in more securely. If you don't have a drill, use a hot glue gun to glue your candles in place and cover with moss.

ADORN YOUR LOG: Drape, pin, or glue greenery along the top and sides.

When the holiday season is over, remember to saw off the bottom 12 to 18 inches of your tree and save it someplace dry and well ventilated for next year's Yule log. This ritual symbolizes the continuity of the wheel of time from one year to the next.

Himmeli

Himmeli is a folk art form from Finland consisting of beautiful geometric shapes made from string and straw. Himmelis are a depiction of the harmonious nature of the cosmos, a talisman that anchors good fortune, peace, and prosperity in your home. Using refuse from the wheat harvest symbolically connects the bounty of the light half of the year with the survival of the dark half. Himmelis seem to have come to Finland by way of Sweden or Germany, since himmel *means "heaven" and "sky" in those languages. It's believed that this art form likely originated in North Africa and spread across Europe where it is known by many regional forms and names.*

If you're using real straw for this craft, you'll discover that working with this material is tricky! Sometimes your straw will split when you create a knot, resulting in some wonky angles and a messy appearance overall. A trick is to prep the straws in advance by cutting them to length, then dipping the ends in white glue. When dried, this creates a transparent stopper against the string that prevents splitting.

12 pieces of straw, in 3 groups of 4 pieces of equal length (or paper straws or brass tubing)

Waxed linen string or dental floss

Scissors

1. Organize your pieces of straw by length. We'll call them groups A, B, and C. The lengths of your straws will determine your final shape. They can be any length you like so long as all pieces within a group are the same length.
2. Thread an A, another A, then a B piece onto your string. Tie a surgeon's knot or double knot here with one end of the twine trailing about 6 inches long. Leave that 6-inch tail alone for now and work with the other longer length of string.
3. Thread two Cs and tie a knot at the corner to make a triangle. Thread on another B, then

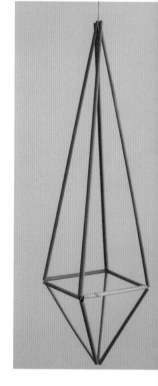

a C, then tie another knot to create another triangle secured at the bottom tip of your himmeli.
4. Thread on another C, then a B.
5. Tie at the corner to create another triangle at the bottom of the himmeli.
6. Thread on two more As and tie off at the corner again.
7. Thread on your remaining B piece and tie the ends of your string together to form the shape of your base, trimming off the trailing ends.
8. Turn your himmeli right-side-up. Take a short piece of string and loop through the two longer diamonds to pull the top of your himmeli together. Make a loop, trim the excess string, and hang your himmeli. You did it!

REGIONAL *Variations*

There are many cultural variations when it comes to straw chandeliers. In Poland, similar straw crafts are called pająki and include ribbons, paper flowers, beads, feathers, even egg shells incorporated at the junctions between straws or tied onto the bottom. For a modern touch, I hang vintage chandelier crystals from the bottom.

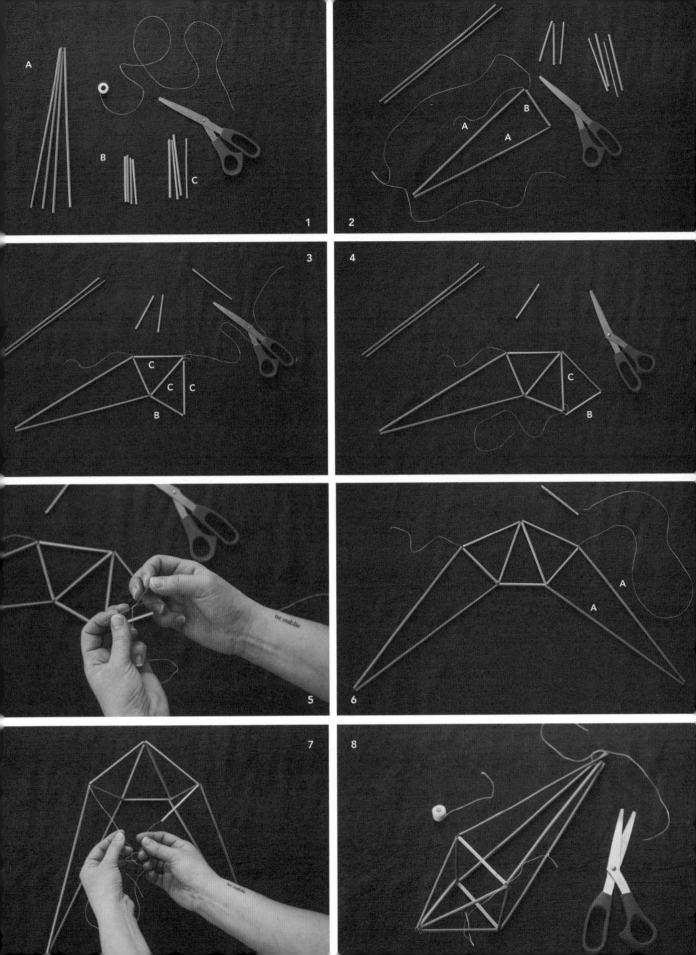

Surprise Balls

Surprise balls are like a blessing ball: When you include items that fit a theme such as "healing," "creativity," or "self-care," the blessings start flowing as the recipient unwraps the gift. Start with your largest or most oddly shaped item at the center and save your flattest prizes for the outer layers. You can shape them into fruits and vegetables, animal faces, Nutcracker Suite characters—anything you can think of! If you decide to paint them, allow at least 24 hours for the paint to dry thoroughly. These can double as place cards or an after-dinner amusement for guests.

MATERIALS
Crepe paper, scissors, glue,
   stickers or acrylic paint

POSSIBLE SURPRISES
Small action figures, stim toys, candy, charms,
   fabric patches, fortune fish, perfume papers,
   stickers, love notes, punch balloons, costume
   jewelry, temporary tattoos, lapel pins.

The first step is to cut your crepe paper across the grain of texture. This way, the paper will stretch, pull taut, and lie flat as you wrap. Glue the ends of the crepe paper strips together with a tacky white craft glue. To keep your glue bottle in ready position and prevent it from drying out, place a damp piece of paper towel in the bottom of a heavy-bottomed glass and keep your glue bottle in there upside down. Allow a few minutes to dry so you have a long paper ribbon. Wrap your first surprise and add more surprises in layers as you go. When you finish wrapping, adhere the end of your paper ribbon with a piece of glue to the bottom of your ball. Decorate with stickers or paint and give with love.

A COMMUNITY FEAST

Yuletide is a time of elaborate hospitality, but it doesn't have to be expensive if we make it a communal effort. But the problem with potlucks for me is that I'm a fairly Type A personality with a very clear and personal sense of the Gaelic "fitness of things." A buffet of deli salads, quinoa side dishes, and store-bought fruit trays does not constitute dinner. What I do instead is design a menu, then ask for help. I send links to the recipes and ask if guests will volunteer to make one. For folks with less capacity, I ask them to bring simpler items like bottled water, wine, or bakery-bought dinner rolls. I handle the critical factors like the meats. It's more pot*planned* than pot*luck*, but everyone ends up well-fed and satisfied. The following menu is for a large gathering and makes for a spectacular buffet.

Mulled Cider with Baked Apples

Apples were said to grant the power to foretell the future and open a portal to the Otherworld, in Welsh tradition known as Avalon or Apple Land. This is a perfect recipe to use for your wassail.

MAKES ABOUT 2 QUARTS

6 small firm baking apples, such as Honeycrisp, Braeburn, Pink Lady, or Jonagold

1 cup demerara sugar

2 teaspoons ground cinnamon

2 teaspoons ground ginger

2 quarts raw pressed apple juice

¼ teaspoon freshly grated nutmeg, plus more for serving

2 cinnamon sticks

10 whole cloves

6 allspice berries

6 whole star anise, plus 6 more for garnish

½ cup brandy (optional)

½ cup bourbon (optional)

Preheat the oven to 350°F. Scoop out the core of each apple without penetrating the bottom so you end up with six little apple buckets that will hold the sugar and spice blend. Mix together the sugar, cinnamon, and half of the ginger. Fill each apple with this mixture and top each with a star anise. Save any of the sugar mixture that's left over. Bake the apples for about 30 to 40 minutes until they are softened but not yet collapsing. Remove from the oven and allow to cool.

Pour the apple juice into a large pot on the stove over medium heat. Add the ground nutmeg, whole spices, and remaining ground ginger, and whisk in any leftover sugar mixture until it has fully dissolved. If you want stronger spice flavors, you can allow the juice to cool to room temperature and refrigerate overnight.

To serve, strain the spices from the juice and reheat to between 160 and 180°F. Pour into a punch bowl or pretty pot and add the baked apples. If you're making a hard apple cider, add the alcohol now or pour a half jigger each of brandy and bourbon into serving glasses and pour the hot cider over top. Sprinkle with freshly grated nutmeg and serve.

Traditional Eggnog

While you can definitely mix this up the day of your party, this recipe can be made in 2 parts, with the egg and alcohol mixture resting in the refrigerator for up to 2 weeks. Soaking your eggs with alcohol not only gives you peace of mind if you're uneasy about consuming raw eggs, it also melds the flavors nicely. This is a potent brew, so serve tiny portions in your daintiest tea cups.

MAKES 3 QUARTS

4 egg yolks

¾ cup maple syrup or granulated sugar

¾ cup white or amber rum

¾ cup Grand Marnier

⅓ cup cognac or brandy

Zest of 1 large orange

1 vanilla bean

4 cups milk

4 egg whites

2¼ cups heavy cream

Freshly grated nutmeg

Twist of orange zest for serving

At least 3 hours prior to serving, beat the egg yolks and maple syrup with an electric mixer until very smooth and light in color. With the mixer on low, add the alcohols and orange zest. Cover and chill at least 2 hours or up to 2 weeks. At least 2 hours before serving, split the vanilla bean and scrape it into the milk. Drop the bean pod into the milk and chill until the next step. (Don't leave the bean pod in the milk more than 30 minutes or so, or it will start to add bitterness.)

Beat the egg whites until stiff. In a separate bowl, whip the heavy cream to a soft peak stage. Take the egg yolk mixture and the vanilla milk out of the fridge and remove the vanilla bean pod. Slowly whisk the milk into the egg yolk mixture until thoroughly blended and smooth. Fold in the whipped cream until only almond-sized lumps remain. Finally, fold in the egg yolks until the mixture is smooth. Serve with freshly grated nutmeg and a twist of orange zest.

Ribeye Roast with
Garlic Herb Crust and Madeira Gravy

The "low and slow with reverse sear" roasting method has become popular lately because it results in perfect evenness of rare meat from the center to the edge of the roast. The problem is that the final step, a flash broil to brown, can cause a potentially embarrassing smoke alarm situation with guests present. I've always found that the traditional method of placing the roast in a very hot oven for a few minutes at the start of roasting then reducing to a low temperature also works beautifully and reduces anxiety at serving time. This recipe will work very well with a standing prime rib roast if you want the bones for broth or your dog, but I choose a ribless roast because it provides more surface area for the delectable garlicky herb crust—a maximum crust-to-meat ratio! (chef's kiss).

A 5-POUND BONELESS ROAST WILL SERVE 6 ADULTS

Ribeye roast (boneless prime rib), about ½ pound per person as part of a large buffet, or more as a main entrée

Salt and freshly ground black pepper

1 small garlic clove per person

1 teaspoon fresh thyme leaves per person

1 teaspoon finely chopped fresh rosemary per person

About ¼ cup olive oil

Madeira Gravy to serve (recipe follows)

ONE DAY AHEAD

Season the roast with salt and pepper, making sure to sprinkle on all sides. Using a mortar and pestle, crush the garlic with the herbs to a chunky paste. You can also use a knife and just keep chopping the herbs and garlic together until it becomes slightly pasty. Slowly stir in the olive oil until you have a chunky but spreadable mixture, about 1 tablespoon of olive oil for every 4 garlic cloves. Using your hands, rub the paste evenly all over the roast, really working it into any seams in the meat. Transfer to a cast-iron skillet (this type of pan is best when it comes time to make the gravy), and place uncovered in the refrigerator overnight.

COOKING DAY

Let the roast stand at room temperature at least an hour before cooking. Set the oven to 450°F. Roast the beef in the center of the oven for 15 minutes. Reduce the oven temperature to 350°F and lightly drape a piece of foil over the top of your roast. (Do not cover completely and especially don't fold the edges over your pan—you're just trying to prevent overcooking the garlic, not steaming the roast.) After 45 minutes, check for doneness with a meat thermometer, and check every 15 minutes after that. A 5-pound roast may not take much longer than an hour, depending on your desired doneness. Remove your roast at 125°F for rare meat, 130°F for medium-rare. Remove the roast from the pan to a cutting board or platter, tent with foil, and allow it to rest at least 30 minutes before carving.

✦ *continued*

Madeira Gravy

MAKES 2 CUPS

2 tablespoons rendered bacon fat or olive oil

4 garlic cloves, smashed

5-inch sprig of thyme

5-inch sprig of rosemary

1 cup Madeira or red wine

2 cups beef stock

6 teaspoons butter

6 teaspoons flour

Salt and freshly ground black pepper

1 teaspoon of something acidic, such as lemon juice or balsamic vinegar (optional)

Add the rendered bacon fat, garlic, and the herbs to a cast-iron pan or roasting pan and place over medium-high heat. Stir and scrape the pan well for about 1 minute then add the Madeira. Continue to stir and scrape until the Madeira has reduced by half. Add the beef stock and continue stirring and scraping occasionally until the liquid has reduced by half again. Turn off the heat and strain the liquid through a sieve to remove all solids. You should have about 1½ cups of liquid. In a small saucepan, melt the butter over low heat. Once it stops foaming, whisk in the flour and continue stirring until well combined. Cook until it darkens to a rich brown color, about 5 minutes. Slowly whisk in the liquid and increase the heat to medium-low. Simmer until you reach your desired thickness. Season to taste, adding salt, pepper, and optional acid, if desired.

Baked Ham with Candied Kumquats and Spiced Sumac Bourbon Glaze

Boar was the prize game of the Wild Hunt, and this recipe serves as a contemporary update. The jewel-like glazed kumquats symbolize the sun and remind us of the return of the light. This recipe has many steps, but each step is super simple. Literally, most of it is just turning the stove on and off. If you can handle basting, you can handle this recipe. Begin this recipe at least 3 days prior to your big event.

SERVES 10 TO 12

CANDIED KUMQUATS

1 pound kumquats, washed, each pierced to their center with a toothpick at least 13 times

1 cup sugar

Plenty of water for multiple changes of water

Pinch of salt

Pinch of cream of tartar

SPICED SUMAC BOURBON GLAZE

2 cups honey, demerara, or light brown sugar

2 cups water

6 to 8 star anise pods (whole stars)

10 to 12 allspice berries

12 whole cloves

1 teaspoon peppercorns

2 tablespoons sumac powder

Kumquat syrup

4 ounces Kentucky bourbon

BAKED HAM

8- to 9-pound fully cooked, bone-in, half ham roast

1 tablespoon whole cloves

Box cutter with a fresh blade

Skewer, metal is ideal but bamboo or a pointy chopstick could work

1 cup unoaked dry white wine or water (optional)

TO MAKE THE CANDIED KUMQUATS

Day 1: After piercing each kumquat, place in a medium pot, cover with cold water, and bring to

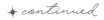

★ continued

a boil. Once the water arrives at boiling, remove from the heat immediately. Set a timer for 30 minutes. When the timer goes off, drain the kumquats and cover with fresh cold water. Bring to a boil again. Once boiling, immediately turn off heat and set a timer for 30 minutes (again). When the timer goes off, drain and cover with fresh water and bring to a boil *one more time*. Same thing: as soon as they're boiling, turn off the heat and set a timer for 30 minutes. The reason for this is to drain off the bitterness and soften the interior of the fruit so it can absorb the sugar syrup completely.

After the third timer, drain out the water and add 1 cup of sugar to the pot. Add 1 cup of water, then the salt and cream of tartar. Bring the fruit and sugar mixture to a boil then immediately reduce the heat to the lowest temperature possible, so there is a slight simmer but it's not moving the fruit. You don't want to stir the fruit because it's very delicate at this stage. If you notice the color is uneven and dark on the bottom but still very light on top, carefully turn the fruit over with a spoon. Allow to simmer very gently, uncovered, on low, for an hour. After an hour, turn off the heat, cover the pan, and allow the fruit to sit in the pot of syrup overnight, or at least 8 hours. By now they will look like tiny balls of amber.

Day 2: Now it is time to coax the syrup all the way into the center of the fruits. Turn the heat up and bring the kumquat and syrup mixture to a low boil. Once boiling, turn off the heat and let it cool for 30 minutes. Do that two more times—just boil, turn off the heat, let sit for 30 minutes. Now you should have tiny balls of amber in thick syrup. Using a slotted spoon, remove the kumquats to a rack placed over parchment paper and allow to dry overnight. While the syrup is still warm, move on to complete the ham glaze preparation, returning to the kumquats the next day.

Day 3: Once the candied kumquats have dried, they will still feel sticky. Roll a few at a time in a plate of white sugar to coat. Serve candied kumquats as a garnish for roast ham or eat as a petit four with after dinner coffee, like candy. Store the candied kumquats in an airtight container with extra white sugar to separate them.

TO MAKE THE SPICED SUMAC BOURBON GLAZE

Add your honey, water, and spices to the kumquat syrup and bring to a simmer, never taking your eyes off of it. Allow it to thicken until it becomes a dark caramel color, and has reduced by half, about 20 minutes. Set aside and allow to cool to room temperature. Fish out the solid spices with a slotted spoon then stir in the bourbon. Use real Kentucky bourbon—corn-based whiskey, not rye, and not Tennessee whiskey. You want to end up with about 2 cups of glaze with the consistency of maple syrup. Taste as you go. It will keep well for a week or more in the fridge.

TO MAKE THE BAKED HAM

Allow the ham to come to room temperature, about 1 hour. Preheat the oven to 325°F. Estimate about 1 pound of meat per person for a bone-in ham, and that it will take about 15 minutes per pound for your ham to reach an internal temperature of 140°F. Hold your box cutter at a 45-degree angle to the surface of the meat. Lightly score a cross hatch design. The most important part of this ham presentation is that you don't cut into the fat or come close to the meat surface—this will explode the design. Where the two lines of your cross hatch form an X intersection, use your box cutter to make a tiny X incision. Press your skewer into the incision all the way down into the meat, even wiggling the skewer around to enlarge the hole. Insert a whole clove into the hole. This will make tiny channels that enable successive washes of glaze to penetrate down to the meat as it expands under heat.

Place the ham in a roasting pan with the flat cut side of the ham down then brush the entire surface with glaze. Add a cup of dry white wine to the pan, if using. Place in the lower third of the oven and roast for about an hour. Remove from the oven and brush with glaze again—make sure you really slather those clove holes. Reserve at least half your remaining glaze for the final portion of cooking and for serving. Do not baste with the pan juices—they're too salty. Add more water if your glaze starts burning to the pan. (Pay atten-tion to the smells coming from your oven—trust your nose to check if things change in the air.) Roast until a meat thermometer inserted into the thickest part of the meat reaches an internal temperature of 140°F. Allow to rest 15 minutes. Brush another flourish of glaze on the sliced meat before it's passed around the table. Garnish with candied kumquats and encourage folks to take one each and add little bits to their mouthfuls of ham.

Baked Salmon with Lemon Confit

The salmon is a supremely sacred animal in Scotland as well as my homeland of Coast Salish territory. In Gaelic lore, the Salmon of Wisdom ate nine hazelnuts, which represent spiritual knowledge. Anyone who partakes of salmon gains this power. The simple yet rich, unctuous lemon confit must be made a month before your feast, but it is well worth the wait.

SERVES 8 TO 10

LEMON CONFIT

1⅔ cups kosher or sea salt

2 tablespoons sugar

2 large lemons, scrubbed and quartered

¼ cup lemon juice (optional)

BAKED SALMON

2 tablespoons extra virgin olive oil

4- to 5-pound side of salmon, skin on

2 tablespoons chopped fresh fennel, dill, parsley, thyme, or a combination

3 tablespoons finely chopped Lemon Confit

Freshly ground black pepper

TO MAKE THE LEMON CONFIT

In a large bowl, mix the salt with the sugar. Toss the lemons with half of the sugar-salt mixture. Pour a small layer of the sugar-salt into a clean quart jar. Layer the lemons in the jar, covering them with the remaining sugar-salt as you go. Let sit on the counter for 3 days, shaking at least twice a day to help release the juices. If the jar isn't at least half-filled with liquid by day 4, add lemon juice to submerge the lemons. Give the jar a good shake and place in the fridge. Refrigerate the lemons for at least 1 month, shaking once a week. To use, rinse the lemons well and use the peel only.

TO MAKE THE BAKED SALMON

Preheat the oven to 275°F. Line a rimmed baking sheet with aluminum foil. Brush with 1 tablespoon olive oil. Place the salmon fillet, skin side down, on the prepared baking sheet. Mix the remaining oil, fennel, and chopped lemon confit in a small bowl. It should be a spreadable paste. Spread three-quarters of the mixture over the salmon. Season with pepper. Let stand for 10 minutes to allow the flavors to meld. Bake the salmon until just opaque in the center, 15 to 18 minutes depending on its thickness. Brush with the remaining confit mixture and serve.

Leek and Camembert Tart

This tart is where leeks end up after slow growing and low-key sulking in my garden for 6 months. Any gardener who loves leeks must cultivate patience and steadfastness, two qualities that serve us well in the depths of winter.

SERVES 4 TO 6

17-ounce package frozen puff pastry, thawed

2 large eggs, 1 beaten for egg wash

2 tablespoons butter

4 leeks (white and pale green parts only), sliced (about 4 cups)

¼ cup water

Salt

⅔ cup whipping cream

4 ounces Camembert cheese, cut into ½-inch pieces

Pinch of cayenne pepper

Pinch of ground nutmeg

¼ cup freshly grated Parmesan cheese

Preheat the oven to 400°F. Roll out the pastry sheet on a large sheet of parchment paper to a square or rectangle of ¼ inch thick fitted to your favorite sheet pan. Trim a straight ¾-inch border off each side. Paint the edge of the pastry base with egg wash and stack the trim on top of the egg wash to create a ½-inch outer rim. Transfer to a baking sheet. Freeze for 10 minutes.

Melt the butter in a large heavy skillet over medium heat. Add the leeks and ¼ cup water. Cook until the leeks are tender, about 15 minutes. Season the leeks with salt then set aside to cool. Bring the cream to a simmer in a saucepan over medium heat. Reduce heat to low. Add the Camembert and stir until mostly melted. Remove from heat and cool for 10 minutes. Whisk in the egg, cayenne, and nutmeg. Set the custard aside.

Sprinkle the Parmesan over the crust, spread the leeks over the top, then drizzle the custard over. Bake until the bottom is golden, about 20 minutes. Transfer to a rack to cool for 10 minutes. Serve warm or at room temperature.

Crushed Baby Turnips and Radishes

Root crops like radish and turnip were once thought to be only fodder for livestock. However, during famine years, which in the Highlands was about every 3 years through the 18th century, these quick-growing crops were lifesavers for farmers to feed their families. A recipe like this can be served to acknowledge the ancient dead and all they went through during life. This recipe can easily be made with any combination of root vegetables, and you can substitute their greens for the Swiss chard.

SERVES 4 TO 6

12 small turnips (about 1 inch in diameter),
    cleaned and trimmed

12 small radishes (about 1 inch in diameter),
    cleaned and trimmed

¾ cup olive oil

Salt and freshly ground black pepper

2 small red onions or shallots,
    peeled and quartered

4 to 6 garlic cloves, peeled

1 small bunch of Swiss chard or kale, stems
    removed and chopped into 1-inch pieces

6 to 8 sprigs thyme

¼ cup butter

⅓ cup maple syrup

In a large heavy-bottomed pot over medium-high heat, cover the turnips with 2 inches of water and bring to a boil. Allow to boil for about 5 minutes then reduce to a simmer and add the radishes to the turnips. Remove the veggies with a slotted spoon when they become fork tender, about 5 more minutes. Allow to cool. When cool enough to handle, smash the root veggies with the bottom of a heavy mug or glass, pressing them to be even in thickness, about ½ inch thick.

Heat the oil in a cast-iron skillet over medium-high heat. Fry the smashed veggies, flipping once, till charred and hot, 5 to 8 minutes. Remove to a paper towel–lined sheet. Season with salt and pepper and cover with foil to keep warm. Drain excess oil from the pan. Add the onions, garlic, and chard stems. Cook over medium-high heat for 2 to 3 minutes until golden and starting to become charred. Add the chard leaves and sprinkle with the leaves of half the thyme sprigs. Stir constantly for 1 minute until the leaves are wilted and become bright green. Push the chard to the side and add the butter. As the butter melts, return the turnips and radishes to the pan for a quick flash fry in the butter and add the remaining whole thyme sprigs. Remove from the heat. Arrange the greens on a platter, top with the root veggies, and drizzle with maple syrup and serve immediately.

Rapini with Garlic Cloves and Parmesan

Rapini is a hardy season-extending crop that gives us bright, bold flavor through the winter months. True rapini looks like broccolini but tastes a bit more like spicy turnip. To tame the hot bitterness of rapini, you need to blanch it first in very salty water. For this recipe, you can substitute broccolini or broccoli rabe, in which case you don't need to blanch for as long.

SERVES 4 TO 6

1 to 2 tablespoons sea salt

1 to 2 pounds rapini

3 tablespoons extra virgin olive oil

⅓ cup peeled whole garlic cloves, slightly crushed flat but still intact

Freshly ground black pepper (optional)

Squeeze of lemon (optional)

½ cup shredded Parmesan cheese

Add the salt to a large pot of water and bring it to a rolling boil. Have a large bowl of very cold water and ice cubes handy to quickly cool your rapini after blanching. Cut off the top 2 inches from the rapini and set aside. Trim off the bottom ends off the stalks, peeling any tough outer skin, and chop into 1-inch bite-sized pieces. Add the stalk pieces to the boiling water and cook for 1 minute then add the tops and blanch until bright green and just tender, another 3 minutes or so more. Scoop out about a half cup of blanching water and set aside. Strain your rapini in a colander and plunge immediately into ice water.

In a sauté pan, warm the olive oil over low-medium heat and add the garlic. Cook gently until the garlic is softened and just beginning to take on a golden color, about 5 minutes. Remove the rapini from ice water and add to the sauté pan with the garlic. Cook and stir until it is warmed through and well coated with olive oil and garlic. If it ever seems too dry and is starting to char, add a splash of the reserved blanching water. Taste to determine doneness; it should be toothsome, not mushy. Adjust seasonings, adding pepper or lemon if desired, and top with Parmesan and serve.

Super Deluxe Potato Gratin

This recipe is really worth doubling because you'll probably want leftovers. If you generally don't like blue cheese, steer away from the very dark blues like Danish blue and Roquefort cheese, but still give some blue a try. The lighter blues of Gorgonzola and Bleu d'Auvergne are made with the less pungent Penicillium glaucum *and have a milder flavor that will nonetheless bring nuance and depth to this dish.*

SERVES 6

½ cup grated and packed aged
    sharp cheddar cheese

⅓ cup crumbled blue cheese

¼ cup packed grated Parmesan cheese

¼ cup very finely sliced sweet onion such
    as Vidalia or Walla Walla varieties

¼ cup finely chopped chives or
    parsley, or a combination of both,
    plus 1 tablespoon for garnish

2 pounds yellow wax potatoes sliced ¼ inch
    thick (use a mandoline if you have one)

¼ cup butter

Salt and freshly ground black pepper

1 heaping tablespoon all-purpose flour

1½ cups whole milk

Butter a 1- to 2-quart casserole dish, 2 to 3 inches deep, and about 8 inches square or round. Preheat the oven to 400°F. Mix the cheeses together and set aside. Toss the onions and chives together in a small bowl and set aside. Line the bottom of your casserole dish with half the potatoes, overlapping neatly. Dot with 2 tablespoons of the butter. Season with salt and pepper, and sprinkle evenly with half the onions and half the cheese mixture. Layer the remaining potatoes on top. Season again with salt and pepper and top with the remaining onions. Save the rest of the cheese to add later in the last few minutes of baking.

In a small saucepan, melt the remaining butter over low-medium heat and add the flour, whisking to remove any lumps. Slowly add the milk while whisking constantly and simmer for about 1 minute until slightly thickened. Remove from heat and gently pour the mixture over the potatoes (they may not be fully submerged and that is all right). Cover with foil and bake in the oven for 45 minutes. Remove the foil and top with the reserved cheese (it's okay if the milk looks curdled at this point). Bake uncovered for another 30 to 45 minutes, until the cheese is nicely browned and the potatoes are tender. Remove from the oven. It's crucial to allow it to sit at least 15 minutes before serving. After sitting, sprinkle with the remaining fresh herbs and serve.

Frisée Salad with Pomegranate Dressing

In Greek myth, Persephone ate 3 pomegranate seeds while in the Underworld. This cursed her to spend 3 months of every year there, resulting in the barren winter months on the earth. We eat pomegranates now to keep vigil for her.

SERVES 6 TO 8

CANDIED PECANS

2 tablespoons water

3 tablespoons sugar

1 tablespoon maple syrup

¼ teaspoon sea salt, plus more if needed

¼ teaspoon cinnamon

¼ teaspoon ground ginger

Pinch of cayenne pepper, or more to taste

½ cup pecan halves, coarsely chopped

FRISÉE SALAD

6 cups (15 ounces) mixed lettuce greens including some bitter frisée or other chicory

Pomegranate Dressing (recipe follows)

Salt and freshly ground black pepper

½ cup pomegranate seeds

TO MAKE THE CANDIED PECANS

Preheat the oven to 325°F. In a small saucepan, bring the water plus the sugar, maple syrup, salt, cinnamon, ginger, and cayenne pepper to boil over medium heat. Reduce the liquid by half so that it becomes nice and syrupy, then stir in the pecans until well coated. There should not be a lot of syrup sitting in the bottom of the saucepan. If there is, you can either add more pecans or continue to cook until the additional liquid evaporates. Transfer to a parchment-lined baking sheet and spread into a single layer. Sprinkle with another pinch of sea salt, if desired. Bake for 7 to 10 minutes until golden and fragrant but not yet blackened. Remove from the oven and let them cool completely.

TO MAKE THE FRISÉE SALAD

Toss your frisée with the dressing, season with salt and pepper, top with the pecans and pomegranate seeds, and serve.

Pomegranate Dressing

MAKES ABOUT 1 CUP

3 tablespoons pomegranate molasses (found in Mediterranean, Southwest Asian, and North African shops)

2 tablespoons red wine vinegar

1 tablespoon honey

2 teaspoons Dijon mustard

⅔ cup olive oil

Whisk together the molasses, vinegar, honey, and Dijon until very well combined. Slowly add the olive oil in a steady trickle while whisking constantly.

Cranberry Custard Tarts

The spiritual significance of cranberries, a staple for Métis, Indigenous, and European fur traders, is related to survival, vibrant well-being, and strong blood. The charm of this recipe is the bright delightful pop in the mouth of the barely cooked berries, which are wonderful on charcuterie boards, too. In summer, top this tart with a mix of fresh berries and apricot jelly glaze for a classic French fruit tart.

SERVES 8 TO 10

PÂTE SABLÉE

2 cups all-purpose flour

⅔ cup granulated white sugar

1 egg

1 teaspoon vanilla extract

Pinch of sea salt

½ cup butter, diced into tiny squares and chilled for 10 minutes

SUGARED CRANBERRIES

½ cup water

1 cup sugar, plus more to coat cranberries

1 cup fresh or thawed cranberries

CRÈME PÂTISSIÈRE

1⅓ cups milk

½ vanilla bean, scraped

⅓ cup granulated sugar

2 tablespoons cornstarch

Pinch of kosher salt

3 large egg yolks

4 teaspoons butter

Mint leaves for garnish

✳ continued

TO MAKE THE PÂTE SABLÉE

Day 1: Make the tart crusts and sugared cranberries.

In a food processor, mix all the pâte sablée ingredients except the butter until they are sandy and homogenous. Add the chilled butter and pulse just until the dough begins to hold together. Transfer to a lightly floured surface and knead a few times to achieve a smooth ball. Flatten to about 1 inch thick, cover tightly with plastic wrap, and chill for just 30 minutes.

Preheat the oven to 375°F. Remove the dough from the fridge and allow it to slightly soften and come to room temperature, about 15 minutes. Lightly flour your work surface and roll out the dough to ¼ inch thick. Drape the dough over your pie tin and press evenly into the bottom of the mold. Run your rolling pin over the top edge to trim the excess dough. Line each dough with parchment paper or foil and fill with pie weights, dried beans, sugar, or rice. Bake for 15 minutes. Gently remove the parchment paper and weights, and continue to bake 5 to 10 minutes more until lightly golden and completely cooked. Allow to cool completely before filling. These can sit in their molds, lightly covered with a clean tea towel, overnight or until ready to fill.

While you wait for the pâte sablée to cool, make the sugared cranberries.

TO MAKE THE SUGARED CRANBERRIES

Bring the water and sugar to a full boil then remove from heat. Add the cranberries and allow to sit in the hot syrup for 3 minutes. Using a slotted spoon, carefully remove the berries from the syrup and place on a wire rack (I use a rack from my dehydrator so they don't fall through). Allow to dry for at least 1 hour. The berries should be relatively dry but sticky. Transfer to a plate of white sugar and coat thoroughly. Allow to dry another

hour in the sugar. Then lift from the sugar and keep in an airtight container until ready to use, up to 2 days

TO MAKE THE CRÈME PÂTISSIÈRE

Day 2: Make the Crème Pâtissière and assemble.

In a medium saucepan, add the milk and the scraped vanilla bean. Bring to a simmer then turn off heat and cover. Let steep for 30 minutes. A few minutes before your milk is finished steeping, in the bowl of a standing mixer whisk together the sugar, cornstarch, and salt. Add the egg yolks all at once and beat for 2 minutes on high speed, scraping the bottom of the bowl halfway through. Remove the vanilla bean from the milk. Turn the standing mixer down to low and in a slow steady stream, add the warm milk to the egg yolk mixture. Then immediately pour the contents of the standing mixer back into the saucepan and return the saucepan to the stove on medium heat.

Whisk continuously without stopping for 5 minutes until you notice the mixture becomes thick like vanilla pudding. Pause your whisking to see if bubbles are beginning to break through. Once you notice bubbles surfacing, continue whisking for a full minute more to allow the starches to fully cook through and transform. Remove from the heat and add the butter, whisking to thoroughly combine. Place the saucepan in a sink of cold water to quickly and completely chill the pastry cream.

TO ASSEMBLE

Whisk the crème pâtissière until smooth, then fill your tarts. Top with sugared cranberries and a tiny leaf of mint. Serve immediately.

Granulated sugar is an excellent pie weight for two reasons: it creates a smooth base, while beans and pie weights can cause dimples, and it is reusable as an ingredient after baking, whereas rice and beans aren't. At higher temperatures, the sugar may toast a bit, but that can add a pleasant layer of complexity and caramel notes to custards and pie fillings.

Chocolate Hazelnut Caramel Tart

The Latin name of cocoa, Theobroma cacao, *means "food of the gods" in Greek. Chocolate has been a sacred medicine for ceremonies and feasting since it was first domesticated by the Olmecs of Mesoamerica at least 5,000 years ago. Cacao contains tryptophan, which can cause warm and fuzzy feelings, and may be helpful at this hectic time of year, no? Besides, chocolate is so synonymous with opulence that a Yuletide celebration without it just seems wrong.*

SERVES 8 TO 10 IN A 14-BY-4-INCH OBLONG TART PAN OR 9-INCH ROUND TART PAN WITH REMOVABLE BOTTOM

GILDED HAZELNUTS

½ cup water

½ cup sugar

12 whole hazelnuts, roast and hulls removed, then cooled

Edible gold leaf

1 recipe Pâte Sablée (page 81)

CARAMEL

⅓ cup sugar

2 tablespoons water

3 tablespoons whipping cream

1 tablespoon butter, cut into small chunks

⅔ cup roasted hazelnuts, coarsely chopped (reserve a few whole hazelnuts for decorative topping)

½ teaspoon fine sea salt

CHOCOLATE GANACHE

⅔ cup whipping cream

8 ounces (225 grams) good quality semisweet chocolate, finely chopped

2 tablespoons butter

TO MAKE THE GILDED HAZELNUTS

In a saucepan, bring the water and sugar to a boil. Then allow it to cool. Add hazelnuts to the syrup, then remove with a slotted spoon to a piece of parchment paper. Allow to dry for 2 hours or overnight. The simple syrup will slip off and each nut will dry in a pool of tacky syrup glue. Press the sticky end of the nut onto the gold leaf. Press into the chocolate ganache–topped tart just before serving.

TO PREPARE THE PÂTE SABLÉE

Preheat the oven to 375°F. Press the pâte sablée into a 14-by-4-inch rectangular tart pan or an 8-inch round tart pan with a removable bottom. Blind bake (lined with parchment paper and filled with pie weights) for about 25 minutes then remove the pie weights and finish baking another 5 to 10 minutes, until the bottom is baked through, dry, and golden brown. Cool completely before starting the caramel.

TO MAKE THE CARAMEL

Stir the sugar and water in a small heavy-bottomed pot over medium heat until the sugar is fully dissolved. Increase the heat and allow to gently boil, without stirring, until the syrup turns an amber color. If you notice crystals forming on the sides of the pan, wash down the sides with a pastry brush dipped in water to dissolve the crystals and prevent burning. This should take no more than 5 to 7 minutes. Remove the pan from the heat and allow it to sit for about 2 minutes to cool slightly. Add the cream, stirring constantly to blend in smoothly. Return to the heat and continue stirring until any bits of caramel dissolve. Add the butter, stirring until the butter is dissolved, then add the ⅔ cup roasted hazelnuts. Pour into the fully baked and cooled tart shell. After half an hour, sprinkle the entire surface with fine sea salt. Chill until fully set, about another hour.

TO MAKE THE CHOCOLATE GANACHE

Heat the cream to a gentle simmer. Remove from heat then add the chocolate and butter. Stir continuously until the chocolate is completely melted and the mixture is smooth. Pour this mixture over the caramel-filled tart shell and smooth the top. Chill until set, another hour. Top with gilded hazelnuts and serve.

Caffè Mocha Bûche de Noël

Is there a more festive holiday dessert than a Yule log jelly roll? Over the years, I've experimented with more than a dozen recipes and flavor combinations. Here, I've combined what I believe are the most satisfying elements with the least amount of fuss. It's basically like tiramisu, but in a jelly roll form. The recipe appears daunting, but give it a try and take your time. If I make it over the course of 3 days, it's so simple I feel like I've cheated when people exclaim how beautiful it looks.

SERVES 8 TO 10

CAKE

5 large eggs, separated and left at room
    temperature for half an hour

1 teaspoon vanilla

½ cup plus 2 tablespoons granulated sugar

½ cup flour

¼ teaspoon salt

¼ teaspoon cream of tartar

¼ cup butter, melted and cooled

2 tablespoons confectioners' sugar

ESPRESSO SYRUP

½ cup espresso or very strong black coffee

2 tablespoons sugar

1 tablespoon coffee liqueur (optional)

CRÈME LÉGÈRE

1⅓ cups milk

½ vanilla bean, scraped

⅓ cup granulated sugar

2 tablespoons cornstarch

Pinch of kosher salt

3 large egg yolks

4 teaspoons butter

1 cup cold whipping cream

✳ *continued*

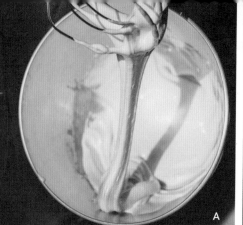

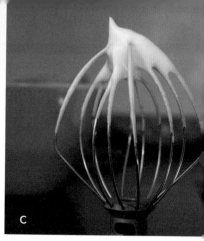

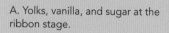

A. Yolks, vanilla, and sugar at the ribbon stage.

B. Scrape and fold in the flour.

C. Egg whites, salt, and cream of tartar at stiff peak stage.

D. Proper pouring consistency.

E., F. & G. Rolling the cake layer into the tea towel to cool.

H. Custard base for the crème légère.

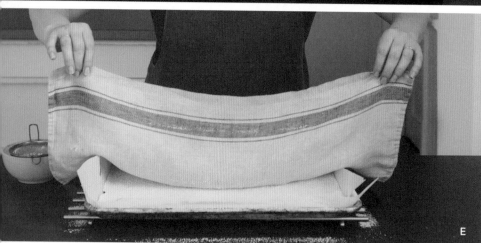

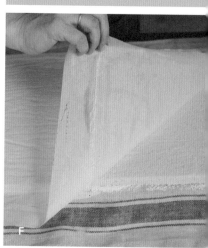

BUTTERCREAM

1 cup butter, room temperature

1 cup high-quality semisweet chocolate, finely chopped

3 cups confectioners' sugar

¾ cup cocoa powder

1 tablespoon coffee liqueur (optional)

¼ cup whole milk, room temperature

TO MAKE THE CAKE

Preheat the oven to 350°F. Butter the edges of a 15-by-10-by-1-inch rimmed jelly roll pan (aka: a cookie sheet with a 1-inch-tall lip on it) and dust with flour, then line the bottom with parchment paper. Beat together the 5 yolks, vanilla, and ½ cup of the sugar until it reaches the ribbon stage, about 8 minutes or more. You'll know when you get there when the mixture turns very pale and fluffy and forms a ribbon that takes at least 3 seconds to dissolve when you lift the beaters. Sift ¼ cup of the flour on top of the mixture and gently fold in by hand with a spatula until just incorporated. Sift the remaining ¼ cup flour on top and continue to gently fold by hand with a spatula. Set aside.

Clean your beater very well until absolutely no grease remains. Beat together the 5 egg whites, salt, and cream of tartar at medium speed just until soft peaks form. Reduce speed to low and add the remaining 2 tablespoons of sugar, a little bit at a time, until the whites begin to hold stiff peaks.

Take about one-quarter of your stiffly beaten egg whites and add them to the yolk mixture. Gently whisk together to lighten the yolk mixture then use a spatula to fold in the remaining whites gently but thoroughly. Take ½ cup of this egg batter and whisk it into the melted butter until smooth. Then use a spatula to fold the butter mixture into the egg mixture until thoroughly combined.

Spread this batter into your sheet pan then give one firm tap of your sheet on the counter to burst any bubbles. Bake until the top of the cake bounces back when pressed with your finger, 8 to 10 minutes.

As soon as you remove the cake from the oven, sprinkle it evenly with the 2 tablespoons confectioners' sugar. Then place a clean, lint-free dish towel on top of the cake. Place a second same-sized cookie sheet on top. Wearing oven mitts, quickly flip the whole thing upside down, so you end up with the hot cake on top of the towel, on top of the cool cookie sheet. Carefully peel off the parchment paper. Starting with the long side nearest you, pick up the towel and roll the cake into a jelly roll so the towel gets tucked into the roll. You don't want the cake to roll onto itself; you want the towel to prevent the cake from sticking to itself. Leave the cake to cool completely on a rack, seam side down, in the towel. If you're making this ahead of time, once it has completely cooled, wrap the entire cake and towel jelly roll in plastic wrap. Leave at room temperature overnight in the tea towel.

TO MAKE THE ESPRESSO SYRUP

Bring the coffee and sugar to a boil, stirring until the sugar dissolves and the liquid is slightly reduced to about ⅓ cup. Remove from heat and add the coffee liqueur. Cool to room temperature.

TO MAKE THE CRÈME LÉGÈRE

Add the milk and the scraped vanilla bean to a medium saucepan. Bring to a simmer then turn off heat and cover. Let steep for 30 minutes. A few minutes before your milk is finished steeping, in the bowl of a standing mixer whisk together the sugar, cornstarch, and salt. Add the egg yolks all at once and beat for 2 minutes on high speed, scraping the bottom of the bowl halfway through. Remove the vanilla bean from the milk. Turn the standing mixer down to low and in a slow steady

continued

stream, add the warm milk to the egg yolk mixture. Then immediately pour the contents of the standing mixer back into the saucepan and return the saucepan to the stove on medium heat.

Whisk continuously without stopping for 5 minutes until you notice the mixture becomes thick like vanilla pudding. Pause your whisking to see if bubbles are beginning to break through. Once you notice bubbles surfacing, continue whisking for a full minute more to allow the starches to fully cook through and transform. Remove from the heat and add the butter, whisking to thoroughly combine. Place the saucepan in a sink of cold water to quickly chill the pastry cream. Alternatively, you can spread it out flat on a parchment-lined cookie sheet and place in the refrigerator for 30 minutes. Allow to cool completely.

When the custard base is completely cooled, whip the cold heavy cream to medium peaks. Take about a quarter of the whipped cream and whisk it into the custard until smooth. Using a spatula, now fold about a cup of the lightened custard into the whipped cream. This gets them a little closer to each other in texture, which will make it easier for them to combine in a smooth, homogenized way. Gently fold the rest of the custard into the whipped cream until just combined.

Gently unwrap your cake layer, pulling out the tea towel and leaving it behind as you go, and brush the cooled espresso syrup over the surface. You don't want to totally soak the cake; you're not making tiramisu. Just brush a light even layer. You'll find that as the cake absorbs the espresso syrup, it makes it easier to unroll, so start wherever it opens easily for you and allow it some time to relax and unfold for you.

Spread the crème légère evenly over the entire surface of the cake, only about ¼ inch thick. If you make it too thick, it can be very oozy when you cut it. Starting with the long edge, which will be the very center of the roll, gently roll the cake back into its final shape, ending with the seam side down. Brush off any excess confectioners' sugar. Cover with plastic wrap and put back in the fridge overnight, or at least a few hours to firm up.

TO MAKE THE BUTTERCREAM

Melt the chocolate over low heat, either over a double boiler or in a microwave. When you see only tiny ant-sized pieces of unmelted chocolate remaining, quickly remove from heat and melt the rest of the way just by whisking. Set aside to cool. In a medium bowl, sift together the confectioners' sugar and cocoa. Beat the butter on high speed with a paddle attachment until very fluffy and light in color. Scrape down the sides and continue to beat well for another minute. Turn down the speed to low and gradually add the cocoa and sugar mixture. Mix well, pause to scrape down the sides again, and continue mixing until well combined. Slowly add the melted chocolate. Again, mix well, pause to scrape down the sides, then beat until very smooth. Add the liqueur and about half of the milk and beat until smooth. Keep adding milk, a splash at a time, until a nice spreadable texture is reached.

TO ASSEMBLE

Trim the ends off your rolled cake at 45 degree angles, 2 or 3 inches long, and reserve for later. Transfer it to your serving platter. Tuck strips of parchment paper under the edges of the cake to prevent the buttercream from smearing on your platter. Spread the buttercream in a thin layer the entire length of the roll but leaving the trimmed ends exposed, saving a bit of buttercream for attaching the trimmed bits like branches onto your log. Once you've attached the trimmed bits, remove the parchment paper strips and finish decorating your platter and Yule log with sprigs of evergreens and a dusting of confectioners' sugar right before serving to give the appearance of snow.

CHAPTER THREE

Imbolc

"Spring grew on . . . and a greenness grew over those brown beds, which, freshening daily, suggested the thought that Hope traversed them at night, and left each morning brighter traces of her steps."
—Charlotte Brontë, *Jane Eyre*

Imbolc is the season of winterspring, when the year itself struggles to be born. The origin of the name Imbolc (pronounced EEM-ol-ck) is a bit uncertain but there are hints that it's associated with lambing season, coinciding with the halfway point between the winter solstice and the spring equinox, usually on or around February 1. An Old Irish term, *imbolc* refers to pregnant ewes. It also means "in the belly." Winter is pregnant with spring soon to come. There is a similar sounding term, *imb-fholc*, which refers to ritually cleansing oneself. Both meanings, pregnant expectation and ritual cleansing, are core components of this festival. Here we have a both/and situation.

This seasonal observance is tinged with a thin, faintly grasping sense of optimism. It's a nascent time when things are not quite fully formed but the potential is showing itself. We're not quite free of the darkness and we yearn for our imminent emergence. Though the dark half of the year is commonly associated with death, it's also a regenerative time, for all the activities of the warm half are planned in winter. As such, we honor deities who've triumphed over cold stagnancy and repression. We attempt to glean some of their courage, will, and rugged resourcefulness in these last gray days of winter.

Surrounding this season is the mythology of Brigid. She is primarily connected with the great trifecta of Gaelic arts: poetry, smithing, and healing. Brigid is strongly associated with the hearth fire, fertility, midwifery, and nurturance. In these fire-oriented aspects, she is similar to the Roman goddess Vesta, and the Greek goddess Hestia. Although some aspects of Brigid are gentle and nurturing, we'd be remiss to paint her as entirely passive. Fire and smithwork are hardly the domains of the genteel. In the Christianized version of her myth, Brigid was born a pagan with the gift of healing and so became a kind of druidic vestal virgin, devoted to maintaining an eternal flame. But then this spirited woman met St. Patrick, converted to Christianity, doused the druidic flame at Kil Dara (Temple of the Oak), and lit a new one consecrated to Christ. She is now known as St. Brigid of Kildare. The Brigid's cross we make this month invokes this deity's devotion, strength, and healing.

In the Hebrides of western Scotland in the 19th century, a doll representing Brigid, called the Bridey doll, was made of rushes, reeds, or wheat straw. She was decorated with flowers, cloth, beads, and shells. A special stone representing the healing powers of the goddess adorned her chest. The Bridey doll was paraded through the village by the young maidens who gathered at a home for food and drink before the menfolk arrived seeking blessings from the goddess. A bed of straw or sheepskin was made where the doll would sleep.

Another deity connected to the emergence from winter to spring is the Cailleach of Ireland and Scotland. The Cailleach (roughly pronounced k-"eye"-ack, which means "the veiled one" and is a synonym for "old woman" in Gaelic), is a supreme deity who creates the landscape and protects nature. On the eve of Imbolc, the Cailleach journeys to the Isle of Youth. Before the first birdsong at dawn, she drinks from a magical spring and is transformed into a young maiden called Bride (*Breed* in Irish, *Breej* in Scottish Gaelic), whose magic wand turns the grass green and causes the yellow and white flowers of spring to grow. Your wheat doll could also be a crone figure that you lay to rest till winter comes again.

As you note the potentiality around you during these weeks, where do you see signs of newness wanting to come to life? What stagnancy are you ready to shake off? How will you ensure you wrap up winter in a good way so you can step fully into your emergence as spring arrives?

The Clootie Tree

Folks in Victorian-era Scotland, Ireland, and England would visit holy wells, sacred stones, and special trees to honor Brigid around this time. These places were chosen as offering sites because they were considered energetically potent. In Scottish Gaelic, the manifest soul essence of a place is called the *buaidh* (boo-aye), a root found in the names of many places and people, including legendary Celtic warrior and mother, Boudicca. Typically, people would leave coins or a Brigid's cross as an offering, or a clootie—a rag ribbon, like a Scottish version of a prayer flag. If you ruin a favorite shirt with a stain that won't come out, tear it into ribbons and use them as clooties. I tie a clootie to my ancestor tree whenever I sense someone is in need of extra prayers and support. On the eve of Imbolc, leave your clooties outside draped on tree branches for Brigid to come bless, endowing the clooties with healing powers in the night. In the morning, bring them back inside to use as needed. I've hung clooties above the dining table for guests to pull down after the meal, which they can take outside to our ancestor tree to leave their wishes and prayers.

Brigid's Crosses

A Brigid's cross is a charming ritual craft that remains important today, in Ireland especially. They're made from rushes (commonly called juncus grass), or other wetland plants like reeds. They can also successfully be made from wheat, straw, ivy, morning glory vines, or grape vines. When harvesting plant materials, first hang them to dry thoroughly, about a week or two. When you're ready to craft, allow them to mellow for about 30 minutes in very warm water, until they are pliable. They need to bend in half without snapping. Sixteen rushes or tubes should suffice.

If you don't have suitable plant material, you can use paper instead. Newspaper or a brown paper shopping bag is perfect. You'll also need glue, a rod for rolling the tubes, and acrylic paint (optional). Your rolling rod must be straight, about ⅛ inch thick.

The length and width of your paper strips depends on the finished size you're aiming for. Using strips of 2¾-by-17 inches results in tubes of about 16 inches long. After folding together, tie and trim the ends to result in a Brigid's Cross of about 12 inches in diameter.

A. Take your paper strip with the long edge nearest you and set a paperweight on the far corner. Hold your rod at a 30-degree angle to the paper and tuck one of the corners closest to you fully around the rod to begin your tube. Make sure the paper is wrapped completely and snugly around the rod.

B. Apply a thin line of glue near the edge of the paper on the short ends and along the long edge farthest from you. Now slowly roll the rod away from you, maintaining your 30-degree angle and keeping the paper snugly fitted around the entire time. Allow the glue to dry. You can paint the tubes now if you like, so the glue and paint dry at the same time. If using acrylic paints, water them down a bit and apply thin coats so the tubes are not too stiff and the paint doesn't crack when bent.

C. To assemble your cross, bend a tube or rush in half. Bend a second tube and interlock them, holding them at a right angle with one arm facing straight up, and the other to your left.

D. Now it changes slightly: take a third tube, bend it in half, and wrap it outside the arm facing upward. Snug it all the way down at the base near the center of your cross. Now rotate the entire thing a quarter turn, 90 degrees, to the left.

E. Do the same again: take a tube and fold it in half, wrap it entirely around the arm facing upward, snug it at the base near the center of the cross, and rotate a quarter turn to the left. Repeat until you've used all your tubes, or it just looks nice to you, with an even number of tubes on each arm. Tie off the ends and trim as you like.

A

B

C

D

E

The Bridey Doll

For this ritual craft, you'll need a handful of dried wheat, rye, or oat stalks, for a total bunch of about 1 inch in diameter. Remove six stalks and set aside. Your stalks can either have the heads still on (the spike that houses the kernels) or they can be trimmed, depending on your aesthetic. Submerge all your grain in a tub of warm water for at least a half hour. It can be helpful to wrap them all in a large towel first in order to keep them submerged. Soaking the grain makes it pliable and easier to work with. After they've mellowed, remove them from the water and unwrap the towel. Squeeze, without twisting, to remove as much water as possible.

A. Tie the end of your straw bundle together with an elastic or twine. Trim the ends evenly to the tie is within a half inch of the trimmed ends.

B. Holding the trimmed end of the bundle, bend the stalks back over themselves, over the place where you've tied them together, until all the stalks are bent over and the tie is no longer visible. Tie another piece of twine around the bundle, about 1½-by-2 inches below the top, and now you have a head. Take your loose stalks and cut them into approximately 6-inch lengths. This bundle will become the arms. Tie the ends with twine, leaving enough excess to look like small hands.

C. Insert the arms into the middle of your bundle and slide up to about a half inch below the neck of your doll.

D. Tie another piece of twine where you'd like the waist to be. Now you're ready to adorn your doll with fabric, dried flowers, ribbons, seashells, stones, and beads. Warm up your glue gun and have fun!

I grow a few square feet of wheat and oats for crafts like this every year. But dried grasses and grains can easily be found through florists and online sources like Etsy.

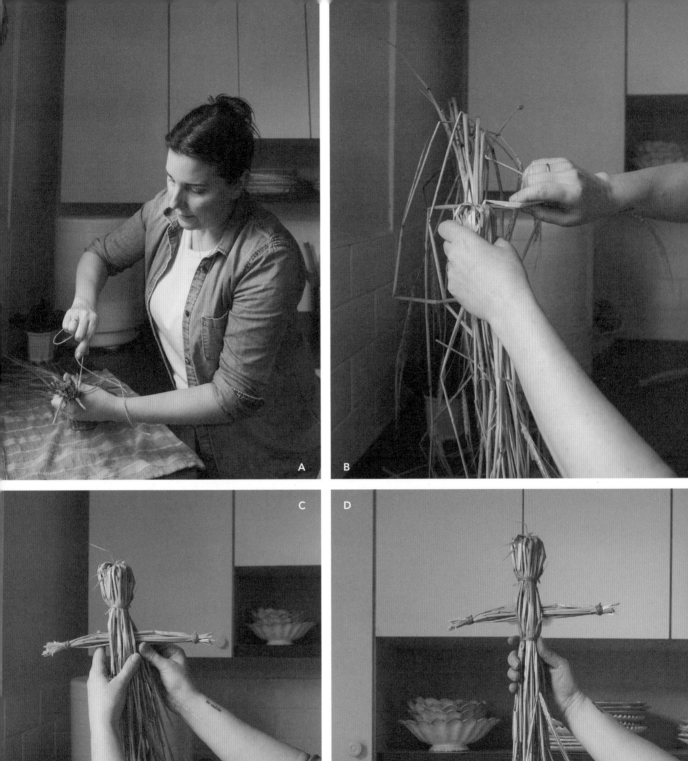

BRUNCH OF SIMPLE SUSTENANCE ———

This menu features ingredients that I'm lucky to be able to forage in this season where I live, which is just below the 49th parallel in a coastal climate. However, you can easily substitute spinach and baby brassicas for dandelion greens and nettles.

This is the type of menu that adapts well to the rhythm of a group—most of the dishes can be precooked. They can then be heated up for service in little more than the time it takes to clear away the craft debris, set the table, and serve drinks.

Gougères

Cheese is a traditional celebratory food at Imbolc because the cows' milk supply is starting to increase. These bite-sized cheese puffs are a charming yet savory way to add substance and style to a humble cheese board. Gougères are made using the pâte à choux technique, which cooks the dough slightly in a pot. The flour and liquid together is called the panade. You'll need to stir the panade continuously over low heat until it reaches 170°F, so have your meat or candy thermometer handy.

MAKES ABOUT 3 DOZEN

1 cup water

½ cup butter, cut into ½-inch cubes

1¼ cups all-purpose flour

4 eggs

Salt and freshly ground black pepper

2 cups grated Emmentaler or Gruyère cheese

Freshly grated nutmeg

1 egg yolk, beaten for egg wash

¼ cup finely grated Parmesan for garnish

1. Preheat the oven to 375°F. In a saucepan over medium-high heat, bring the water and butter to a boil. Remove from the heat and add all the flour at once, stirring quickly to remove lumps.

2. Turn down the heat to low and return the saucepan, stirring the dough for another full minute, until the dough pulls away from the sides of the pan and forms a ball. Use a meat or candy thermometer to test the center of your ball of dough: you're finished this step when it reads 170°F. Turn off the heat and keep stirring to cool the dough slightly before you add the eggs.

3. Add the eggs one at a time, stirring to fully incorporate between each one. You may feel despair that you've ruined the pastry dough, that it will never come back together again, but keep stirring briskly and it will. You can do this part in a stand mixer on medium speed; just make sure you still add the eggs slowly, one at a time, fully incorporating between each addition.

4. Once you've added all the eggs, you should have a smooth, dewy, thick, sticky batter.

5. Once the dough is of uniform consistency, sticky and smooth, then you can incorporate the cheese and nutmeg. Do not overmix from here, just stir the cheese in lightly. You don't want it fully melted—we like chunks of cheese! Season with some salt and pepper.

6. Fit a piping bag with a round tip and fill the bag with your dough. Alternatively, you can use the 2-spoon method and drop balls of dough onto a parchment-lined baking sheet. Pipe balls about the size of a walnut, about 2 inches apart. Glaze with egg wash, top with some Parmesan and more pepper, then place in the oven on the top rack. Do not open the door for the next 25 minutes. The gougères are finished when they are a deep golden color. Serve immediately or allow to cool, then freeze. To reheat, simply place frozen gougères in a hot oven for 5 to 7 minutes.

✦ *continued*

Juniper "Saffron" Syrup

This syrup honors the spring crocus, the flower that alerted Demeter that her daughter Persephone would soon be home from her long winter journey through the Underworld. Whenever I make myself this drink, a voice whispers in my mind, Persephone returns! Most North American gardeners are familiar with Crocus vernus, the spring-blooming crocus with stamens that are safe for human consumption. This is not true of autumn flowering crocuses, Colchicum autumnale, which are toxic. Spring crocus stamens have a very similar though less concentrated flavor than true saffron, Crocus sativus, which blooms in fall.

MAKES ABOUT 12 OUNCES OF SYRUP

1 cup water

1 cup sugar

5 dried juniper berries, crushed

Stamens from 10 to 12 spring crocus flowers

Bring the water and sugar to a boil, stirring to completely dissolve the sugar. Once boiling, remove from the heat, add the juniper and crocus stamens, and allow to cool. Taste to determine whether you'd like a stronger flavor. You could remove the juniper and add more crocus stamens, for instance, or vice versa. If you choose to add more flavoring, simply bring to a simmer then remove from the heat and allow to cool again. Once you've landed on a flavor profile you enjoy, strain into a glass jar with a well-fitted lid. This will keep for at least a month refrigerated.

A refreshing way to enjoy this syrup is to pour 1 to 2 ounces over ice and top with 4 to 6 ounces of soda water. Add 1 ounce of vodka or gin to create a botanical cocktail. This syrup can also be brushed on pound cake or drizzled over cheese and crackers.

Dandelion and Pine Nut Tart

Milk-producing plants are representative of Brigid and earth goddesses. Dandelions are often included in this holiday as both decor and mealtime fare due to the milky sap from their cut stems. I grow Italian red dandelions from seed in pots on the windowsill through winter to hurry spring along.

I like to use a 14-by-4-inch-long rectangular tart pan for this, which is equivalent to a 9-inch round. You'll blind bake this tart crust first, which you can do a day in advance. This crust recipe, adapted from chef and food writer J. Kenji López-Alt, is modified for savory pies with slightly different ratios to create a bit more toothsome mouthfeel.

SERVES 6 TO 8 AS PART OF A BUFFET, OR 4 AS AN ENTRÉE. MAKES 1 STANDARD-SIZED PIE OR TART

SAVORY TART DOUGH

1¼ cups all-purpose flour

½ teaspoon fine sea salt

1 cup very cold butter cut into ¼-inch cubes

2 to 3 tablespoons very cold water

DANDELION AND PINE NUT FILLING

2 cups chopped leeks

2 tablespoons butter

2 tablespoons olive oil

1 cup full fat milk (at least 3%)

Salt and freshly ground black pepper

Herbs for seasoning

2 to 3 cups tender dandelion leaves, cleaned and roughly chopped

3 eggs

½ cup pine nuts

✦ *continued*

TO MAKE THE SAVORY
TART DOUGH

Add ⅔ cup of the flour plus the salt to the bowl of a food processor. Pulse a few times to combine. Then add all the butter in an evenly distributed layer and pulse about a dozen times. Scrape the edges of the bowl and continue to pulse until the dough begins to gather into itself in clumps. The butter chunks will be quite a bit smaller than the usual pea-sized chunks of traditional methods. Sprinkle with the remaining flour and pulse four or five times, just until the dough has broken up again. By this point, the dough will look somewhat shaggy. Transfer to a mixing bowl.

Sprinkle the water evenly over the surface of the dough and fold it onto itself, pressing it together into a ball as you incorporate the water. Turn your dough out onto a well-floured surface. Roll out to your needed shape to line your tart pan. Don't be afraid to use plenty of additional flour for sprinkling. Once you've lined your tart pan, wrap with plastic wrap, and chill for at least 2 hours before baking.

Preheat the oven to 350°F. To bake, remove the tart pan from the fridge and line the surface with aluminum foil or parchment, allowing the edge to overhang your crust, protecting the top edge from over-browning. You can use rice, beans, or plain white sugar for your pie weights—the advantage of sugar being that you can use it again for cooking, but you'll need to throw out rice or beans (or reuse them for blind baking). Bake for 30 minutes. Remove the foil and bake 15 minutes more until the bottom of the tart shell is dry. Remove from the oven and cool completely before filling.

TO MAKE THE DANDELION
AND PINE NUT FILLING

Sauté the leeks in the butter and olive oil on low heat until well softened but not browned, 15 to 20 minutes. Add the milk and bring to a simmer then remove from heat. (Can be made a day ahead.)

Preheat the oven to 400°F. Use a fork to remove the leeks from the milk and spread evenly along the bottom of the prebaked crust, reserving the milk for later. Season with salt and pepper and your favorite herbs if you like. Sprinkle the chopped dandelion greens evenly over top.

Break the eggs into the reserved milk and whisk until thoroughly blended and smooth. Carefully pour over your crust fillings. Use as much custard as you can without risking spills. Transfer the pan to the oven. Sprinkle the pine nuts evenly on top and place in the oven. Bake until the top has nicely browned and the nuts are toasty, about 35 minutes.

IMBOLC

Mushroom, Nettle, and Barley Soup

Mushrooms are associated with otherworldly wisdom, a gift we hope to bring back with us as we emerge from the Underworld. Fresh button, cremini, and porcini mushrooms are best for this soup. Special and delicate varieties such as oyster and chanterelle can be dry sautéed separately and added to individual dishes right before service. If you don't have access to nettles to forage, ask at your farmers' market or substitute Swiss chard.

The method I lay out here is the best format for entertaining. The barley isn't added from the beginning because it's an endless absorber—over time it will become mushy and over-thicken your soup. If you want to cook everything together for a quick meal-à-la-minute, then add the barley at the same time as the mushroom stock.

Makes about 12 servings

1 cup pearl barley

1 teaspoon sea salt

¼ cup olive oil or butter, or blend of both

2 cups chopped sweet onions (Vidalia, Maui, or Walla Walla variety)

Salt

6 garlic cloves, finely chopped

2 tablespoons fresh thyme leaves, or 1 tablespoon dried

3 cups mixed brown mushrooms, sliced if small, roughly chopped if large

2 quarts mushroom or beef stock

Freshly ground black pepper

Herbs for seasoning (optional)

Mushroom or beef bouillon paste for flavoring (optional)

2 to 3 cups nettle leaves, cleaned and stems removed, roughly chopped to ½-inch pieces

½ cup finely grated pecorino or Parmesan cheese (optional)

Bring a liter of water to boil then add the barley plus the sea salt. Reduce to a vigorous simmer and cook until the barley is tender, approximately 30 minutes. When chewy but not hard, drain and rinse with cold water. (Can be made a few days in advance, kept refrigerated until ready to assemble your soup for service.)

Heat the oil over low heat in a soup pot with a well-fitting lid. Add the onions and season with salt, then cover. Allow to cook, stirring occasionally, until the onions are very soft and slightly caramelized, about 15 minutes. Stir in the garlic and thyme and continue to cook another 2 minutes. Meanwhile, dry cook the mushrooms over medium-high heat in a large enough frying pan that they are no more than 1 inch deep in the pan. Stir frequently enough that they don't burn, but allow them to rest long enough on the heat to develop some nice, dark charred colors. You want them to expel all their moisture and become nicely browned. Remove from heat when finished. (Can be made a few days in advance and kept tightly sealed in the refrigerator.)

When both the onions and mushrooms are ready, add the mushrooms to the pot full of onions and combine well. Add the mushroom stock and bring to a boil. Check the flavorings and season to taste with more salt, pepper, herbs, or bouillon paste to your preference. When ready to serve, add the nettles and stir well, allowing them a moment to wilt. Add the barley to the soup pot or individual serving dishes and ladle the broth over top. Pass the grated cheese for guests to garnish as desired.

No-Knead Seed Bread

MAKES ONE 8- TO 10-INCH LOAF

1½ cups warm water (no hotter than 110°F)

3 tablespoons honey

2 teaspoons salt

1 tablespoon active dry yeast

⅓ cup sunflower seeds, toasted

3 tablespoons pumpkin seeds, toasted

¼ cup small seed mix, such as black or white sesame, millet, flax, poppy, or chia

3 cups flour, plus extra flour for dusting (you can add up to ¾ cup whole wheat flour for a nuttier flavor, but more than that won't work for this method)

Brigid and Imbolc are strongly associated with seeds since they carry our dreams for the future, which makes this bread as perfect for the altar as it is to accompany soup. No-knead-style breads require a Dutch oven with a well-fitted lid and often require a 24-hour ferment. This recipe uses more yeast and a shorter rest time. Your Dutch oven should be at least 5 quarts (about 4 inches deep and 10-by-12 inches in diameter).

Measure a piece of parchment paper to fit into your Dutch oven, like a little basket with a 1-inch overhang all around. This is used to lift your bread out and prevent it from sticking to your pot. Once you've measured the parchment paper, remove the

paper from the Dutch oven and set it flat on the countertop for later.

Combine the warm water, honey, and salt in a large bowl. Stir to dissolve the honey then sprinkle the yeast in a single layer on top. Leave untouched in a warm place for 5 minutes. Mix the seeds all together and set aside 2 tablespoons for later. Add the flour and seeds to the yeast mixture and stir with a spatula until well combined. It will be very sticky and that's just fine. Loosely cover with a clean tea towel or plastic wrap and let sit until tripled in volume, probably about 2 hours or more at standard room temperature.

Use a spatula to fold the dough in half then fold in half again. Sprinkle generously with flour. With well-floured hands, lift up the dough and form a ball in your hands, turning the loaf over and tucking the folds into the center of the underside. Place on your parchment paper on the countertop, seam side down. Sprinkle with your reserved seed blend. Let rise uncovered at room temp for 45 minutes.

Put the lid on your Dutch oven and place it in the oven while it preheats to 450°F.

Once preheated, remove the Dutch oven and place it on the stove. This pot will be absolutely molten hot—do not touch without oven mitts! Holding the parchment paper "basket," lift the dough and carefully place it in your Dutch oven. Cover it with the lid and place it in the oven for 30 minutes. Remove the hot lid and bake the loaf another 5 minutes, or until the top is golden brown. Remove from the oven and carefully use the parchment to lift the bread out of the pot. It must be almost completely cool before you slice into it or the crumb will not set up properly. Tempting as it is, it's better to completely cool and reheat the loaf than to slice it warm but too early.

Oatcakes with Orange Blossom Cream

Brigid is known for transforming seed to grain with the help of the sun, represented here by oranges. This recipe is both perfect for the season and a nostalgic homage to my family. My grandmother's signature brunch dish was Crêpes Suzette, which she doused in Grand Marnier and 80 proof rum and set aflame. It was all a little much for my young palate and possibly not quite legal. This is my all-ages alternative.

Oatcakes are not as thick as pancakes, not as eggy as crêpes, but a toothsome middle ground inspired by Scottish historian F. Marian McNeill's sooty bannocks.

MAKES ABOUT A DOZEN 8-INCH OATCAKES

OATCAKES

1½ cups oats

1¼ to 1½ cups milk

3 eggs

½ cup melted butter

2 tablespoons demerara sugar

1 tablespoon orange flower water

½ teaspoon vanilla or 1 inch of vanilla bean pod scraped, pod reserved for the whipping cream

½ teaspoon cinnamon

Zest of 1 orange

1 teaspoon butter

VANILLA ORANGES

4 sweet and juicy oranges, peeled, seeds removed, and chopped into ¼-inch pieces, about 3 cups

2 to 3 inches of vanilla bean pod, scraped (again, pop that scraped pod into the cream for added aroma)

2 tablespoons orange flower water

1 tablespoon confectioners' sugar

ORANGE BLOSSOM CREAM

1 cup whipping cream (vanilla pods removed and discarded)

1 teaspoon confectioners' sugar

½ to 1 teaspoon orange flower water

½ teaspoon vanilla extract

TO MAKE THE OAT CAKES

Blend all the ingredients except the 1 teaspoon unmelted butter in a high speed mixer until very smooth. Drop the vanilla bean pod into your whipping cream to infuse until you're ready to whip it.

Melt a teaspoon of butter into a wide cast-iron or non-stick pan. Pour ⅓ cup of batter into the center of your hot pan. Use a spatula to pull the edges of the batter outward. Keep gently pulling the batter into any gaps or tears, smoothing out the surface of your oatcake, until there's no more wet batter remaining on the top of your oatcake. When the edges start to brown, flip your oatcake to briefly brown the other side. This whole process should take about 3 minutes. Place on a warm cookie sheet in the oven when it's done, covering it with tin foil to prevent it drying out.

TO MAKE THE VANILLA ORANGES

Mix all the ingredients together and place in the refrigerator for an hour or overnight.

TO MAKE THE ORANGE BLOSSOM CREAM

Remove the vanilla bean pod and whip together all the ingredients until just a little past the soft peak stage but not yet stiff.

Serve the oatcakes with the vanilla oranges inside the rolled up oatcake and on top, with a big dollop of scented whipped cream.

CHAPTER FOUR

Ostara

"The beautiful spring came; and when Nature resumes her loveliness, the human soul is apt to revive also."
—Harriet Jacobs

Now is the time for a fresh start, a new chapter, and a chance to renew our dreams. Like the Persian New Year festival, Nowruz (meaning "new day"), Ostara is celebrated at the vernal equinox on March 20 or 21, and heralds a preparatory season of hope and new life. The work of spring is to initiate what will be the rewards of summer. The equinox is the moment we weave the details of our plans together. The emphasis now is on capability, competency, and working toward a brighter future for the collective. We celebrate new beginnings, the stirrings of growth, and signs of vitality. Green shoots are pushing up through the soil, chickens are laying more eggs, and it's time to sow the wheat.

Now is a perfect time for the spellcraft of daily life. Domestic tasks and crafts have always lent themselves to ritualization because of their transformative effects: roadside plants become a basket to manifest abundance, flour and eggs become a love magic dessert. Opportunities for practical magic abound. Our everyday tools, choice food stuffs, special bowls, bottles, and baskets become our ritual apparatus. Almost every mundane chore can be made potent by layering it with spiritual significance, which is exactly what we'll do as we weave a small basket for the altar.

This season, we celebrate deities who possess a good work ethic, a cheerful outpouring of generosity, and bring fertility, such as the Norse goddess Freya. We call those who help lay the groundwork for abundance, such as Hathor, the Egyptian cow goddess who labors to deliver her calf, the sun, every morning. We might honor Anna Perenna, the Roman goddess of spring who spins the Wheel of the Year. The spell jars you create this season can combine mundane ingredients in symbolic ways to invoke the power of a spring deity to support your endeavors.

Ostara is the name of an Anglo-Saxon spring goddess connected with agriculture and the dawn. Actually, that's pretty much all we can say about her for certain. She's related linguistically to Eostre, the Germanic pagan goddess who is first mentioned in the 8th century in a text by the Venerable Bede. Ostara is associated with fertility, rejoicing, and triumph over winter, and has come to be linked with the rabbit as her escort and colored eggs as her symbol.

The rabbit is a commonsense symbol of spring because of their high reproduction rate and large spring litters. But there's more than this to their symbolism. Because rabbits are so fast and difficult to hunt, quickly disappearing in hedges and underground tunnels, they carry a mythology around shape-shifting. The connection between the Easter bunny and shape-shifting is recorded in Germany in the mid-1880s when stories were told of a bird that laid the most beautiful colored eggs. The goddess Ostara changed this bird into a hare that took on the role of her swift messenger. Every spring this rabbit lays colorful eggs in remembrance of their earlier form.

Like many of the symbols associated with seasonal festivals, rabbits and eggs are connected to Ostara less because of ancient goddess cults and more because of the everyday lived experience of our agrarian ancestors—eggs and rabbits are abundant in springtime. Take a look outside your window. What are the signs that herald spring where you are? Remember, if any aspect of the celebrations as I describe them seem out of touch with where you're at, use what you have where you are. Worship the sacred in your local little brown birds, swelling waterways, or emerging plants. Ask the wind to inspire the right deity to come to you, bringing with them hope and renewal.

Spell Jars

Vessel spells are a form of folk magic common to Anglo-American, African American, African, European, as well as Latinx cultures, making them a fairly pan-cultural magical working. To create a spell jar, begin with a strong and clear intention. Then gather the items and elements that match and amplify your intention, plus a lidded vessel to contain them.

Spell jars are like seeds of magic you plant to grow an intention. Expect the work of spring equinox spell jars to develop over time and bear fruit on or before the autumn equinox. You place symbolic ingredients in a vessel and bind them with a wish, then the magic incubates inside and reveals itself in the material world over time. Use a spell jar to attract a deity or a life circumstance you desire, such as calmness, prosperity, or companionship. The vessel and everything that goes inside must be absolutely dry. I like to balance the elements by adding a feather for air, a dead bee to represent the sun and fire, a seashell for water, and a stone or dried flowers for earth. I use bones and dried snapdragon seed pods (because they look like little skulls) to represent ancestors generally, and dried heather or oat florets for my Scottish heritage specifically. To amplify the magic, I sometimes place a coil of copper wire inside or use it to wrap around the bottle if I'm going to hang it from a tree.

The charms and color of wax I use to seal the magic are especially important to me. I buy vintage charm bracelets and deconstruct thrift shop jewelry to find my charms. The charm is like a homing beacon for the deity or guide I'm calling in, and the color of the wax seal signals the emotional note I want to hit with the spell. See the "Magical Correspondences" section on page 235 for more guidance on ingredients. You might want to write in your grimoire: "My intention with regard to [current troubling situation] is to experience [desired outcome]. I fill this spell jar with [ingredient] to represent [magical correspondence], and [ingredient] to represent [magical correspondence], as well as . . . etc."

Think about your ideal outcome as you fill the jar. Bind your spell with an affirmation as you seal the vessel, such as a phrase like, *My word is firm.* You can keep your jar on your altar, bury it outside, or hang it like an ornament on a sacred tree.

COMPLEMENTARY
Stones

When obtaining stones for magical purposes, it's prudent to be mindful of some ethical considerations. How do you feel, emotionally and energetically, about harvesting stones from the earth and the context in which that happens? I used to love attending mineral shows and buying crystals. I get it—I love shiny things, too! But now I can't help thinking about the extractive violence rampant in the global mineral mining industry.

If I purchase crystals, I do so from family-run businesses where I've developed an honest working relationship with someone who cares about where their product comes from and who purchases directly from small family-owned mines. I buy from countries where enslaved labor, including prison labor, is illegal and unlikely. (This narrows the field quite a lot.) I've started swapping stones and crystals with friends. Why not organize a stone swap on social media? Everybody loves snail mail! That way, nobody is buying more crystals and everyone periodically gets to spend time with new rock friends.

Offering Baskets

Basket weaving is both meditative and fulfilling. It connects us to ancestors from around the world who wove grasses and wood fibers into containers, sleeping mats, shields, clothing, and almost anything else you can think of—even entire homes! The weaving technique we're using here is called "twining," where long dried grasses are twisted around flat spokes of rush.

As you weave, contemplate your intention as you work. In this way, the process becomes a manifestation ritual. You'll end up with an object that anchors your intention in the physical world. While basket weaving lends itself well to Virgo tendencies, I personally just want to develop basic competence that enables me to pick up whatever materials I have on hand and fashion something I could humbly place on the altar, as my ancestors might have done. In other words, don't get too caught up trying to make the most flawless basket. Focus on your intention as much as execution.

A collection of long dried grasses such as daylily leaves, iris leaves, long dandelion stems, morning glory vines, thin plantain stems, the outer fiber from long rhubarb stalks (for pink twine), or sedge grasses (see Note)

8 to 16 pieces, about 10 to 12 inches long, of dried rush (also called freshwater bulrush; see Note)

A thicker piece of material for the rim, such as a piece of dried vine

A spray bottle of water

Scissors

Wrap your dried weaving materials in a towel and submerge the towel in a basin or bathtub of warm water for at least 30 minutes or up to an hour. Remove from the water and squeeze to expel as much water as possible, but keep the materials in the towel so they don't dry out. If you notice your materials starting to get papery feeling while you're weaving, spray them with water.

A. The dried rush will become the base and spokes of your basket. Lay two of them horizontally on your work surface and weave two of them in vertically, alternating in a check weave. Keep adding spokes evenly around all four sides, weaving over one, under one. Make sure you tighten the weave after each new spoke is added and try to keep your rushes centered in length so you don't have one short side and one long side.

B. To start twining material onto your spokes, tie the ends of two pieces of long dried grass together in a knot.

C. Loop the grasses around one of the spokes.

D. Take the left piece of material and cross over the spoke you just looped it around, and tuck it

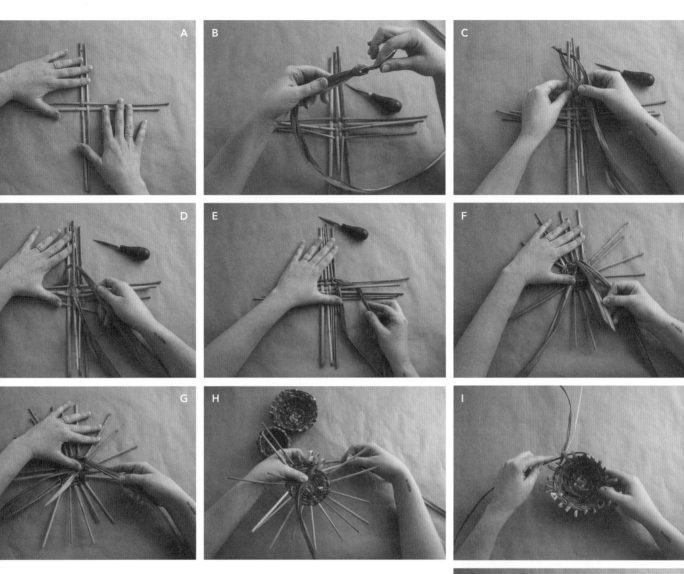

 _____

You can substitute another plant here, but the key is that it's both spongy and flexible. It needs to be spongy so it forms a flat base for your basket, and flexible so the spokes don't break when you bend them up to create the sides of your vessel. Plantain stems can work for small baskets, or tender cattail with outer leaves removed.

How much dried material you need depends on how big you want your offering basket to be. For a basket about 6 to 8 inches in diameter, the diameter of your bundle of materials should be at least 1 inch thick.

_____

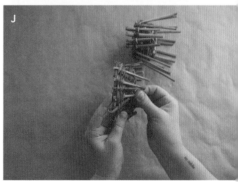

* continued

OSTARA

behind the next spoke to the right, then bring it back in front.

The piece you've just moved has now moved to the forward position. Keep working with the left piece of material, pulling it across the front of the central spoke and looping it behind and around the next spoke to the right, coming back to rest in the forward (right) position. Continue with this until you reach the corner.

E. At the corners, you're still following this same weave pattern, but grab two spokes at a time. This will help you put a curve on the corner. Continue grabbing two spokes at a time at the corners until you have the height and diameter you want, then go back to weaving each spoke individually if you like. For the first few rows, you might even want to weave more tightly around corners to achieve a stronger circular shape off your square base. Corners are a place where you can experiment and play with your design.

F. When your piece of twining material is becoming short and almost running out, just 2 inches left or so, simply layer a fresh piece of material over top and blend it into the usual weave pattern. You will wind up with wayward ends that can be trimmed later. If you have a spoke that breaks, the fix is to unweave a couple of rows and tuck a new spoke in, overlapping the broken one by at least ¾ inch, then weave it securely into place.

G. Eventually, you'll want to start creating the sides of your basket. Just bend the spokes up to the angle degree you'd like and continue weaving.

H. When you have only about 3 to 4 inches of spoke remaining, fold it down to create a loop and weave that into place.

I. Thread your vine or rim piece through the looped spokes. Add at least three more rows of weaving to secure the loops and rim in place.

J. Now pull the spokes down tightly. Allow the basket to dry completely before cutting the excess material away, including the overhang from the spokes. Your basket is ready for your altar!

WEAVING

Intentions

Possible intentions to weave into your baskets, repeating to yourself like a mantra as you work:

I am open to receiving more abundance in my life.
I am weaving more joy into my life.
I am worthy of more support and ease in my life.
I gratefully receive blessings and prosperity in my life.

Botanical Print Eggs

Decorated eggs are a form of prayer. Like a prayer, they are ephemeral and impermanent. After your egg has adorned your altar, you can bury it like a seed so your prayer comes to pass.

Full eggs are easier to handle when it comes to dyeing, so I dye mine first, then blow them out. You'll want to purchase free-range organic eggs for this craft because factory eggs have very thin shells and will often explode when you blow them out, which is especially vexing after you've done so much work to color them. Ideally, your eggs will come from the farmer washed only with water, not soap, and only wiped gently, not scrubbed. Your dye will penetrate just a thin layer of the shell, and if soap is used it may leave a film that prevents the dye from absorbing and reveal any scratches in the final result.

DYEING SOLUTIONS

1 quart water

3 tablespoons turmeric (makes yellow)

4 cups finely chopped red beets (makes pink)

4 cups roughly chopped red cabbage (makes blue)

4 packed cups yellow onion skins, about a dozen medium onions (makes orange-gold)

Add the water and dye ingredients to a large pot. Bring to a boil, then lower the heat and simmer for 1 hour. Strain the dye into a glass jar or stainless steel bowl and allow to come to room temperature.

BOTANICAL PRINTS

A few herbs, leaves, or flowers

A small paintbrush

Well-beaten egg white

Some nylons

Scissors

Paint the foliage with some egg white, then paste it onto the egg. Make a knot in the end of the nylon and place the egg inside, making sure that the knot doesn't cover the foliage. Make a knot on the other end, pulling the nylon so it is flat and firmly pressed against the egg, but not pulled super tight. Cut off the nylon, make another loop knot, and continue wrapping the eggs this way. Place the wrapped eggs in your dyeing solution. The colors you choose are symbolic of your hopes for the year ahead: yellows and oranges for solar blessings, hope, joy, strength, and endurance; pink for love and connection; light blue for the sky

✦ continued

and expansion; dark blue for wisdom and grace; greens for health and renewal; and purples for faith, patience, and wealth.

> Pale yellow: turmeric solution, 30 minutes.
> Light pink: beet solution, 30 minutes.
> Light blue: cabbage solution, 30 minutes.
> Royal blue: cabbage solution overnight.
> Lavender: beet solution, 30 minutes, followed by cabbage solution, 30 seconds.
> Chartreuse: turmeric solution, 30 minutes, followed by cabbage solution, 5 seconds.
> Salmon: turmeric solution, 30 minutes, followed by onion skin solution, 30 minutes.

Check your eggs periodically to see if you like their color. When you feel they're finished, remove with a slotted spoon and place on a baking rack to dry. Once completely dried, remove the nylon and foliage. Now you can blow them out.

Make a hole on the top of an egg with a strong, sharp needle. Then unfold a paper clip and insert it all the way into the egg and whip the contents as much as possible. Cover the hole with your finger and vigorously shake the egg to help liquefy the contents. Turn the egg over, hold it above a clean bowl, and create the bottom hole. Either use your mouth or a nasal aspirator to blow the contents of the egg into the bowl (and perhaps set in the refrigerator to use for the Deep Dish Nettle Quiche, page 133). Allow the shells to dry for at least an hour. The egg shells are ready for your altar, or they can be threaded onto a ribbon to create a garland.

COVEN LUNCHEON

This menu is ideal for a casual "crafternoon" with friends since every recipe is an easy make-ahead dish. This meal invokes the magical properties of herbs, eggs, and spring flowers, all key ingredients in fertility and/or creativity magic. Plus, quiche is a perfect choice since you'll have blown all those eggs for dyeing!

Floral Syrup

After a long winter, spring flowers are so precious and hopeful. This recipe can be used to connect with flower energies as they come into season, such as foraged gorse blossoms (also known as whin), early violets, or plum blossoms at Ostara, lilacs at Beltane, roses and lavender at Midsummer, and jasmine at Lughnasadh. Floral syrups are irresistible, easy-to-make love potions.

2 cups water

1 cup superfine white sugar

⅛ teaspoon citric acid (optional)

1 cup packed flower petals, stems and green parts completely removed (see Note)

Bring the water and sugar to a simmer, stirring the sugar to dissolve completely. Remove from the heat, stir in the citric acid to dissolve, and let sit for 5 minutes. Add petals and allow to sit uncovered until completely cooled then pour everything into a jar and place it in the fridge to continue infusing. After a week, use a funnel to strain the syrup into an easy-pour bottle with a tight-fitting lid.

Note: For flowers with very strong aromas such as lavender and gorse, as little as ¼ cup of flowers will suffice. Most important, all green parts of the flower must be completely removed or your results may be bitter and astringent.

This syrup can be added to soda, sparkling wine, and cocktails, or brushed onto white cake or drizzled over vanilla ice cream.

Golden Dip for Crudités

This golden dip invokes solar energies of vitality and radiance. It's a variation of Hollyhock Salad Dressing, named after the famous learning center on Cortes Island not too far from where I live, that seems to pair well with every vegetable.

MAKES ABOUT 2 CUPS

½ cup nutritional yeast flakes

¼ cup unsalted cashews

¼ cup apple cider or white wine vinegar, or a combination of both

¼ cup tamari or soy sauce

2 garlic cloves

1 cup light oil such as avocado, grapeseed, or sunflower

Salt and freshly ground black pepper (optional)

Place all the ingredients except the oil, salt, and pepper in a high-speed blender or a jar that your stick blender easily fits into and puree on high speed until smooth. With the blender running, slowly add the oil in a steady stream. Continue adding the oil until you are happy with the consistency. Taste-test using whatever vegetable you'll be serving with the dip and adjust seasonings as necessary. If you want a brighter flavor, add a touch more vinegar. Add salt or pepper, if using. If you find it too thick, you can always add a bit of water, 1 tablespoon at a time.

Duck and Rabbit Pâté en Croute

Ducks are magically associated with adaptability and freedom, since they're comfortable in all three realms of earth, sea, and sky. Like rabbits, they're also communal animals that symbolize strong social bonds and nurturance, which are good energies to invoke in spring or any time.

Make this in stages starting at least 2 days before you plan to serve. Remember, this is peasant food, so don't stress out about all the steps and ingredients. It's really just blended meat wrapped in pie dough. The Instacure or pink salt in this recipe will keep your pâté looking attractively pink, but as this is a fully cooked dish, it's okay to omit (your pâté will just look a little more gray in color when serving). Pink salt is very salty, so measure carefully.

MAKES A SMALL LOAF, APPROXIMATELY 8-BY-4-BY-3 INCHES

DUCK AND RABBIT FILLING

7 ounces skinless duck breast meat, cut into 1-inch cubes

4 ounces rabbit meat, roughly cut into ½-inch cubes, though if you have the tenderloin, that can be left whole (you can substitute chicken breast)

3 ounces chicken or rabbit livers, cubed

2 egg yolks

2 tablespoons cream

2 teaspoons fresh thyme leaves

½ teaspoon fennel seeds, crushed with a mortar and pestle or roughly ground in a spice grinder

½ teaspoon crushed juniper berries

½ teaspoon freshly ground black pepper

Scant ¼ teaspoon Instacure #1 or Prague Powder #1 or pink salt #1

¼ cup raw unsalted pistachios, roughly chopped

¼ cup fresh or dried cranberries, roughly chopped

PASTRY DOUGH

1¾ cups all-purpose flour

1 tablespoon plus 1 teaspoon kosher salt

½ cup chilled butter, cut into ½-inch cubes

2 egg yolks plus 1 egg, lightly beaten together

1 whole egg for decorative egg wash, well beaten (or you can use the extra egg whites, though you will end up with a lighter-colored pastry crust in the end without yolk or cream in the egg wash)

GELATIN

1 tablespoon unflavored gelatin powder or gelatin sheets following the manufacturer's instructions

1 cup chicken stock, cool or room temperature

TO MAKE THE DUCK AND RABBIT FILLING

Place all the meats except the rabbit tenderloin, if using, in a food processor. Pulse until the mixture looks like sausage meat—not whipped or pureed, but chunky and just beginning to emulsify slightly. Remove to a bowl and add all the remaining ingredients except the pistachios and cranberries. Using a wooden spoon, stir vigorously for at least a minute until very well combined. Toss the rabbit tenderloin on top, cover tightly, and allow it to rest overnight in the fridge.

 *continued*

TO MAKE THE PASTRY

In a food processor, pulse the flour and 1 tablespoon of kosher salt until combined. Add the butter and pulse until it forms large pea-sized crumbs (not tiny peas). Add the beaten eggs and continue pulsing just until the dough comes together. Transfer to a clean work surface and knead until smooth, about 2 minutes. Cut off about a third of the dough and flatten into a disc. Wrap separately; this will become the lid. Wrap all the dough in plastic wrap, and refrigerate for half an hour.

Preheat the oven to 350°F. Grease your loaf pan by brushing with oil, then line with a strip of parchment paper equal to the length of the pan, leaving several inches of overhang on the sides. These "wings" will become like a basket or lifter that will help you pull the pâté out of the pan when it's time to serve.

Roll the larger disc of dough out into a rectangle between ⅛ and ¼ inch thick and drop into your loaf pan, leaving at least a 1-inch overhang around the edges. Fix any cracks by pressing more dough into them.

Take the meat mixture from the fridge. Add the pistachios and cranberries to the meat and stir well to combine. Press half the meat mixture into the loaf pan. Make sure it is firmly pressed in and there are no gaps between the meat and the walls of the pastry. Lay the rabbit tenderloin down the center. Top with the remaining meat mixture, again ensuring there are no gaps along the sides between the meat and the pastry. You want to make sure that when you pour in the chicken stock, it remains on the top of the meat, not draining down little gaps in the sides of the terrine. The meat will shrink, so it won't be perfect, but do your best.

Roll out the smaller disc of pastry to the same thickness and lay it over the top of the meat mixture like a lid. Trim and crimp the edges so they stand proud and decorative above the edge of your loaf pan. Using a straw or just the tip of a knife, cut a few small holes into the pastry lid, each at least ¼ inch in diameter. This will release steam as the pâté cooks, helping to prevent cracks in your pastry. It's also how you will get the gelatin into your pâté after it has been baked and chilled. Cut shapes out of the remaining pastry dough and use a well-beaten egg wash to attach. Brush the entire top of the loaf in egg wash to finish.

Bake until the pastry is golden in color and the internal temperature reaches at least 165°F, about an hour. Remove from the oven and cool to room temperature, then transfer to the refrigerator.

TO MAKE THE GELATIN

In a small bowl, combine the gelatin powder with ¼ cup of chicken stock and whisk until completely combined. Bring the rest of the stock to a simmer in a small pot, then remove from heat and add the gelatin-stock mixture, whisking well until the gelatin is completely dissolved. Remove from heat and cool to room temperature.

Using a small funnel or a homemade foil chimney, carefully pour the stock into the vent holes of the pastry. Return to the refrigerator and chill until set, at least 8 hours, preferably overnight. To serve, run a knife around the top edge of the loaf pan to free any pastry that might have baked on. Holding the parchment paper "wings" carefully lift the pâté en croute from the loaf pan. Cut into ½-inch slabs and serve with a selection of mustards and pickles.

Stout Onion Soup

Onions carry the same protective magic as other alliums, such as garlic, but with an additional emotional depth. Not only does their name derive from the Latin unio *(meaning "unity or wholeness"), but they also have the unique ability to elicit our tears. As such, they're connected to spiritual purification and healing.*

MAKES ABOUT 8 CUPS

3 medium onions

½ cup butter

¼ cup flour

6 cups beef broth

1 cup stout or sherry

Salt and freshly ground black pepper

Grated Parmesan or Swiss cheese

Fresh bread

Peel and finely slice the onions into half-moons. Slice these in half again. Heat the butter over medium heat then add the onions. Stir and cook over medium heat until they are slightly caramelized and soft, about 15 minutes. Don't let them get too dark or the soup will be bitter.

Add the flour and stir until the onions are coated. Add the broth and stout, and bring to a boil. Lower the heat to a simmer and cover the soup. Let it simmer for another 10 minutes or so, lifting the lid at the end to let it reduce a little. Taste and season with salt and pepper. Serve with grated cheese and fresh bread.

Spring Zing Vinaigrette

Serve a salad of spring greens and edible flowers such as violets, pansies, and early bachelor's buttons, and toss with this brightly flavored vinaigrette.

1 small finely minced shallot

1 tablespoon finely minced dill

1 tablespoon finely minced chives

1 tablespoon finely minced chervil, if available

2 teaspoons sherry vinegar

½ teaspoon Dijon mustard

¼ teaspoon sea salt

Pinch of sugar

Freshly cracked black pepper

3 tablespoons olive oil

Combine all the ingredients except for the olive oil and allow to marinate for 10 minutes to meld the flavors and temper the shallot. Then slowly add the olive oil while stirring with a fork, or simply add to a jar, seal the lid, and shake vigorously. If it's too thick, you can add a teaspoon of water. Toss your greens right before serving; ensure they are evenly coated with herbs, and season with salt and pepper.

Deep Dish Nettle Quiche

Stinging nettles are a favorite plant ally of mine, but you can substitute spinach, chard, or dandelion leaves in this recipe. Magically speaking, nettles bless us with communal resilience, something we might need after a long winter stuck indoors. Nettles for eating should be harvested when they're under a foot tall. And, does it need to be said? I suppose it does: Be careful, they sting! Wear thick leather gloves and loose-fitting long sleeves and pants.

Double the Savory Tart Dough recipe from the Dandelion and Pine Nut Tart (page 105) and follow the instructions in that recipe to roll out and line the pie pan. Be sure to give the edge a nice high decorative crimp. Chill for at least 2 hours before filling.

MAKES A 9-INCH PIE, 3 INCHES DEEP

1½ cups grated semi-hard cheese (cheddar, Edam, Gruyère, or a combination of many kinds is fine)

1 tablespoon flour

Savory Tart Dough (page 105) doubled, chilled in a pie pan

2 tablespoons butter

1 small onion, finely chopped

2 packed cups fresh stinging nettles, washed and roughly chopped (use rubber dishwashing gloves)

1 tablespoon fresh thyme leaves

½ teaspoon salt, plus an an extra pinch

6 eggs

1½ cups light cream

1 tablespoon Dijon mustard

Pinch of nutmeg

¼ teaspoon freshly ground black pepper

Preheat the oven to 400°F. Toss the cheese and flour together and place in the bottom of the pastry-lined pie pan. Melt the butter in a saucepan over medium heat and add the onion. Sauté, stirring frequently, until the onions are soft and beginning to brown, about 5 minutes. Add the nettles and stir constantly, until they are wilted and soft but still bright green in color. Add the thyme and cook for 1 more minute. Sprinkle with a pinch of salt and remove from heat. Allow to cool slightly so it won't immediately melt the cheese when you place it in the pie. Whisk the eggs in a medium bowl until completely smooth and frothy. Add the cream, Dijon, nutmeg, salt, and pepper, and mix together well.

Scatter the sautéed nettles and onions evenly in the bottom of the pie dish. Pour the egg mixture evenly on top, to within ½ inch of the lip of your crust. Bake for 45 minutes to an hour, until the pie is puffed, golden, the filling is beginning to crack at the outside edge, and the center is dry and no longer jiggly when you move the pie. Remove from the oven and allow to sit 15 minutes before slicing.

Note: If you want to use this as a make-ahead recipe, simply freeze the pie once you've filled it with custard, wrapping well in plastic wrap. It will easily keep for a month in the freezer. Then bake from frozen, simply adding about 45 to 60 minutes of cooking time.

Macarons Violettes

This quintessential French patisserie is actually Italian, dating back to the Renaissance and the court of Catherine de' Medici. But here again, we find connections to Nowruz since almond cakes were baked to celebrate the Zoroastrian New Year. It's via Persian contact in Sicily in the 800s that these cakes with sweet almond cream inside migrated into Italian culinary tradition. Almond desserts in spring are an ancient idea that we should definitely carry forward in every form imaginable.

You can make candied violets up to a week in advance. Violas and pansies will also look cute but they don't have the distinct perfume and flavor that violets do.

This recipe will easily double or triple without requiring modification, but if you're a beginner with macarons, it's really best to practice with just a small recipe. This is one of the few times when I follow a recipe exactly to the letter and use a kitchen scale to measure. Anything that touches your egg whites must be absolutely grease-free or your macarons will not succeed. So be sure to wipe down your spatula, the bowl and whisk of your standing mixer, and whatever you're cracking your eggs into, with a paper towel soaked with a bit of lemon juice.

Okay. Ready? Let's do this!

MAKES 1 DOZEN FILLED MACARONS

Focus

Note that macarons are not the type of thing you can start and then pause midway through the recipe. Once you press start on your mixer, you are committed and there should be no interruptions. Macarons require your focused attention—one might even say, devotion.

CANDIED VIOLETS

2 teaspoons meringue powder

2 tablespoons water

12 violets or other edible flowers

¼ cup superfine sugar (or granulated sugar pulsed in a food processor for 30 seconds)

MACARONS

75 grams room temperature egg whites (best if they are at least 2 weeks old—do not use carton egg whites)

95 grams confectioners' sugar

100 grams almond flour or meal

⅛ teaspoon cream of tartar

75 grams superfine granulated sugar (sometimes called berry sugar)

Gel food coloring

VIOLET BUTTERCREAM

¼ cup very soft unsalted butter

¾ cup confectioners' sugar

2 teaspoons Crème de Violette liqueur or 2 tablespoons homemade violet syrup (Floral Syrup, page 124, with or without petals strained out), or 1 teaspoon rosewater to make rose macarons

Gel food coloring (optional)

TO MAKE THE CANDIED VIOLETS

Mix the meringue powder in the water until completely dissolved. Hold the violet by the stem and use a paintbrush to coat the flower petals with the mixture, then sprinkle with superfine sugar. Place on a parchment-lined baking sheet and pinch the stem off. Allow them to dry overnight.

✦ continued

135

OSTARA

The figure 8 test

TO MAKE THE MACARONS

Make sure your egg whites are at room temperature: Leave them out on the counter for at least an hour.

In a food processor, pulse the confectioners' sugar and almond flour until very fine and all lumps are broken up. Sift this mixture into a mixing bowl and set aside.

Add the room temperature egg whites to the bowl of your standing mixer and blend on medium speed until frothy. Add the cream of tartar and continue to blend on medium for 1 minute. Slowly pour in the granulated sugar. After another minute of incorporation, pause mixing to scrape down the sides and bottom of your mixing bowl with *an absolutely grease-free* spatula. Then turn the mixer up to high speed and whisk until stiff peaks form, about 8 minutes more. It has to be really stiff! You should see sharp, pointy peaks.

Your meringue should be puffing up like a cloud in the center of the bowl rather than a smooth wave from edge to center. In fact, the meringue should be pulling away from the sides of the bowl and gathering into itself in the center of your whisk. If you remove your whisk from the mixer, the meringue should stick to it in a fairly solid mass and seem almost like a marshmallow texture.

Now STOP.

Color your meringue with gel food coloring, a little bolder than you want it to be in the end. Mix the food coloring in thoroughly with the mixer on high speed.

Now add about a third of the almond mixture into the meringue. Using a spatula, fold 10 times. Do not stir—*fold*. Scrape the entire edge of your bowl in a 360-degree rotation to count as one fold.

Gently incorporate the almond flour mixture, making sure you're scraping the bottom of the bowl, as well. Add another third of the almond flour mixture and fold another 10 complete times. Add the remaining almond flour mixture and continue to fold 10 more times, making sure you mash the spatula against the sides of the bowl to help deflate the mixture somewhat. Keep folding until the mixture is homogeneous, which should be about 30 more folds.

By now, your wrist will probably need a break, but don't walk away from your batter! Have a stretch and shake out your hands, but don't let your batter sit for more than a minute. Test consistency by scooping the mixture and allowing it to drop: Does it flow off the spatula smoothly? If not, the mixture is too thick and undermixed. In this case, keep folding to deflate the batter some more, otherwise you will have hollow shells. Retest your ribbon every second or third fold. The consistency is perfect when the batter runs slowly like lava from your spatula. If you overmix your batter, your macarons will be too runny when you pipe them and will have sunken middles after baking. Do a ribbon test: When the batter drops from your spatula, the edges should be tapered and even a little frayed looking, like a ribbon; and if you make a figure 8, you can connect the start and end of your 8 before the ribbon disappears.

If the 8 doesn't disappear for several seconds, your batter is probably still a bit too thick—try giving it two or three more folds. Now move immediately to piping.

Fit your piping bag with a round tip, for instance a #12 Wilton size is great. Twist at the top of the bag and hold over your parchment paper at a square angle. Pipe 2-inch circles, 1 inch apart.

If you have peaks on your macarons, gently flatten them with your fingertip. Tap your cookie sheet hard on the counter to deflate any air bubbles, and poke any remaining bubbles with a toothpick.

Allow to rest 45 minutes to an hour to form a skin.

Preheat the oven to 300°F. Bake for 16 to 18 minutes, rotating your pans halfway through. Remove your macarons from the oven before they begin to brown. Cool completely before filling.

TO MAKE THE VIOLET BUTTERCREAM

Whip the butter until light and fluffy, about 5 minutes on high speed. Turn off the mixer, add half the sugar, and continue to beat on low until well incorporated. Add the remaining sugar and blend well, then turn the mixer up to high and continue to beat for another 5 minutes. Turn the speed down to low and slowly pour in your flavoring, continuing to beat until thoroughly combined. Taste and add more flavoring or coloring to suit yourself.

Use a medium to large round piping tip to pipe the filling onto half of the cookies. Be careful as you sandwich the second cookie onto the filling. They can be very delicate! After filling and making your little macaron sandwiches, place in the fridge in an airtight container for 24 hours before serving. Macarons are much better after a day of mellowing in the fridge.

CHAPTER FIVE
Beltane

"It being springtime there were sexual and generational as well as political energies coursing wildly about, not to mention Dionysus with his overflowing cups."
—Peter Linebaugh

The 19th-century essayist Leigh Hunt wrote that May Day is "the union of the two best things in the world, the love of nature, and the love of each other." May Day, coinciding and comingling with the folk celebration of Beltane, occurs in this vigorous and vibrant month. Beltane is named after the fire god of the Gauls, Bel, whose symbols include the horse and the wheel because he rides the sun across the sky in a horse-drawn chariot. The actual celebration date can vary widely from April 30 to May 15, depending on whether you're aiming for the true midpoint between spring equinox and summer solstice, or the nearest full moon in May.

While this time is often associated with the fire rites of the Druids, there also remains a strong memory of the flower rites of the ancient Roman festival Floralia. We see this carried forward in adornment of doorways, tables, and Maypoles with branches of greenery and roses, wearing flower and ivy crowns, and carpeting the ground with petals. Beltane, known as the time of sap rising, has an exuberant spirit coupled with an energy of transformative force. In Beltane myth and ritual, the Sun and the Earth join in lusty union to bring fruitful blessings to the community.

Beltane signals a critically important turn of the Wheel of the Year in the agricultural calendar. At least as early as the 14th century in northwest Europe, May was the time when young single members of the community, mostly young women, would spend a few weeks driving livestock up into the mountain pastures for summer. In Scotland, they called it "flitting to the shielings." The youth would look forward to this time of temporary independence as an opportunity for courtship. There might potentially be a rendezvous in one of the shielings in the hills, far away from the spying eyes of their home village.

However, all was not love and freedom. Beltane is a rest day, because the hardest working half of

the year is about to kick off. From the first foot of flitting in May, through the last cut of grain at Samhain, folks were concerned with cycles of of communal labor revolving around cattle, sheep, pigs, grain, flax, vegetables, fruits, nuts, and bees. The rituals at this time are about preparing us for our role in the collective well-being.

In the Highlands, large Beltane bonfires were lit from hilltops at daybreak. Livestock would be blessed and protected from maleficent forces by walking between two fires before departure because shieling sites were considered liminal places where supernatural forces could cause trouble. Burn bundles offered to the bonfire are another way to ask valiant spirits for protection. Jumping over the Beltane fire as you make a wish or declare an intention is a common adaptation from ancient fire rituals.

At its heart, Beltane is a fertility festival that celebrates the marriage of our deliberate *intention* with visionary *action*. Beltane is not just about heterosexual coupling; this is the time of unleashing pleasure and ecstasy in *all* its forms. It's about an erotic relationship with the sensuousness of life and the body as a site of creativity and passion. In that communion, we can also find a *philia* type of love—often translated from the Greek as the highest, most altruistic form of love. This is where our Beltane rituals intersect with the affiliative movements of May Day.

The historian Peter Linebaugh writes, "May Day is about affirmation, the love of life, and the start of spring, so it has to be about the beginning of the end of the capitalist system of exploitation, oppression, misery, toil, and moil." May Day was historically a celebration of all that is free and life giving in the world, so it makes sense that since the enclosures of the 15th century when the commons were privatized, it's also been a day of strike and revolution. This festival has always tended to be the most boisterous of the year, sort of like Valentine's Day, Mardi Gras, and a protest march all mixed together. But during the Celtic Revival period of the 19th century, a more Victorian attitude sought to quell the agitation of the underclass. Beltane was rebranded with very young children's games and demure May Queen pageants. But leftists, resisting repression by the industrialist class, began to call their May Day competitions the Robin Hood games. The May Queen and the Green Man became Maid Marian and Little John, part of a band of outlaws who steal from the rich and give to the poor. Such is Beltane with its irrepressible, life-giving quality—it carries the overarching message that *change cannot be stopped.*

Now we commit seed to soil. We rejoice that summer has triumphed over winter. We step into our power to create, reclaim the commons, and declare our sovereignty. We celebrate with fulsome appetites and frisky play. At the altar, we honor Milk Lines and movements that embody the potent energies of love and freedom together: Boudica, Elen of the Ways, Mother Jones, Lucy Parsons, John Brown, Louis Riel and the Métis, Romani Resistance, the Zapatistas, the Arab Spring, the Black Panthers, and the American Indian Movement. Now is the time to channel your energy and commitment to create something powerful and meaningful for yourself and the collective.

RITUALS

Burn Bundles

A burn bundle is a small parcel of magical ingredients that you place on the fire so the smoke can carry your wishes to every corner of the cosmos, alerting helpful allies of your desire. Add dried herbs and flowers that represent the energies you wish to invoke in the season ahead. The Beltane bonfire can be lit with a burn bundle made of the Nine Sacred Woods as a way to infuse their blessings into the smoke. These particularly venerated trees include alder, ash, birch, hawthorn, hazel, oak, rowan, willow, and yew. The smoke will cleanse the animals and people who pass near, and especially those brave souls who make a wish as they leap across the flames. See the "Magical Correspondences" section on page 235 for ideas about which woods and plants to add to your burn bundle to match your intention and desires.

Rowan Cross

It's customary to refresh your house charms on all quarter days, but Beltane is the only time when rowan wood should be cut, it being unlucky to do so any other time. In Scotland in the 19th century, rowan crosses with lucky, protective red thread were hung to protect folks from bad luck, the livestock from illness, and the land from unfortunate harvests. All you need are 2 small sticks of rowan and about 3 yards of thread.

Simply tie the twigs of rowan together in a cross. As you do, whisper a petition of protection, finishing with "a rowan charm between this house and harm." To make your cross more elaborate, you can string a few overwintered rowan berries onto red thread and pull them tightly into a circle, wrapping them on each end of your rowan twigs. Pull tightly as they will loosen a bit as they dry. Or you can simply string some berries onto threads and let them dangle like beads from the bottom of your cross.

Maypole Chandelier

Many scholars connect the Maypole to the archetypal World Tree, also known as the Tree of Life, representing the connection between the celestial realm of spirit in its branches, with the earthly realm as its trunk and the roots as the mysterious Underworld of soul. However, sometimes dancing around the Maypole can seem a bit like the worship of a gigantic phallic symbol. While I've found no scholarship to support that suspicion, it's just not a tradition that resonates for me. However, I do hang a ribbon chandelier as a gesture toward the importance of the circle of connection and continuity, to ritualize being bound together in community by seasonal cycles in the Wheel of the Year. For this, I take a metal peony ring from my garden, tie lengths of ribbon onto it, and suspend it with garden twine above our dining table.

Consecration Oils

For millennia, ceremonial oils have been sacred conduits for blessing, prosperity, and healing. Jewish holy anointing oils are described in the Book of Exodus. Aleister Crowley, a Victorian-era occultist and founder of Thelema witchcraft, repopularized consecration oils in esoteric circles. Conjure oils are common in African American folk magic and rootwork. They're easy to make and use, but their simplicity belies their power—these potent amplifiers need only be used in small amounts. They're often used in manifestation spells; perfect magic for this time of year.

Your vessel should be very clean and dry. The base is commonly olive oil. However, if you're using essential oils for aromatics, a lighter carrier oil such as grapeseed or jojoba is more appropriate. The main use of consecration oils is on your ritual candles, though some people anoint their sacred tools such as knife handles, leather medicine bags, wands, or wooden spoons to impart characteristics of the sacred oil.

As always, you'll want to begin with a strong, clear intention for your desired outcome. Be sure to check the "Magical Correspondences" section on page 235 to discover which ingredients best support that. Once your oil is complete, rub it on the outside of a pillar candle, light it, and spend time meditating on how you'll feel when your intention is reality.

Anointing

Consecration oils are not for consumption, so you can use any combination of dried herbs, flowers, barks and roots, stones and metals, as well as essential oils. If you wish to anoint your body with your oil, you'll want to research your ingredients more carefully for possible toxicity or allergenic qualities. Applying an anointing oil is a good substitute for walking through two Beltane bonfires as a protection ritual.

WILD GODS GARDEN PARTY ——————

After a long winter-spring, the magic of eating flowers seems obvious: *Put the life back in my body, please.* This menu celebrates all that is springing up in the garden right now. Add a giant bowl of baby greens tossed with a ravishing amount of colorful petals as a nod to Floralia. Bachelor's buttons, pansies, violas, borage, calendula, cherry blossoms, and rose petals can often be found by now.

Lavender Beltane Bannock

This is a variation of my favorite recipe from forager, historian, and epicurean extraordinaire, Danielle Prohom Olson of the blog Gather Victoria. *What I love about this recipe is that no matter how you modify it, it always works and is always delicious! This version is like a giant lavender oatmeal cookie you make with your hands.*

MAKES TWO 8-INCH CAKES

2 cups old-fashioned rolled oats

2 cups oat flour (see Note)

½ cup sugar, plus more for sprinkling

½ teaspoon sea salt

1 tablespoon dried lavender buds

¾ cup chilled butter, cut into 1-inch cubes

2 teaspoons vanilla extract

1 cup milk

Preheat the oven to 400°F. Line a baking sheet with parchment paper. Place the oats, oat flour, sugar, salt, and lavender into a large bowl and stir to thoroughly combine. Sprinkle the pieces of butter evenly over the top and use your clean hands to mash the butter into the dry ingredients. Working quickly, continue to blend until the mixture is sandy and there are no large bits of butter. Add the vanilla to the milk, stir, and pour evenly over the flour mixture. Blend with your hands to combine. Allow it to rest for a minute to soak up the liquid.

Gather the dough and gently knead until it reaches a consistent texture and holds together well. Divide the dough in half and pat each half out into a flat circle on your parchment-lined baking sheet, about ¼ to ½ inch thick. Mark it with a vertical and horizontal line to represent the four quarters of the year and say a blessing upon your household as you do, such as, "May the love and affection of the sun be with us." Sprinkle with sugar and bake until the edges are golden brown, about 20 minutes. As soon as you remove it from the oven, cut it into wedges with a long sharp knife. Allow to cool before handling further.

 ────────────────────────

Note: You can put rolled oats in a blender on high speed to turn it into flour.

Maywine

This alluring libation, known as maiwein *in its homeland of Germany, is made when sweet woodruff, a woodland herb, is added to sweet white wine from the Rhine region. Woodruff can be found at garden centers. It grows as a groundcover in full or part shade, and it also grows quite easily in a pot on a north-facing windowsill. It doesn't have an aroma when fresh, but after a day in the dehydrator, or a half hour in a 250°F oven, it smells like a combination of vanilla and freshly mown hay.*

    Riesling is traditional, but I think the stone fruit notes of a Pinot Auxerrois or a Gewürztraminer give this beverage an ambrosial quality. Is it just me or is this how an aphrodisiac smells? So lusty and exuberant! Floating strawberries are the customary garnish.

MAKES 6 SERVINGS

12 sprigs dried woodruff

1 (750 ml) your preferred wine

Strawberries for garnish

Add the woodruff sprigs and your preferred wine to a carafe. Place it in the fridge for a few hours or up to a few days. Strain (if you like) and top it off with a few fresh strawberries—it's ready to enjoy!

Elderflower Lemonade Syrup

Blue elderberry and American black elderberry, with their flat umbels of flowers, grow east of the Cascade Mountains. Where I live on the West Coast, we have red elderberry whose flowers have the same intoxicating fragrance but with a pyramidal flower cluster. You definitely need a very detailed guidebook before you go foraging, because there are poisonous look-alikes like water hemlock, which is no joke. As always, do not over harvest—if you take the flowers, they can't become fruit for birds and other animals, so take only what you need, about 25 umbels, and pick no more than 20 percent of a tree's flowers. If elderflowers aren't blooming yet, violets or lilacs work really well here, too. This beverage is like drinking sunshine.

MAKES 3 PINTS OF SYRUP

2 cups packed elderflowers (not washed
    or you'll lose the flavorsome pollen)

Zest of 2 lemons

2 tablespoons citric acid

Juice of 2 lemons

4 cups sugar

1 quart water

Snip off the elderflowers from the stalks into a large bowl or bucket that will hold everything. Try to remove as much of the stems as you can; they are toxic. A few stray bits of stem will not hurt you, but you want to minimize it flavor-wise. Add the lemon zest to the bowl, then the citric acid and lemon juice, then set aside. In a large pot over high heat, bring the sugar and water to a boil, stirring occasionally to dissolve. Let the syrup cool enough so that you can stick your finger in it without getting burned. Pour the syrup over the flowers and lemons mixture and stir to combine. Cover the bowl or bucket with a towel and leave it for 2 or 3 days.

When you're ready, strain it through a fine-meshed sieve lined with cheesecloth or a paper towel into a clean mason jar. Seal the jar and store in the fridge.

 _____

Note: To serve, pour the syrup into a glass until it's about one-quarter full, then add water or seltzer. It's also lovely in sparkling wine or cocktails.

Spring Tonic Syrup

Since our body is an altar to our ancestors, this tonic offers medicine to your ancestors by adding astringency to the diet. This ancestral norm has largely gone missing from the world since the advent of industrial sugar manufacture. This recipe is made from ingredients that have a burst of growth in our yard in May, so I know for sure they haven't been sprayed by any chemicals. Make sure all your ingredients are thoroughly rinsed so that they are free of dirt and bugs. Use whatever combination of edible flowers and foliage appear in your neck of the woods this time of year at a ratio of about 4 cups of forage to 1 quart of water.

MAKES ABOUT 4 CUPS

3 cups stinging nettle leaves, stems removed

1 cup red raspberry leaf, stems removed

3 to 4 packed cups of spring greens such as fennel fronds, dandelion leaves, lemon balm, chickweed, dead nettle, red flowering currant blossoms, primroses, violet leaves and blooms, thyme

½ cup rhubarb stalk, roughly chopped

4 inches wormwood (artemisia) leaf

¼ cup dried rosehips

Zest of 1 large orange, removed in large strips with no pith

2 quarts water

1 cup liquid golden honey

Add all of your foraged ingredients plus the orange zest to a pot and top with the water. Bring to a boil, then reduce to a simmer. Reduce to about 3 to 4 cups. This could take over an hour depending on your heat setting. Strain all the solids out of the reduced liquid and pour the liquid back into the pot. Add the honey and stir to dissolve completely. Allow to cool completely before transferring to a bottle or jar to chill in the refrigerator for up to 3 months.

Note: To serve, pour an ounce or more, according to your taste, over ice and top up with 4 ounces of soda water. Add a squeeze of fresh lemon to brighten and balance the flavors.

Buttered Baby Radishes

Check your farmers' market for first-of-the-season mini morsels of radishy goodness! Baby radishes have less heat than later-picked, larger ones. Keep a few leaves attached to them for easy and adorable serving. Root vegetables are grounding and should be eaten whenever you're feeling adrift or unfocused.

2 dozen baby radishes with
    greens attached

½ cup salted butter, the best quality you
    can find, cut into very small cubes

Flaked sea salt

Finely chopped dill or
    fennel fronds (optional)

Clean the radishes and dry them well. Trim off their root tips and remove any wilty greenery, leaving a few fresh leaves on each. Line a baking sheet with parchment and place a cooling rack on top. Place the butter in a small saucepan on very low heat, continually stir it until just half of it melts. It has to stay creamy looking the whole time—you don't want it to separate or clarify. Immediately remove from the heat. Allow it to cool, stirring frequently until it becomes thickened again, like a thin chip dip. Dip each radish in the butter and immediately sprinkle with a bit of salt and the dill, if using. Place on the baking rack. When the radishes have stopped dripping, move directly onto the parchment and place in the refrigerator until ready to serve.

Soupe aux Primeurs with Chicken Polpettine

SERVES 6 TO 8

CHICKEN POLPETTINE

½ pound ground chicken

½ cup fine bread crumbs

½ cup finely grated Parmesan cheese

1 egg

2 tablespoons chopped chives

2 garlic cloves, finely minced

½ teaspoon salt

¼ teaspoon freshly ground black pepper

BROTH

2 tablespoons olive oil

1 large yellow onion, chopped
 (about 2 to 3 cups)

Salt

1½ cups thinly sliced leeks,
 white and green parts

1 medium carrot cut in julienne strips

6 cups chicken or vegetable broth

2 cups of early spring greens (beet
 greens, turnip greens, kale,
 spinach), in bite-sized pieces

½ cup sliced green onions,
 white and green parts

Freshly ground black pepper

2 tablespoons lemon juice

2 tablespoons chopped fresh dill

¼ cup chopped fennel greens

Finely grated Parmesan (optional)

A handful of pea shoots, cut to 2-inch lengths

Chicken symbolizes creativity and renewal and is combined here with ingredients that capture the essence of the season. A soupe aux primeurs is a simple broth made with the earliest spring vegetables. Polpettine means "small meatballs" in Italian.

TO MAKE THE CHICKEN POLPETTINE

Preheat the oven to 375°F. Mix all the ingredients together until very well blended. Roll into tiny ½-inch balls and place on a parchment-lined baking sheet. Bake about 15 minutes then stir the balls to rotate them for more even cooking. Cook about 5 to 10 minutes more, until they are golden brown and reach an internal temperature of 145°F. You may need to skewer a few onto your thermometer at a time to get an accurate temperature reading. These can be cooled and frozen for later use if you like.

TO MAKE THE BROTH

Heat the olive oil in a large saucepan, add the onions, and season with salt. Soften over low-medium heat, stirring frequently for about 20 minutes. Add the leeks and continue doing the same for another 10 minutes, until the leeks are very soft. Add the carrots and broth and turn up the heat to bring to a low boil. Turn off the heat, add the spring greens and green onions. Taste, adjusting the flavors with salt and pepper. Add the lemon juice 1 teaspoon at a time until the flavors brighten, but don't yet taste tart. Arrange the warm polpettine in serving bowls. Pour the broth over the polpettine and top with a sprinkling of fresh dill, fennel, and Parmesan cheese, if desired. Top with a swirl of pea shoots and serve.

Notes: Make sure your polpettine are teeny tiny so they easily fit on a soup spoon.

Since beets are sacred to Aphrodite, goddess of love, if you select beet greens and combine them with fennel for fertility and virility—plus dill for mental clarity—this soup becomes a potent potion for wise choices in love.

Ruben's Soft Buns

There's something so sensual about bread—the smoothness of the dough, the springy softness in the hand, the comfort when it's warm. Bread making has long been associated with folk magic because the transformation of flour and water to bread represents life itself and human survival. Evidence dates to 3rd-century Greece of ritual breadstuffs shaped into effigies, but here the jolly shape of rolls can represent whatever your heart desires.

MAKES A 6- TO 8-INCH CAST-IRON PAN OF BUNS, OR ABOUT 8 LARGE BUNS

Half package (4 grams) active dry yeast

½ teaspoon sugar

2 tablespoons warm water, no more than 110°F

3 cups all-purpose flour, plus 2 tablespoons if needed

1 cup buttermilk, at room temperature (see Note)

1 teaspoon salt

1 tablespoon honey

1 egg for wash

Poppy, sesame, or other seeds for topping (optional)

Salt and freshly ground black pepper (optional)

Combine the yeast, sugar, and water and allow to rest for a few minutes to proof. You should see the yeast bloom and liquefy, showing that it is active. After the yeast has proofed, combine the flour, buttermilk, yeast, salt, and honey in the bowl of a stand mixer. Mix on medium until the dough is smooth, about 10 minutes. Halfway through, check for stickiness and correct with a couple of tablespoons of flour, as needed. You want it to be smooth dough, not sticky or shaggy.

Cover the dough and let rise until doubled in volume. This will take about 2 hours—the temperature of your kitchen will have a huge influence on how long it takes to rise. After the dough has doubled, lightly flour the counter and knead the dough into a smooth ball. Divide into eight equal portions and roll again into tight, smooth little dough balls.

Butter the cast-iron pan and put one ball in the middle and seven around the edge in a circle. Cover the pan with a tea towel and let rise until doubled again, probably at least an hour.

Preheat the oven to 375°F. Whisk the egg until smooth. When risen, brush the rolls with the egg wash. At this point, you can top with seeds, if desired, or sprinkle with salt and pepper, if you like. Bake for 40 to 45 minutes until browned and a thermometer inserted inside reaches 200°F. Serve (carefully!) in the cast-iron pan.

Note: If you don't have buttermilk handy, you can use regular milk clabbered with a tablespoon of lemon juice. You will also need to add about ⅓ cup more flour. And if you don't have lemon juice, plain milk works, too—there will just be less tang to the bread.

Green Goddess Salad

Ancient Egyptians considered asparagus a sacred, even ceremonial vegetable, and the Greeks connected it to Aphrodite as a symbol of fertility. Serve asparagus to direct and focus your energy and to enhance manifestation magic.

SERVES 4 TO 6

Salt

1 cup shelled fava or edamame beans

1 pound of asparagus, 1 inch of ends trimmed off, cut into 3-inch pieces

½ pound haricot verts, the small thin French variety of green beans, trimmed

½ cup extra-virgin olive oil

4 garlic cloves, thinly sliced

2 lemons, peeled, taking care to leave white pith behind, zest sliced into long thin strips; then juice the lemons

4 sprigs thyme

2 sprigs rosemary

2 teaspoons honey

1 teaspoon chopped mint, dill, or fennel, chopped

Freshly ground black pepper

1 tablespoon edible spring flower petals, such as bachelor's buttons, violas, or plum blossoms

Bring a large pot of heavily salted water to the boil. Add the fava beans and blanch until bright green and cooked through, about 5 minutes. Remove with a slotted spoon to a large bowl of ice water. Add the asparagus and green beans to the water and blanch for about 3 minutes until bright green. Remove to the ice water to chill quickly and completely. Strain and allow the veggies to drip dry. Warm the olive oil over medium heat and add the garlic. Stir until fragrant but not yet beginning to brown, less than a minute. Add the strips of lemon zest, thyme and rosemary herb sprigs, and honey. Stir for 30 more seconds to combine, then remove from the heat. Allow to cool to room temperature, at least 30 minutes. Once cooled, remove the sprigs and add the mint. Whisk in the lemon juice. Pour the dressing over the vegetables. Sprinkle with salt and pepper to taste. Chill at least 4 hours before serving. When it's time to serve, garnish with edible flower petals.

Lemon Tart with Almond Crust

Lemon symbolizes optimism and action, a perfect blend of energies for Beltane. When it comes to lemon juice, this is one of those rare times when a packaged product actually can be much better than fresh. The secret to my mouth-puckering lemony desserts is that I use only ReaLemon brand lemon juice, which contains lemon oil. Other brands can have synthetic flavors, and fresh lemon may contain lower acid levels than ideal.

The whipped cream paired with this recipe uses gelatin, which allows it to be piped high and hold its shape for hours. I generally use European-style gelatin sheets, but you can also use powder for this. Either option will result in show-stopping, whipped-to-perfection peaks, the perfect dessert to round out a May celebration.

MAKES A 9-INCH TART

ALMOND CRUST

3 cups almond flour (finely ground almond meal)

6 tablespoons butter

¼ cup sugar, white or cane

1 teaspoon fine sea salt

½ teaspoon vanilla bean seeds or 1 teaspoon vanilla bean paste

2 teaspoons cold water

LEMON FILLING

Zest of 3 lemons

¾ cup lemon juice

1¼ cups sugar, white or cane

½ cup butter

4 large eggs

4 egg yolks

STABILIZED WHIPPED CREAM

Gelatin sheet or powder to thicken

1 cup cold liquid

2 to 3 tablespoons of water to make the gelatin

1 cup heavy cream

¼ cup confectioners' sugar

½ teaspoon pure vanilla extract or vanilla beans

Edible flower petals (optional)

TO MAKE THE ALMOND CRUST

Preheat the oven to 350°F. In a food processor, blend all the ingredients except the water, until they are well combined and crumbly. Slowly add the cold water, 1 tablespoon at a time, and pulse until the mixture holds together when you press it between your fingers. Add up to 1 more table-spoon if necessary. Press into the tart pan to less than ¼ inch thick. Chill for 20 minutes. Bake for 10 minutes to par-bake. Remove from the oven and cool.

TO MAKE THE LEMON FILLING

Zest the lemons with a microplane. In a saucepan, combine the zest with the lemon juice, sugar, and butter. Place over medium heat, stirring occasion-ally, until the butter melts and sugar dissolves. Combine the eggs and yolks in a blender and blend on high until smooth. Switch the blender to low speed and gradually add the hot lemon mixture. Pour the mixture from the blender back into the saucepan. Cook on low-medium heat, whisking constantly till thickened, 5 to 7 minutes. This

will be a dramatic change so watch carefully. It will be slowly thickening, thickening, thickening, and then suddenly it will lose its opaqueness, turn bright vibrant yellow, and quickly thicken so your whisk will leave streaks. Remove from the heat immediately.

Pour into par-baked crust and smooth the top. Wrap the edge of the tart in foil to prevent over-browning, taking care not to touch the custard. It's a bit like making an awning—imagine you're trying to protect the edge of the pie from rain. Bake for 25 minutes until set but still shiny and slightly puffy. Remove the tart before you see cracks in the edge—it can become a bit rubbery if overcooked. Allow to cool to room temperature, about an hour, then refrigerate until chilled and firm, about another hour.

TO MAKE THE STABILIZED WHIPPED CREAM

Follow the instructions to reconstitute the gela-tin and set aside. The gelatin should be pourable liquid but no more than 2 or 3 tablespoons. In the bowl of a standing mixer, combine the cream, sugar, and vanilla together and whip on medium speed until soft peaks form. This could take up to 5 minutes. Don't be tempted to turn up the speed because cream can turn to butter very suddenly. In a slow, steady stream, add the gelatin mixture and continue to beat until stiff peaks form, but stop before it starts to look grainy. Add mountainous dollops of cream to your tart or use your favorite piping tip to create giant rosettes and stars. Sprin-kle with edible flowers, if using.

CHAPTER SIX

Midsummer

To Hestia,
Incense and aromatic herbs.
Queen Hestia,
Daughter of mighty Kronos,
You dwell in the center of the home
With your vast everlasting fire.
Purify the initiates of these rites.
Inspire endless youth, wealth,
Benevolences and holiness.
You are the dwelling place of the blessed gods,
And the strong support of mankind.
Eternal, many-formed, beloved and verdant,
Smiling and happy one, accept these offerings with kindness.
Breathe upon us with weal and soothing health.
—Orphic Hymn to Hestia

Astrologically, I was born under a trio of asteroids, Vesta, Lilith, and Athena, three rather singular energies that work well together as uncompromising defenders of the sacred. I feel a strong duty of care toward these celestial ancestors. Therefore, at the summer solstice our family observes Vestalia, the Roman festival celebrated in June honoring Vesta, the goddess of the hearth. June is named after Juno, the Roman goddess of motherhood, placing emphasis on governing the domestic sphere this month. This makes sense when we consider midyear as a metaphor for midlife and maturity.

Summer solstice is the time for powerful matriarchs to shine. The personal characteristics of hearth goddesses are synonymous with the element of fire: Life-giving and all-powerful, they command respect yet also provision us with nurturance, comfort, and illumination. Hearth goddesses are potent, well organized, capable, protective, wealthy, and wise when wielding power and magic. Hearth goddesses we might honor this season include Hestia, Brigid, Maman Brigitte, Baba Yaga, Frigga, Holle, and Áine.

There are multiple links between the sun, the chariot wheel of time, and celestial horses now. Helios, the sun god of ancient Rome, and the Egyptian god Horus were each said to be carried across the sky by a horse-drawn chariot. The same is true in Old Norse mythology, with the sun goddess Sunna. One day during her ride across the sky, Sunna discovers that Baldur the Beautiful's foal is injured. She sings a magical charm that cures the animal. This links the sun with the miracle of healing powers.

Small replica chariot wheels, votive offerings sometimes known as roulettes, are found at many archaeological sites across Europe, in the Levant, and in North Africa. In more recent centuries in Scotland and Ireland, during Midsummer games, youth would line up on the high side of a riverbank to chase a burning cart wheel downhill, racing each other down to where the wheel splashed into the water with a hiss. Modern pagans can ritualize this by making four-spoke sun wheels from vines and sticks and place them on the Midsummer bonfire to carry their wishes through the sky.

This mystical time is associated with water and flowers as much as with fire. In ancient Gaul, Midsummer was connected with the Feast of Epona, a

Yet along with feats of strength and skill, many rituals have a more gentle, nurturing quality to them. Yarrow and vervain are commonly harvested now and added to burn bundles for smoke divination. In Scandinavia, seven flowers under your pillow on Midsummer eve ensures you dream of your future spouse. In Wales, rubbing your hand on the bark of an oak tree this day keeps you healthy all year. In the Scottish isles during the 19th century, youth spent days leading up to solstice collecting large bundles of heather. On Midsummer Eve, farmers with their families and farm hands circled the land sunwise with the burning heather torch, blessing the land, ensuring to complete the circuit before the flame went out. It's said this made the hills light up with halos.

MAKING

Flower Essence

A simple water ritual for Midsummer would be to harvest flowers early in the morning on solstice eve and let them sit out all day under the full sun in a glass vessel full of pure spring water or filtered tap water. Later on, take a sprig of mugwort or whatever is growing in abundance, dip it into the water, and sprinkle the holy water all over you to be purified and blessed with well-being in the season ahead. If you strain and save the water, you will have a flower essence for use in your rituals throughout the year. I made an essence of St. John's wort (for healing) with phlox (for partnership, harmony, and agreement), shown here with a portrait of Baba Yaga by the artist, Rima Staines.

tribute to a horse goddess who originally sprung from a river. In Ireland, this was a time to visit sacred wells, streams, and rivers associated with supernaturally obtained wisdom—a magic that's intensified around waterfalls and whirlpools. Midsummer water rites were later overlaid by the feast of St. John the Baptist, he being a famously water-loving fellow. His sacred herb, St. John's wort, is customarily harvested on this day for medicine.

Rituals of Midsummer are concerned with pursuit of excellence and worthy challenges, of nurturing the inner flame, and of self-expression.

Homemade Incense

Forest Incense

This blend can be used to consecrate sacred space or tools, feed ancestors, purify, or bless. Add some banishing herbs for releasement or to reverse psychic attack. All your ingredients should be thoroughly dried out, except for the needles—the oils of the needles can add pleasant aromas. Caution: Some ingredients such as mugwort and wormwood are mildly psychoactive when burnt.

1 part punk wood or crushed conifer bark such as pine, cedar, fir, hemlock, spruce, juniper, or cypress

1 part minced evergreen needles such as pine, cedar, fir, hemlock, spruce, juniper, or cypress

1 part dried herbs such as vanilla leaf (*Achlys triphylla;* see Note), mugwort (European: *Artemisia vulgaris,* or Coastal: *Artemisia suksdorfii*), wormwood (*Artemisia absinthium*), or sweetgrass (*Hierochloe odorata*)

1 part dried flowers such as elderflowers (*Sambucus nigra*), Nootka rose (*Rosa nutkana*), violet (*Viola sororia*), goldenrod (*Solidago*), or yarrow (*Achillea millefolium*)

1 part dried crushed juniper berry (*Juniperus communis*)

1 part Douglas fir resin, lodgepole pine resin, bee propolis resin (see Note), or a combination of these

✦ *continued*

Blend everything *except the resin* together in a mortar with pestle. Add the resin last and mix thoroughly. Your incense may smell different burned than fresh so test it on a piece of self-igniting charcoal and adjust ratios to your preference.

Keep homemade incense in a glass jar, well-sealed, in a cool, dark place. Clean your hands and tools with rubbing alcohol as needed.

Notes: Vanilla leaf (see photo on page 161, upper right corner of tray) is not commonly used in Western herbalism. But it has been used by Indigenous peoples on the West Coast of North America since forever as a treatment for respiratory issues and hung in the home as insect repellent. When dried, it has a soft, hay-like aroma not unlike sweetgrass. It's usually found in the shady undergrowth of a temperate rainforest.

Bee propolis that you find at health food stores is not the same *as bee propolis resin* (see photo on page 161, right side of tray, piled on top of a dried vanilla leaf), which can be scraped from the edges of beehives. When you're at the farmers' market, ask a beekeeper to bring you a few tablespoons of bee propolis resin next time! It burns wonderfully and smells heavenly.

Hymn to Hestia Incense Blend

In the Orphic Hymn to Hestia, recorded between 200 BCE. and 200 CE, the first line references an offering of aromatic herbs—incense. This is a recipe blend I've created to honor Hestia, the Greek predecessor to Vesta.

3 parts bee propolis resin or a tree resin

1 part fir, pine, or cedar bark or punk wood

1 part dried calendula petals, goldenrod, or other orange and yellow flowers

1 part dried yarrow

1 part dried thyme leaves

1 part frankincense or myrrh (optional)

Stir everything together in a mortar then crush lightly with a pestle.

✦ continued

This is a page from my grimoire where I've transcribed the Homeric Hymn to Hestia, written in the 6th or 7th century CE.

with the honey
Nourished, I wil
The Bee-song
The long-forgo
Of praise to thee.

Hymn to Hestia

Hestia,
You who have received the highest honour,
to have your seat forever
in the enormous houses of all the gods
and the humble places of men who walk the earth.
Receive this offering
As a gift of beauty to honour you.
Without you,
Humankind would have no feasts
since no one could begin the first
and last drink of honeyed wine
without first an offering to Hestia

Hekate's Incense

1 part wheat bran

1 part crushed dried bay laurel

1 part tree resin or high-quality myrrh or frankincense such as Royal Hojari

1 part rue seeds

1 part storax (also known as styrax or benzoin)

1 part dried juniper berries

1 part dried vanilla leaf

This blend is adapted from a recipe by Theocritus around 325 BCE. Though Hekate is often associated with the dark half of the year, fire is known as the first element and Soul of the World, which connects with Hekate in her anima mundi aspect.

Crush all the ingredients together into a coarse powder using a mortar and pestle.

USING Loose Incense

If you have a sacred fire going, you can toss your incense into the flame or pull a small piece of charcoal out to the side and sprinkle the incense on top to release the smoke. For a longer ritual, you'll want to use charcoal discs.

A fire-proof container

Sand, salt, or white ash to fill your container halfway

Self-lighting charcoal discs (found at most spirituality stores or online)

Tongs

Barbecue lighter

Fill your fireproof container halfway with sand or salt. Hold a charcoal disc with tongs and apply flame to it with a lighter. Stay alert: The disc will spark a bit. After half a minute or so, the disc will be thoroughly heated through. Place it on the sand. Sprinkle a little bit of your incense on the charcoal to release the smoke. Continue to sprinkle incense on top a little bit at a time without smothering the disc. The disc will burn for about an hour, but you can smother it with sand to douse it whenever you please.

A NOTE ON *Foraging*

Making your own incense and teas connects you to centuries of ancestors who found their medicines, both physical and spiritual, in their direct surroundings. I highly recommend you invest in a foraging guide for your local area. It's crucial that you correctly identify a plant before harvesting. Better yet, take a course from an Indigenous expert in your area so you know what's sacred, what's safe, when to harvest it and how, and what is toxic or endangered. Nurture the relationship with your guide and practice reciprocity. In the future, if you run across something you're not certain about, you'll have a trusted advisor you can ask.

Get to know the area where you're harvesting: Whose land is it? What is its history? Should you be concerned about toxins or overspray from nearby agricultural activity? Is it at least 300 yards from a highway or 150 yards from a busy road? Have you observed it over time to know whether this is a "good" year for the plants or if they're struggling?

A general guideline when harvesting from a healthy and abundant ecosystem is to harvest from only 10 percent of a grouping of plants, and less than 20 percent of the aerial parts of any single plant including leaves, flowers, and seeds. For example, when harvesting wild roses, you'd only take two petals from each flower head, rather than the whole bloom, otherwise it won't be able to produce a rose hip. Leave the biggest, best, and strongest parts of the plant to keep it vital and maintain a healthy population. Spread your harvest over as wide an area as possible.

When gathering tree resins, look for the hardened liquid that naturally emerges from a wound in the wood of evergreens. Do not cut into the wood looking for it. Sap is different. Sap is generally a sugary, watery liquid (think maple tree sap, which becomes syrup), whereas resin is more unctuous, sticky, and prone to solidify at cooler temperatures. Resin doesn't play a role in the fundamental processes of the tree's life and is considered a waste product, so it's okay to remove as much as you can so long as you don't reopen the wound. Clean your hands of residue with alcohol sanitizer. Frankincense and myrrh are common resins in Southwest Asia and North Africa, whereas where I live on the western coast of Canada, Douglas fir resin has been burned as lamps and for smoke cleansing for thousands of years.

When gathering barks, look on the ground. Don't take from standing wood. There's usually bark and punky wood to be found by looking down. Punk wood is soft rotted wood, often found in the center of a dead tree or the core of stumps—it's perfect for incense because it creates so much smoke when burned. Certain woods provide both light and spiritual cleansing with their resinous aromatics, such as tjärved from Scandinavia, similar to firwood in Scotland, and fatwood in North America. In South America, there is a sacred wood by the name of palo santo, which translates to "holy wood." However, there's no need to import sacred woods from other places or cultures when your local trees and shrubs will do perfectly.

Sun Wheel Burnt Offerings

The cross-in-a-circle symbol has been used to depict the wheel of time since the Bronze Age. Gather vines and thin, flexible branches. Bend them into a circle, tying them into shape. Cut smaller lengths and tie them on as the center cross. Place it in a window in the sun to dry for a week so they'll burn well on the fire. Write the name of the deity you wish to honor on a small piece of paper. Roll it into a scroll and affix it to the wheel. Adorn the wheel with dried herbs and flowers as gifts. Add your wheel to the sacred fire, offering gratitude to this deity.

Poppets

Poppets are magical dolls that often appear in folklore. An example is the Russian fairy tale of Vasalisa the Beautiful. In this Cinderella-style story, poor Vasalisa is ordered to go fetch fire from Baba Yaga in the forest. Baba Yaga entraps the girl, saying she must first complete a series of arduous tasks before she can have the fire. Each night Vasalisa falls into bed exhausted, unable to complete her tasks. Fortunately, Vasalisa has a little doll her mother gave her before she died. She always gives the doll a bit of her food each day so the doll loves her and completes all Vasalisa's tasks each night. When Baba Yaga demands to know how Vasalisa successfully completes all the tasks, she replies, "By my mother's blessing." Baba Yaga is furious, gives Vasalisa the sacred fire, and sends her home.

Healing dolls connect us to strength, willpower, and matriarchal love. While this ritual craft can be done at any time of year, here we harness the potency of the time around Midsummer's fiery peak. Healing dolls can be made for yourself, of course, but I've found that friends in need appreciate them very much.

A tiny scroll of paper and jewelry jump ring for a blessing

Wool roving or other stuffing

2-inch stick for the torso

A scrap of fabric about 10 to 12 inches square, which could be dyed by soaking for 1 to 10 hours in tea

Embroidery floss

Scissors

Air dry clay or a bead for the heart

2- to 3-inch sticks for arms

A tiny healing stone for the belly

Ball of yarn to wrap the doll into shape

3- to 4-inch Y-shaped stick for legs (if you want them to be able to stand)

Fabric, ribbons, buttons, beads, and jewelry for adornment

Wool roving or yarn for hair

Needle and thread

A. Begin by writing a blessing on your tiny scroll of paper. Tuck this into the stuffing so the message stays in its mind. Tuck the torso stick into the bundle of roving that will become the head.

B. Drape the center of the fabric square over top. Use the embroidery floss to tie the fabric securely into place, shaping the head into a nice round ball.

C. Cut from the corners of the fabric up to the body; this will create separate sections of fabric from which to shape arms and legs.

D. Place more wool along the torso to shape the body. Place the heart here, plus the stick for the arms, and add a little more stuffing.

E. Secure the arms and heart in place with more floss.

F. Place the healing stone in the belly area and tie the fabric below with more floss.

G. Now fold the fabric around the doll's arm and wrap it into place with yarn. Do this for each arm. The yarn will not only secure the fabric but also add some more bulk and shape. Tie off wherever convenient. There's no specific technique to this, just whatever works. If you like, you can do the same for the legs to create pants, or you can skip wrapping with yarn and simply cover them with a fabric skirt. Sew the hair into place using a needle and thread.

Make an outfit and accessories that fit the personality your doll. Place the doll on your altar, at your bedside, or in your kitchen, wherever suits it. The poppet will hold your healing vision for you, even when it's hard for you to believe in it.

 ✦ continued

FIRESIDE FEAST

In recent years where I live, there's been a shorter and shorter window of summery weather before the fire bans are announced. If there's an ideal time for a Vestalia live fire feast, it's going to be on or near the solstice. We live in an urban area where enclosed fires are a must, so we use a portable firepit with a lid. This menu offers a chance to worship fire and sun in a safe and relaxed way.

Midsummer Tea

Pineapple weed is the urban forager's friend because it grows in hard-packed soil and gravel lots. The stems can be disagreeable for digestion so stick with flower heads only—they smell like their name! After flowering, nettles can be hard on the kidneys. However, the harmful compound is destroyed after drying, so the dried leaves can still be consumed as tea. If you don't have a food dehydrator, hang the foliage upside down in a warm, dark place with good air circulation for at least a week.

2 parts pineapple weed flower heads

1 part dried stinging nettle leaves

1 part dried mint leaves

1 part dried rose petals

1 part dried calendula petals

Honey

Lemon

Combine all the dried herbs and flower petals. Steep 1 tablespoon of tea in a mug of hot water for 5 minutes. Add honey and lemon to taste. Serve hot or cold over ice.

Vin d'Orange

If you like an Aperol spritz on a summer day, this recipe is for you. An apéro, to use the colloquial French term, is a predinner drink to stimulate the appetite. They're not too sweet, even pleasantly bitter, with a crisp refreshing quality. This aperitif recipe should be started by Beltane if you'd like to enjoy it during your solstice celebration. If you can't find Seville oranges, use half oranges and half pink grapefruit. Drink straight on ice or topped with soda water.

MAKES 1 (750 ML) BOTTLE

2 blood oranges

2 Seville oranges

1 navel orange

1 pink grapefruit

1 lemon

¾ cup of cane sugar

3 cloves

3 peppercorns

½ vanilla bean, split open

1 (750 ml) bottle of white or rosé wine

½ cup vodka

Chop each citrus into eight pieces and place in a large lidded container. Sprinkle the sugar over top and add the cloves, peppercorns, and vanilla. Pour in the wine and vodka and stir to blend well. Seal your container and leave in a cool dark place, shaking or stirring every other day for a week. Let it sit for 40 days. If your fruit was very juicy, your beverage may be a bit cloudy but still taste lovely. Strain into an empty wine bottle and keep in the fridge for up to a year.

Calendula Chicken with Gravy

Calendula might be the ultimate Midsummer edible flower, here coupled with chicken, a symbol of luck and abundance. Cook the chicken in the same pan you'll make the gravy to ensure you capture all the flavorful bits and juices.

SERVES 4 TO 6

3-pound farm-raised chicken

1 teaspoon salt, plus more to taste

¼ teaspoon freshly ground black pepper, plus more to taste

2 teaspoons fresh thyme leaves

2 tablespoons fruity white wine, unoaked like a Sauvignon Blanc, Viognier, Orvieto, or Pinot Grigio

½ teaspoon Dijon mustard

¼ cup chicken stock, if needed

1 teaspoon cold butter

2 tablespoons melted butter

1 tablespoon fresh calendula petals

Preheat the oven to 450°F. Rinse the chicken and dry it well with paper towels. Cut in half and remove the spine then lay the halves in a cast-iron pan. Rub the salt and pepper evenly over the entire surface of the bird. Roast for at least an hour or until the internal temperature reaches 165°F. Take the chicken out of the oven and remove from the cast-iron pan to a cutting board to rest for 15 minutes. Turning back to the gravy, place the cast-iron pan on the stove on a medium heat and add the thyme, white wine, and Dijon mustard. Whisk to combine, scraping up any caramelized or charred bits on the bottom of the pan. Add the chicken stock if you need a bit more liquid, tasting as you go and seasoning as desired. At the last moment before serving, whisk in a teaspoon of cold butter to add a velvety texture to your gravy. Place the chicken halves on your serving dish, baste with the melted butter, and sprinkle the calendula petals over the entire surface. Serve with gravy on the side.

Rainbow Trout with
Orange Butter, Capers, and Mint

SERVES 4

FRIED CAPERS (MAKE AHEAD)

¼ cup olive oil

¼ cup capers, rinsed and dried very well

ORANGE SAUCE (MAKE AHEAD)

1 tablespoon olive oil

1 tablespoon very finely minced
shallot or white onion

¼ cup white wine (unoaked such as
Sauvignon Blanc or Pinot Grigio)

¼ cup orange juice plus zest of the orange

½ teaspoon sugar

¼ cup cold butter

1 tablespoon finely minced mint, ideally
orange mint (*Menta piperita citrata*)

ROASTED TROUT

1½- to 2-pound whole gutted and cleaned
rainbow trout, head removed

2 teaspoons salt

¼ cup olive oil

Handful of mint for stuffing the cavity, plus
1 tablespoon finely minced for garnish

4 thick slices of juicy orange

4 tablespoons butter

This recipe is a form of "fire in water" magic. Trout represents the spiritual quest, which in turn is connected to the element of fire—double potent for a solstice feast!

Live fire cooking requires some comfort and intuition with fire. Many foods require plenty of hot coals to cook properly, which can't easily be achieved in an urban backyard. However, if you want to give live fire cooking a try, a small fish is a great option since they cook quickly and don't require very intense, continuous heat.

If using the oven, preheat to 300°F.

TO MAKE THE CAPERS

Heat ¼ cup of olive oil over medium heat on the stovetop. Carefully add the capers and fry until golden brown, swirling periodically, for about 1 minute, 2 minutes if the capers are very large. Turn off the heat and remove the capers with a slotted spoon. Allow to dry on a paper towel.

TO MAKE THE ORANGE SAUCE

Begin the orange sauce by adding 1 tablespoon of olive oil to a small saucepan over medium heat. Add the shallots and stir constantly for 1 minute. Add the white wine, orange juice and zest, and reduce by half. Add the sugar and stir to dissolve, then turn off the heat. Add the cold butter, 1 teaspoon at a time, whisking constantly until fully melted and combined. Do not allow the sauce to boil or it will separate. Stir in the mint and set aside.

continued

TO MAKE THE TROUT

Wash the fish then dry with a paper towel. Make three score marks across each side of the fish to allow for penetration of salt and butter. Slather the fish with the olive oil and sprinkle it all over with kosher salt, inside and out. Stuff a handful of mint leaves and orange slices into the body cavity. Tie with kitchen twine into a nice tidy bundle. Place a large cast-iron pan over medium-high heat or live fire and add the butter.

Once the butter begins to brown a bit, quickly sear the fish for 1 minute on each side until lightly browned. You want this to be a flash browning for crispness and appearance, not deep cooking of the flesh.

If oven cooking, place the pan in the oven and continue cooking the fish for 15 to 20 minutes depending on its thickness.

If live fire cooking, cover the fish with aluminum foil to retain as much heat as possible. After about 5 minutes, flip the fish over and re-cover with foil. Repeat every 5 minutes until the fish starts to become flaky.

You can check for doneness by poking the thickest part of the fish with a fork. It should be slightly flaky but still moist in the center. When fully cooked, the entire skeleton with all the tiny little bones will easily lift out in one piece. Pour the orange sauce over the top, sprinkle with minced mint, and garnish with crispy capers to serve. Serve extra orange sauce on the side.

Fava, Mint, and Pancetta Salad

Ovid tells us it's customary in June to eat bacon and beans to protect us from the striges—evil witches. Why bacon and beans? In ancient Rome, not only were pigs sacred to Vesta, they were also used as a substitution rite—the death of a pig averted disaster befalling the family—and fava beans were customary offerings to appease the gods. This makes a wonderful side dish but can also be served as a salad entrée atop lettuce with feta, olives, hazelnuts, and poached egg.

SERVES 4 TO 6

1½ pounds fresh fava beans (you can substitute frozen edamame beans if necessary)

¼ cup olive oil plus 1 tablespoon

1 cup (8 ounces) pancetta or smoked bacon lardons ("lardon" is a matchstick shape, about 1 inch long)

1½ teaspoons Dijon mustard

1 teaspoon sugar

2 tablespoons white wine vinegar

Salt and freshly ground black pepper

½ cup shredded mint

Peel the fava beans and blanch in a large pot of boiling water for 2 minutes. Drain and transfer to an ice water bath. Young fava beans do not need a second peeling but older ones have a coat around them that will need to be removed. Heat 1 tablespoon of the olive oil over medium-high heat in a heavy skillet. Add the pancetta and cook until crispy. Remove and drain well on paper towels. In a small bowl, whisk together the mustard, sugar, and vinegar. Whisk in the remaining ¼ cup of olive oil until well combined. Add salt and pepper to taste. Combine this dressing with the fava beans. Add the pancetta, toss with the mint, and allow the flavors to mingle for at least 15 minutes before serving.

French Lentil Pilaf with Vinaigrette

Lentils are associated with wealth and abundance. They don't need to be soaked ahead of time and should not be salted during cooking or they'll become tough. This side dish can be served warm, room temperature, or chilled.

SERVES 4 TO 6

1 cup black beluga lentils (or some other whole, not split, lentil)

6 cups low-salt chicken stock

1 small sweet onion, finely chopped

1 small garlic clove, finely chopped

⅛ teaspoon salt, plus more to taste

1 tablespoon red wine or sherry vinegar, plus more if needed

½ teaspoon Dijon mustard

3 tablespoons high-quality olive oil

Freshly ground black pepper

Pat of butter (optional)

Rinse the lentils to clean off any dust and debris and place in a large pot with the chicken stock. Be sure to use a large pot since the lentils will at least double in size and they should be able to float freely in the boiling liquid. Bring to a boil then reduce the heat to a simmer and cover with a tight lid. Check for doneness after about 15 minutes. They should be firm and not mushy. Simmer 5 minutes more if they don't seem quite cooked enough. Strain and rinse and replace in the pot, fluffing with a fork. Shake the remaining ingredients together in a jar to make a vinaigrette and pour over the lentils. Season to taste with salt and pepper, more vinegar, or even a pat of butter if you like.

Sautéed Fennel

Fennel is mentioned in the old Anglo-Saxon preparation called the Nine Herbs Charm from the 10th century. The charm is said to bestow confidence and eloquence. In the Highlands, hanging a frond of fennel over the doorway at Midsummer protects the inhabitants, similar to France and Haiti where fennel hung over the keyhole is a classic protection from the loup-garou, *or werewolf.*

SERVES 4 TO 6

1 tablespoon crushed fennel seeds

2 tablespoons butter

2 fennel bulbs, sliced in ¼-inch slices

½ cup water

¼ cup chopped fennel fronds

¼ cup minced shallots

¼ cup Pernod

Salt and freshly ground black pepper

Place the fennel seeds in a dry pan and heat on medium for 2 minutes until fragrant. Remove a pinch or two for garnishing later. Add the butter and melt over medium heat, then add all the fennel slices to brown for a couple minutes. Add the remaining ingredients. Turn down the heat slightly and simmer for 8 minutes covered, then uncover and finish for 2 more minutes, or until the liquid has evaporated and the fennel is softened. Season to taste and serve.

Sun Wheel Puff Pastry

Here we ritually swallow the sun, symbolizing our intimate reliance on this celestial ally for survival. Make this recipe savory with grated cheese, or make it more breakfast-like with jam. It's also lovely with chocolate to accompany after-dinner coffee.

SERVES 1 SELFISH ADULT (LIKE ME) OR
4 DECENT HUMANS WILLING TO SHARE

1 pound package frozen puff pastry, thawed

1 egg, beaten

½ cup chocolate hazelnut spread

Preheat the oven to 375°F. Roll out the pastry to about ¼ inch thick. Use a plate as a guide to cut two equally sized circles. Brush the outer edge of one-half with some of the egg wash. Spread the chocolate hazelnut evenly from the center to the edge of the egg wash. Cover with the second disc of pastry dough and press the edges together. Press a standard-sized mason jar into the center, upside down, pressing firmly to seal the dough halves to each other. Use a sharp knife to cut through the pastry dough in equally spaced rays, from the mason jar to the edge. Gently twist the end of each ray a full rotation and press down to connect with the ray beside it. Place in the refrigerator to rest for 15 minutes. When you're ready to bake it, brush lightly with egg wash and bake for 15 to 20 minutes, until it reaches a deep golden color. Allow to cool slightly before serving.

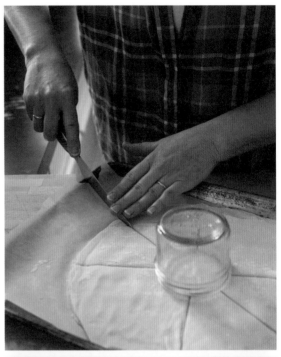

Paris-Brest

SERVES 8

PRALINE PASTE

⅛ teaspoon salt

⅛ teaspoon baking soda

2 tablespoons water

2 tablespoons light corn syrup

4 tablespoons sugar

¼ cup toasted and skinned hazelnuts,
   reserving 1 tablespoon for garnish

¼ cup sliced almonds, reserving
   1 tablespoon for garnish

CRÈME PÂTISSIÈRE

¾ cup milk

¼ vanilla bean, split, scraped

3 tablespoons granulated sugar

1 tablespoon cornstarch

Pinch of salt

2 medium egg yolks

2 teaspoons butter

CRÈME MOUSSELINE PRALINÉ

⅓ cup soft butter

Praline Paste

Crème Pâtissière

PÂTE À CHOUX

¼ cup water

¼ cup milk

3 tablespoons butter, in small pieces

2 teaspoons granulated sugar

¼ teaspoon salt

½ cup all-purpose flour

3 large eggs (1 is for egg wash)

Confectioners' sugar for topping

This spectacularly delicious dessert is an homage to the bicycle wheel, but for our purposes, let's say it's a chariot wheel! It's named after a long-distance cycling event in France that began in 1891 and, notably, has always allowed women to race. This dessert can seem overwhelming if you try to tackle it all in 1 day. But if you allow 3 days like I do, it becomes a leisurely, sensual pleasure. In fact, a little extra time yields better results: Making the mousseline cream the night before assembly allows the flavor to deepen overnight.

This pastry can handle only a little time in the summer heat, so assemble it as close to serving time as possible. It should not be refrigerated fully assembled or the pastry will become soggy. You'll need a candy thermometer for this recipe.

DAY 1:
TO MAKE THE PRALINE PASTE

Butter a baking sheet. Stir the salt into the baking soda and set aside. In a small saucepan, heat the water, corn syrup, and sugar over medium heat without stirring but constantly swirling the pot, until the caramel turns a golden brown. Once it starts turning slightly tawny-colored, do not take your eyes off it. When it begins to turn amber colored, it can transform very quickly, and one little section turning to black will ruin the whole batch. To take the temperature, briefly remove the pot from the heat and slightly tip it so you can insert the thermometer in at least 1 inch. Move to the next step when a candy thermometer registers 250°F (116°C). Add all the nuts (except the nuts for garnish) at once and then the baking soda mixture, and using a silicone spatula, *very quickly* fold until you have a foamy caramel of consistent tex-

✦ continued

ture. Move swiftly to pour the mixture out onto the buttered baking sheet. Do not be tempted to use your finger to unstick the lava-like caramel from your spatula: *You will regret it.* Allow to sit for 30 minutes, no longer. Break the praline into pieces into the bowl of a food processor. Process until it's spreadable, like smooth peanut butter. Place in a covered bowl overnight.

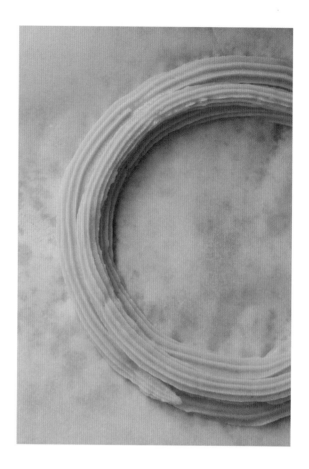

DAY 2:
TO MAKE THE CRÈME PÂTISSIÈRE AND CRÈME MOUSSELINE PRALINÉ

In a medium saucepan, add the milk, vanilla bean seeds, and scraped pod. Bring to a simmer then turn off heat and cover. Let steep for 30 minutes. A few minutes before your milk is finished steeping, in the bowl of a standing mixer whisk together the sugar, cornstarch, and salt. Add the egg yolks all at once and beat for 2 minutes on high speed, scraping the bottom of the bowl halfway through. Remove the vanilla bean pod from the milk. Turn the standing mixer down to low and in a slow steady stream, add the warm milk to the egg yolk mixture. Then immediately pour the contents of the standing mixer back into the saucepan and return the saucepan to the stove on low heat. Whisk continuously without stopping for 5 minutes until the mixture becomes thick like vanilla pudding. Pause your whisking to see if bubbles are beginning to break through. Once you notice bubbles surfacing, continue whisking for a minute more to allow the starches to fully cook. Remove from the heat and add the 2 teaspoons butter, whisking to thoroughly combine. Place the saucepan in a sink of cold water to quickly chill the pastry cream.

Using the whisk attachment, whip the ⅓ cup butter in a stand mixer until light and fluffy, about 3 minutes. Add in the praline paste and whip 3 minutes more. Reduce the speed to low and gradually pour in the fully cooled crème pâtissière. Cover and place in the fridge overnight.

DAY 3:
TO MAKE THE PÂTE À CHOUX

Preheat the oven to 500°F. In a medium saucepan, combine the water, milk, butter, sugar, and salt. Bring to a boil over medium-high heat, stirring so that the butter melts quickly. As soon as it boils, remove from the heat and add the flour, stirring constantly with a wooden spoon until it is a very smooth paste. Return the pan to low heat and continue stirring the paste until it stays together easily in a ball and is becoming a bit dried out, about 2 minutes. Remove from the heat and continue stirring quickly for 1 minute to cool the mixture somewhat. Set it aside for 5 more minutes to cool. Add 1 egg and stir like crazy until it is fairly smoothly blended into the paste. Repeat with the second egg. The paste should be very smooth, but not slick, and hold a stiff peak. If not, allow it to chill in the refrigerator for 30 minutes so it can stiffen up for piping. Put the pâte à choux in a pastry bag fitted with a large round or star tip. Either use right away or allow to rest for up to 2 hours before piping.

Draw a circle about 9 inches in diameter, or four smaller circles about 4 inches in diameter for individual servings, onto your parchment and flip the sheet over. Hold your piping tip at a right angle to the baking sheet and pipe out the pâte à choux following your lines. If you're doing one large circle, pipe another circle inside the first one. Then finish by piping a third and final ring on top of the first layer.

Beat the third egg. Brush with the egg wash.

Chop the reserved 1 tablespoon each hazelnuts and almonds and sprinkle on top. Place in the oven and immediately reduce the temperature to 375°F. Set a timer for 35 minutes. Do not open the oven during this time! When the pastry appears evenly browned, turn off the oven and leave the oven door slightly ajar to dry out the pastry even further. Set a timer for 30 more minutes. Remove from the oven and allow to cool completely on a baking rack.

To assemble, use a serrated knife to slice the top third off the wheel of pastry. Fit a pastry bag with a large star tip and fill with crème mousseline praliné. Pipe the filling into the bottom of the pastry, lightly put the top in place, then dust with confectioners' sugar right before serving.

Lughnasadh

The first harvest festival of the year, known in Gaelic cultures as Lughnasadh (pronounced LOO-na-sah and variously spelled Lughnasad, or Lùnasdal depending on where you are), occurs on the first of August or thereabouts. This is a time for generosity, compassion, and community spirit; a moment when we offer our labor, talent, and effort to the collective. In agricultural communities, people would go out to whichever neighbor's wheat was coming on earliest to help reap the first grain harvest, moving from field to field, inning the crops. There's a subtle yet urgent pulsing, a desire to preserve this season's fleeting beauty and surplus, and quickly. Lughnasadh comes in like dahlias and blackberries; you spend months in eager anticipation, waiting, waiting, waiting for the big show, then all of a sudden it's lush and blowsy, on the edge of overgrown and a bit unwieldy. Lughnasadh festivities are an opportunity to showcase all that is overflowing and abundant, plump, lush, juicy, and quintessentially summer.

Lugh (lew) is a prominent deity in Irish mythology and a member of the Tuatha Dé Danann (TOO-ah duh DAN-an), the tribe of the gods. Lugh, is known as The Many Skilled, with talents in those areas most highly valued by the Gaels: oration, crafts, warriorship, and magic. He's also the god of social contracts. His festival dates back to at least 1600 BCE. It was said to feature great assemblies for entertainment and merrymaking, gatherings of bards to disseminate news and legal pronouncements, competitions among artisans including goldsmiths and weavers, as well as chariot races, archery, and sword fighting. The atmosphere of this medieval festival seems not unlike today's county fairs.

By now the rate of milking would have fallen significantly at the shielings, and so many of the milkmaids would have returned to their villages from the summer pastures. With the return of the eligible singles, now began the season of handfasting and marriage. It's therefore a festival of feasting, alliances, and community celebration. But it's also one of sacrifice. The tradition of offering first fruits of the harvest to a deity ensures a long season of abundance, and stretches back at least to ancient Greece. The early Christian name for this festival was Lammas, from "loaf mass" when special breads would be blessed in church. Since this is the first cutting of the grain, many of the rituals honor the sanctity of grain and bread, the staff of life.

This was also the season of bee transhumance. In August, young boys would make trips to the summer pastures to help the women with sheep shearing. They'd bring bee skeps with them so the bees could make heather honey. The bee charms we make remind us to include our more than human kin in our celebrations.

There are many cleansing and blessing rituals done now, known in Scottish folklore as saining rites. Saining is usually done with smoke or water. Other cleansing traditions use perfumed waters,

for example Florida Water or No. 4711 Eau de Cologne, for similar purposes. The smoke wands you create this month can be used to cleanse or bless in the same way.

Creating your own rituals is part of spiritual maturation and an important aspect of folk magic continuity. The rituals needed during the 11th or 19th century are not necessarily the rituals needed today. Each year at Lughnasadh, I carve the first potato I find into a goddess and bury it in the spot where I plan to plant potatoes next. It's a First Fruits offering to encourage the Wheel of the Year to keep spinning. The idea came to me from the land itself. An image of a little potato goddess popped into my mind while I was digging in the garden and I had the thought to bury her there. I've since discovered that yes, of course, this is a very common ritual found in many parts of the world. If you listen, the land will tell you what ritual to do.

Bee Charms

Bees have long been considered sacred to the sun, representing vitality and the sweetness of life. Bee magic is perfect for this time when both bees and humans tend to be at their most active. A bee charm in the home draws in the positive, resourceful energy of the sun. In the Highlands, this charm was simply made of three dead bees in a pouch. If you can't find any dead bees, use bee-shaped beads or sculpt them from air dry clay. Include other ingredients in your bag such as herbs for health, grain for sustenance, and a crystal for love. Hang your charm bag in your home or carry it with you.

Smoke Wands

Smoke is used to purify, bless, banish, protect, or invoke a plant spirit you'd like to work with. To know how your ancestors used smoke for spiritual cleansing, look to the culinary herbs and native plants of their homelands. For instance, from North Africa to the Hebrides, wild thyme has been a common smoke cleanser since antiquity. Look outside your door to forage or to the garden for herbs. Gather 6 to 12 stems of foliage and flowers such as lavender, rosemary, wormwood, coastal mugwort, yarrow, echinacea, eucalyptus, culinary sage, thyme, mugwort, chamomile, calendula, cedar, juniper, heather, or cypress. Note that these items will smell different when dried and burned—the mint family is notably unpleasant. We're aiming more for their magical and antiseptic qualities than their aromatics.

Gather stems about as long as your hand. Once you have your material collected, tie it all together snugly with a natural fiber twine (so it burns cleanly) and trim the stray ends. The wand will shrink significantly as it dries. Leave to air dry for about a month or in your dehydrator for a week. Light the end of your wand and blow it out to release the smoke, then pass it around your body or room. Keep a burning candle at hand to relight your wand as often as necessary.

Corn Dollies

Lughnasadh is a busy season that's known as the time of "bringing in the corn." This might sound strange considering it's a western European observance. You might be wondering, Does corn even grow in England? In Old Europe, kern meant "single grain," like kernel, so it is thought that the word corn is a derivative of old Anglo-Saxon, rather than a reference to maize. One is hard-pressed to buy sheaves of wheat in the city these days, whereas bags of corn husks are often readily available wherever you find Mexican groceries. If you're a person of European heritage making corn dollies, it's an opportunity to sit for a moment with the grief of imperialism and industrial agriculture. If you're Latinx or Indigenous Mesoamerican, a corn dolly may be part grief ritual acknowledging the continued fight for sovereignty. It's also a ritual of pride and self-honoring. We live in complex and grief-filled times, no doubt. Crafting a corn dolly can be an act of beauty-making while grappling the impacts of globalization.

6 to 10 husks per dolly,
  plus an extra husk for making the arms

A. Soak your husks for 10 minutes in warm water. Remove and blot with a towel. Lay your husks (always an even number) on top of each other in the same direction.
B. Using twine, tie the husks together about 1 inch from the narrow end.

✴ continued

C. Separate the husks into two equal portions, and fold downward over the tie, half to the front and half to the back.

D. Make a head by tying again about 1 inch down from the rolled-over top. Tear the extra husk into three strands and braid them together, tying at both ends to make arms.

E. Place it below the neck knot between equal portions of husks.

F. Tie the waist. To make legs, cut the husks up the center and tie at the groin, knee, and ankle of each leg. Use a glue gun to adorn your corn dolly with fabric, ribbons, dried flowers, and leaves.

THE SPIRITED KITCHEN

THE FABULOUS FEAST

All grains are considered sacred, always, but especially at Lughnasadh. Bread, cakes, beer, and baked goods with barley, oats, rye, millet, and wheat are traditional. Berries are in season and copious quantities connote wealth and abundance—pile them high! And honey should be used liberally to sweeten relations as much as the food.

Hibiscus Rose Lemonade

Dried hibiscus flower, known in Mexican culinary traditions as flor de Jamaica, *can be found in tea shops and Mexican groceries. Hibiscus and rose are flowers that drip with passion and extravagance—a perfect combination of Lughnasadh energies.*

MAKES ABOUT 2 QUARTS

7 cups water (4 cups boiling, 3 cups cold)

1 to 2 cups sugar or honey, to taste

⅓ cup dried hibiscus petals, also known as hibiscus tea or tisane (available at most fine tea shops)

2 cups lemon juice

1 to 2 tablespoons rose water, to taste

¼ teaspoon citric acid (optional)

Unsprayed fresh rose petals for garnish

Bring 4 cups of water to a boil in a saucepan and add the sugar, stirring continuously to dissolve. Turn off the heat and add the hibiscus leaves. Steep for 5 to 30 minutes, depending on how deep the color you wish. Meanwhile, in a large serving pitcher, stir together the cold water and lemon juice. Strain the sweet hibiscus mixture into the lemon water, add the rose water, and stir well. If you'd like it more tart, add citric acid and stir to dissolve. Sprinkle with rose petals as garnish.

Salted Honey Shortbread

Beeswax and honey take this shortbread to an etheric new level. This recipe works well when doubled or even tripled (as pictured).

MAKES AN 8- OR 9-INCH TART

PAN COATING
2 tablespoons butter

2 tablespoons food grade beeswax

SHORTBREAD DOUGH
½ cup very soft butter

⅓ cup confectioners' sugar

¼ teaspoon vanilla

1 cup flour

2 tablespoons honey

½ teaspoon fine sea salt

TO MAKE THE PAN COATING
Melt the 2 tablespoons butter in a small saucepan over low heat. Add the beeswax and stir until mostly melted. Remove the pan from the heat to finish melting the wax. Use a pastry brush to completely cover the inside of your shortbread pan with a thin layer of wax mixture. Place in the fridge to chill while you make the cookie dough. Wipe the saucepan and pastry brush with a paper towel to remove excess butter and beeswax—you do *not* want that going down your drain.

TO MAKE THE SHORTBREAD DOUGH
Preheat the oven to 325°F. Using a wooden spoon, cream the butter until it's light and fluffy, then add the confectioners' sugar and vanilla. Continue to beat another minute until smooth. Add the flour and mix until well blended. Turn out onto a lightly floured surface and knead a few times until smooth. Press the dough evenly into the chilled shortbread pan and pierce all over with a fork. Bake until slightly brown around the edges, about 30 minutes. Heat the honey until warm and liquefied but not yet simmering. Remove the shortbread from the oven and brush the entire surface with honey. Sprinkle with sea salt. Put it back in the oven for another 5 minutes more. Remove the pan from the oven and set a timer for 10 minutes while you let the shortbread cool on a rack. Then turn out onto a cutting board and cut while still warm into individual servings.

Purple Potatoes with Green Beans and Pink Onion Pickle

In ancient Scotland, beans were associated with immortality and the soul, so that walking through a bean patch was considered akin to walking through a cemetery. It was believed ancestors inhabited the plants.

SERVES 6 TO 8 AS A SIDE DISH

PINK ONION PICKLE

1 cup thinly sliced red onion

6 peppercorns

½ cup water

½ cup apple cider or white wine vinegar

2 teaspoons salt

2 teaspoons sugar

SALAD

1 pound fresh green beans, ends trimmed

1 pound purple potatoes, well cleaned and chopped into 1-inch pieces

Salt for the pot

2 green onions, finely chopped

VINAIGRETTE

1 tablespoon Dijon mustard

3 tablespoons lemon juice

¼ cup sherry vinegar

Freshly cracked black pepper

Pinch of kosher salt

3 garlic cloves, minced

2 tablespoons capers, finely chopped

⅔ cups extra virgin olive oil

TO MAKE THE PINK ONION PICKLE

Make at least 2 days ahead. Place the sliced onion and peppercorns in a half-pint jar. In a small saucepan, boil the water, vinegar, salt, and sugar, stirring to dissolve. When fully dissolved, pour the brine over the onions to within half an inch of the lip of the jar. Stir with a fork to remove all the air bubbles. Cover and place in the refrigerator. This will make more than you'll need for this salad, but will last up to a month.

TO MAKE THE SALAD

Bring a large pot of unsalted water to a rolling boil. Prepare a large bowl of ice water. Add the green beans and blanch until they're bright green yet still crisp, about 2 minutes. Strain and plunge directly into the ice water. Let sit until completely cold, then strain into a colander. Allow to air dry for half an hour. Meanwhile, put the potatoes in a large pot and cover with at least 1 inch of water. Add enough salt that the water tastes like the sea. Set over medium heat and simmer, but never boil, about 15 minutes. Cook until the potatoes are just fork tender, testing frequently. Turn off the heat and strain, allowing the potatoes to sit until thoroughly dried. Keep the beans and potatoes separately in the fridge until ready to assemble.

TO MAKE THE VINAIGRETTE

Whisk the mustard, lemon juice, and vinegar together until smooth, add some pepper and pinch of kosher salt. Add the garlic and capers. Slowly add the olive oil while whisking steadily.

TO ASSEMBLE

Place the potatoes in your serving dish and pour half the vinaigrette over top. Add the green onions and stir carefully to fully coat the potatoes. Add the green beans, then the remaining dressing. Use tongs to thoroughly coat and blend the beans with the potatoes. Strain your desired amount of pink onion pickle and distribute them evenly over top of the dish. Serve at room temperature or chilled.

Farro, Tomato, and Mozzarella Salad

Farro is an ancient grain popular in Italy. If you choose pearled farro, it will cook quickly. If you use whole-grain farro, soak it overnight first. Substituting barley for farro is quite suitable, since Lughnasadh marked the first harvest of barley in ancient times.

SERVES 6 TO 8 AS A SIDE DISH

SALAD

2 cups uncooked pearled farro
   or whole-grain farro

1 medium red onion, cut in half

2 garlic cloves, slightly crushed

Handful of parsley, full stems,
   plus 1 tablespoon finely chopped parsley

½ teaspoon salt, plus more to taste

6 cups water or chicken broth

1½ cups fresh buffalo mozzarella
   cheese, ¼-inch dice

½ cup minced Kalamata olives

1 pint grape tomatoes, cut into halves

2 tablespoons finely chopped fresh basil

Freshly ground black pepper

DRESSING

½ cup extra virgin olive oil

2 tablespoons red wine vinegar

1 tablespoon balsamic vinegar

1 tablespoon honey

Add the farro, half of the onion, garlic, handful of parsley, salt, and 6 cups of water to a pot. Bring to a boil, then cover, reduce to a simmer, and cook for 10 minutes. Turn off the burner and let sit for another 5 minutes. Test for doneness. The farro should be al dente but not at all crunchy, still firm and not mushy. If it tastes at all uncooked or is too firm for your liking, you can turn up the heat again, simmer for another 10 minutes, and retest. Strain the farro through a sieve. Discard the onion, garlic, and large pieces of parsley. Spread the farro on a cookie sheet to cool completely—if it's hot, the mozzarella will melt and disappear in your salad.

Whisk together all the dressing ingredients. Finely chop the remaining half onion. In a serving dish, toss the onion, farro, mozzarella, olives, tomatoes, and basil together. Pour the dressing over top and stir well to combine all of the ingredients. Top with chopped parsley, season with salt and pepper, and serve chilled or at room temperature.

Panzanella

This Tuscan recipe helps deal with the bucketloads of tomatoes and cucumbers coming on in the garden at this time of year. Your bread should be dry, not stale. Toasting it will produce a richer, nuttier flavor.

MAKES 6 TO 8 SERVINGS

⅓ cup extra virgin olive oil

¼ cup red wine vinegar

2 pounds assorted varieties of tomatoes, chopped into large chunks

1 small red onion, thinly sliced

2 garlic cloves, 1 finely chopped and 1 sliced in half

Salt and freshly ground black pepper

4 pieces of ½-inch-thick, day-old Italian bread

1 cup packed fresh basil leaves, torn into bite-sized pieces

1 large English cucumber, diced

Shake the oil and vinegar together in a small jar with a well-sealed lid. In a large bowl, place the tomatoes, onions, and chopped garlic. Pour the dressing over top and mix well. Take care not to crush the tomatoes. Season with salt and pepper. Allow to sit, covered, on the counter for at least an hour at room temperature. Toast the bread slices under a broiler until slightly charred. While they're still warm from the oven, rub the surfaces with the garlic halves. Finely chop that garlic and add to the marinating tomatoes. Chop the bread into bite-sized cubes and set aside. At least 15 minutes before serving, add the bread cubes to the tomato mixture. Toss well to coat with the marinating liquid. Add the basil and cucumbers. Toss to combine, adjust seasoning, and serve.

Boeuf en Croûte with Olive Tapenade

Cattle are associated with both the moon and with Lughnasadh fire festival blessings, but few of us have resident livestock these days. Instead, we can prepare roast beef in a reverential way. For this recipe, I use a mix of pitted Niçoise olives with green Castelvetrano and Cerignola olives, plus a few trusty Kalamata olives thrown in. The longer you chill your pastry-covered meat, the longer it will take to get the internal temperature up. This is actually a benefit because you're less likely to over-cook the meat before the pastry is fully browned.

When scoring the puff pastry for decoration, make sure you apply the egg wash first, then score. If you apply the wash after scoring, it will seal the pastry to itself and you won't achieve a nice picture in your puff. If the pastry is becoming too darkened before the internal temperature is to your liking, simply tent it with foil. Better too-dark pastry than too-done meat.

SERVES 6

1½ to 2 pounds beef tenderloin
   roast of even thickness

Olive oil for coating meat

Salt and freshly ground black pepper

1 pound puff pastry

5 to 6 thin slices of prosciutto

½ to 1½ cups pitted olives (the
   amount is entirely dependent on
   how much you love olives)

1 tablespoon capers

2 teaspoons thyme leaves

1 egg

1 tablespoon milk or cream (optional)

Dijon mustard or horseradish for serving

Dry your tenderloin, rub with olive oil, and season with salt and pepper. Place a cast-iron pan over very high heat. Sear all sides of the roast until they have a nice color on them. You're just searing, not cooking, so this whole operation should take only about 5 minutes. Remove the roast from the pan and let it rest until cool enough to handle.

Roll out your puff pastry until it's a rectangle about 1 inch longer than your roast, and wide enough to wrap around it. Lay the prosciutto slices on top, slightly overlapping. Keep them about a half inch away from the edges of the pastry. Chop the olives and capers together so they are finely blended but not a paste. Arrange in an even layer over the prosciutto, then sprinkle with thyme.

Prepare the egg wash: If you just beat an egg white for your wash, the resulting pastry will be evenly browned with a more matte-look finish. If you use a whole egg beaten with a bit of milk, you'll achieve a nicely browned look with a touch of glossiness. For the deepest brown and the most gloss, use just the egg yolk with some cream. Lift up the pastry along the long edge and roll over the meat into a pastry bundle until the seam side is down. Tuck the ends in neatly, like you're wrapping a present. Brush over the entire surface of the wrapped roast with the well-beaten egg wash. Save some of the wash for a second coating. Chill for at least 30 minutes.

Preheat the oven to 450°F. Brush the pastry all over again with egg wash. If you want to score the pastry for decorative effect, make sure you don't cut too deeply or your pastry will split and all the juices will spill out and make a mess of your design. I like to make score marks where I'm going to slice the meat. If you're going to apply pastry cut-outs, stick them on now and then brush those with egg wash, as well. Sprinkle with kosher salt.

Place in the middle of the oven and set a timer for 15 minutes. When the timer goes off, turn down the oven to 350°F and continue cooking until a meat thermometer placed in the center of the roast registers 130°F for medium-rare, probably at least 25 to 30 minutes more depending on how chilled the meat was going into the oven. Once your desired temperature is reached, remove from the oven and allow to rest at least 15 minutes before slicing. Serve with Dijon mustard or horseradish.

Vanilla Pound Cake
with Fresh Summer Fruits

MAKES A 9-BY-13-INCH CAKE,
SERVES 12 TO 20

VANILLA POUND CAKE

2 tablespoons baking powder

1½ teaspoons salt

4 cups all-purpose flour

1¼ cups butter, room temperature

2½ cups sugar

4 eggs

1 tablespoon pure vanilla extract

2 cups milk

TOPPING

3 tablespoons milk

1 teaspoon almond extract

¼ vanilla bean pod, split and scraped

2 cups confectioners' sugar, sifted

2 pints mixed berries such as blackberries,
   raspberries, blueberries, and strawberries

2 perfectly ripe peaches, thinly sliced

What elevates this cake from humble to spectacular is the riot of fruit and luscious icing spilling over the sides. Don't be afraid to really heap the fruit high—it's a magnificent effect that evokes a horn of plenty vibe.

Preheat the oven to 325°F. Butter and flour your cake pan. Line the bottom with parchment paper. Whisk the baking powder and salt into the flour and set aside. In the bowl of a standing mixer, beat the butter on medium speed until smooth then scrape down the sides of the bowl. Add the sugar and beat on high until very fluffy and light in color, 5 to 7 minutes. Turn off the mixer, add the eggs and vanilla, and resume at low speed. Once the batter is very smooth, turn the mixer to low and add a third of the flour mixture, quickly followed by half of the milk, then a third of the flour mixture, then the remaining milk. Add the last of the flour and stop the mixer as soon as no dry streaks are visible. Pour into the prepared pan and bake at the center of the oven until a toothpick inserted in the center comes out clean, about an hour. If the cake seems to be browning too much before it is done, cover lightly with foil. Cool for 15 minutes on a rack, then turn out the cake and leave on the rack until completely cooled.

For the topping, whisk the milk, almond extract, and vanilla bean seeds into the confectioners' sugar until smooth. Pour slowly over the cooled cake, starting along the edges and allowing it to spill over the sides a bit. Top evenly with half the berries, then the peach slices, then the remaining berries, and serve.

Cranachan

Because of their heart shape and red color, raspberries are associated with love and kindness. Their Latin name, Rubus idaeus, comes from Ida, the tenderhearted and protective nursemaid of Zeus. This traditional Scottish dessert pairs raspberries and honey—the perfect spell to seal the bonds of friendship and affection.

MAKES 6 SERVINGS

1 cup old-fashioned oats

6 tablespoons honey, heather honey preferred, plus a few more teaspoons for garnish

¼ cup plus a light splash Glenmorangie Scotch or some other high-quality, fruity, easy drinking whisky

2 cups fresh ripe raspberries

1 cup heavy whipping cream

1 teaspoon vanilla extract

A small scraping of vanilla bean (optional)

Toast the oats in a small skillet over medium heat until they are fragrant and slightly golden. Take off the heat and reserve about 2 tablespoons for garnishing at service time. In a small bowl, whisk 2 tablespoons of honey into the whisky until it is well blended. Stir in the toasted oats and allow to soak, covered, for a few hours or overnight.

Take 1 cup of raspberries and crush them slightly to release their juices. Stir in 2 tablespoons of honey, a light splash of whisky, and mix well. Carefully fold in the remaining whole raspberries, setting aside a few of the prettiest ones for garnish. Place the raspberry mixture in the fridge, covered, until ready to assemble your dessert.

When you're ready to serve, whip the cream until it starts to thicken, then add 2 tablespoons of honey, vanilla, plus a wee scrape of vanilla bean, if using. Continue to whip until you reach stiff peak stage, then fold in the whisky-soaked oats by hand. Place half the raspberry mixture in the bottom of the serving dish, layer with a bit of whipped cream, then the remaining raspberry mixture, and a final dollop of the whipped cream. Garnish with a few fresh raspberries and a sprinkling of the reserved toasted oats. Drizzle with a bit of honey and serve.

CHAPTER EIGHT

Harvest Home

> *"Gratitude and reciprocity are the currency of a gift economy, and they have the remarkable property of multiplying with every exchange, their energy concentrating as they pass from hand to hand, a truly renewable resource. I accept the gift from the bush and then spread that gift with a dish of berries to my neighbor, who makes a pie to share with his friend, who feels so wealthy in food and friendship that he volunteers at the food pantry. You know how it goes."*
> —Robin Wall Kimmerer, *Braiding Sweetgrass*

In September, there's still much work to do to close out the year, but we pause now to appreciate how far we've come through these many seasons and how much has been accomplished. Autumn is spiritually connected to the west, the direction of the setting sun, and to dusk. It's time to down tools. It's the twilight of the year when edges soften and blur, and the psychic undertow of impending darkness quickens the imagination and attunes our senses to the endings of things. The autumn equinox is a chance to settle our spirits, come home to ourselves, and give thanks for the blessings of the final harvest of the year.

So many cultures observe a major celebration in the fall near the autumn equinox. In China, the Mid-Autumn Festival is the second most important holiday of the year. Slavic people celebrate with Dożynki, the English have Ingathering, and the Germans celebrate Oktoberfest. Michaelmas is the Christian festival more recently layered over this time, yet many pagan customs survive. The Witches' Ladders we'll make are in honor of all the witches down the ages who also celebrated with autumnal rites, often in secrecy for their own safety.

Now we save seeds to secure our future abundance. The activist Vandana Shiva said, "The seed, for the farmer, is not merely the source of future plants and food, it is the storage place of culture and history." In many places, it was believed that during the harvest, the magical, life-giving qualities of the grain leaped from stalk to stalk as the field workers cut, until the entire spirit of the grain was transferred to the last stalks standing. This last sheaf would be treated with extraordinary care, woven into a sacred object to hold the seed until the next year's planting, as we will do with our wheat weaving ritual. In cultures across Europe, the last stalks of grain would be fashioned into Harvest Mothers or Corn Maidens, a nod to Demeter and Persephone.

For a period of two thousand years, roughly 1450 BCE to 400 CE, autumn heralded the annual performance of the Greater Mysteries at Eleusis, celebrating the story of the great goddess Demeter and her daughter, Persephone, who began her Underworld voyage through winter at this time. The Greeks believed that these rituals, which involved the reenactment of the death and rebirth of the crops and therefore the perpetuation of the human race, enshrined the natural order of the cosmos and held society together. To them, life without these rituals would be unlivable. Cicero said the Eleusinian Mysteries gave "a reason not only to live in joy, but also to die with better hope."

Outside Demeter's temple, offerings were made at shrines to Hekate of the Crossroads and Artemis of the Portals. Libations were given to the *Demetrioi*—the ancestors—and sweet minted barley water was drunk by participants. Finally, a reenactment depicted the reunion of Mother and Child, who were then joined by the loving and devoted crone aspect of Hekate. In the *Hymn to Demeter*, the Homeric poet writes, "Happy at long last together, held close in each other's arms,

each receives joy from the other, each gives joy in return! Hekate comes near to embrace, and welcome back with great love, Holy Demeter's daughter. Now to Persephone, this elder Queen, Hekate, will become priestess and devoted companion."

And so, the cycle is complete. The Wheel turns and another year begins again.

Flying Ointment

Flying ointments are salves containing psychoactive ingredients that can cause hallucinations and the sense of flying. My recipe calls for milder yet no less magical ingredients. Use this ointment to ceremonially anoint yourself before ritual or trance journeys, much in the way that the brave initiates at Eleusis ritually prepared themselves for revelatory states. This recipe would typically be applied to your wrists, temples, or slathered onto a stone if you have sensitive skin.

Certain plants offer the power of eons of history: roses have existed for over 30 million years, fossilized yarrow pollen has been discovered in tombs in Iraq dating over 60,000 years, and ancient Egyptians used lavender in the mummification process. Don't be fooled into thinking of these botanicals as ordinary. They are, in fact, noble ancestral medicines. The herbs noted here have each been mentioned in historic grimoires as a flying ointment component.

4 teaspoons dried herb blend in your preferred combination of mugwort, lavender, rose petals, vervain, hyssop, valerian, sage, parsley, poplar buds, or yarrow

3 tablespoons neutral oil such as grapeseed, canola, coconut, or a mild olive oil

2 to 3 teaspoons grated beeswax or beeswax pastilles, plus more if needed

6 drops floral essential oil such as rose or lavender (optional)

Mix the herbs and oil together in a jar and set in a bain-marie or crock pot of hot water that can hold the water temperature at about 120°F for an hour without simmering or boiling. Once the oil is infused and aromatic, either skim out the solids or strain through cloth and compost the used herbs. Place the infused oil back in the jar.

Add the beeswax to the infused oil and return the jar to the bain-marie until the beeswax is melted. This could take as much as another hour depending on the fineness of your beeswax pieces. Once the wax has melted, test the consistency by dropping some mixture onto parchment paper and allowing it to cool. Add more beeswax if you want it more solid. Once you've reached the desired consistency, remove from the heat and stir in the essential oil, if using. Pour into the final container such as a jar, cosmetics tin, or a special locket. Allow to cool completely before placing the lid on the container. The shelf life for this ointment is about 1 year in a cool dark place.

 *continued*

WORKING WITH
Baneful Herbs

Poison plants in the witch's apothecary, sometimes referred to as baneful herbs, include monkshood, belladonna, mandrake, foxglove, datura, brugmansia, henbane, and wormwood. You should never work with baneful herbs unless under the tutelage of an experienced herbalist who specializes in the poison path. I'm not saying, *Never work with them*, but I am saying, *Take a course first*. There are other plants you could choose for similar effects that are powerful but not outright poisonous. In autumn, we commonly collect the roots of herbs and plants that have died back, when their magical properties have moved down from the leaves and back into the earth. But with this recipe, we'll stick with the aerial parts of potent plant allies that carry less risk of toxic effects. If you want to dip your toe in the waters of working with poison plants, use a teaspoon of wormwood leaves in your recipe.

Wheat Weaving

Wheat weaving is a near global tradition with deep roots in Africa, Europe, Asia, and Latin America. This 12-straw braid, called a Glory Braid, is an old English design used to ward off evil and invite in friends. Thicker varieties of grain such as black bearded wheat or oats are recommended. I grow a little patch of grain for this purpose each year, but you can also inquire at your farmers' market or check online sources like Etsy for dried floral art supplies.

**12 thick, large straws of dried wheat,
   oats, barley, or rye, heads left on**

Twine

Scissors

Ribbon

A. First, mellow your grain in very hot water to render it pliable. Thinner varieties of wheat will soften in half an hour but thick varieties such as oats can take a couple hours. Keep the stalks submerged in your bathtub by placing a thick towel on top of them. You can test them by bending the thick bottom of a stalk to see if it snaps. If it's pliable, you're ready to weave.

B. Tie your straws together with twine at one end and separate them into three groups of four. Begin to braid in a classic hair-braid fashion, the inside straw on the right bending over the center and resting parallel to the group on the left. Do this one at a time with all four straws on the right moving across the center to the left.

C. Go slowly, keep them snug to each other, at times perhaps even using an awl to tighten and straighten your weave, and shape your braid. Watch where your bend lies—you want the outside edge to create a straight vertical line.

D. Keep going until you reach eight folds on each side or you reach the end of your straws.

E. To finish it off, fold the middle group behind, then the side groups, and tie off with twine. Secure the bundle to itself with a small knot threaded to the main body of the braid so now you have a loop to attach a ribbon hanger. This makes a lovely hostess gift as a house blessing.

✤ continued

213

HARVEST HOME

B

C

D

E

Witches' Ladders

This ritual is a form of knot magic where an intention is methodically bound to a talismanic object. As always, a strong, clear intention strengthens the spell significantly. A charm is spoken for each knot you make.

Distill your intention to a short phrase you can easily remember and repeat. For instance, to call in Persephone, you might say, "I honor you, Persephone. Please be with me now." Repeat this as you tie each knot. Or you might have a more elaborate intention such as, "This home is filled with love, trust, and harmony. Our bonds are secure. We nurture a culture of repair. We honor each other's spirit." For each knot, you'd repeat a key word such as, "love," "harmony," "secure." The magic is bound at the end of the working with a declaration such as, "And so it is," or "My word is firm."

To make your ladder, you'll need:

Twine

Scissors

A few sticks that carry the right energy for your magical working

Corresponding materials such as flowers and herbs, feathers, antlers, bones, nuts with holes drilled through them, dried apple or orange slices, beads, ribbons in symbolic colors, locks of hair, mementos, or heirlooms

Tie the sticks together, using either one piece or two parallel lengths of twine, as is your preference. Your correspondences can be threaded onto the twine as you go along, or you can tie all the sticks together for your ladder first, then attach the correspondences after. Hang your ladder to anchor this energy in your space.

LEVEL UP YOUR

Knot Magic

I use a specific knot called the constrictor knot which is easy, elegant, and very secure. Find a how-to demonstration at Animated Knots (animatedknots.com).

KITCHEN CÈILIDH SUPPER

A cèilidh (pronounced kay-lee) is an Irish or Scottish house party that usually involves music, storytelling, drinking, and dancing. Smaller than a barn dance but louder than a dinner party, it's not too many steps from a typical gathering of friends to a cèilidh. Just add some singing and a bright, boisterous spirit of conviviality. Perhaps the carefree kitchen party has become less rowdy and smaller in scale lately, but this is why we do ritual: to retain the essence of a thing and carry it forward in a form that serves the need of the moment. This menu features gastropub-style comfort food. All you need to add are music and memories.

THE SPIRITED KITCHEN

Sweet Minted Barley Water

In ancient texts, barley water was named as the ritual drink of the Eleusinian Mysteries. It has been posited that the grain was infected with fungal ergot, a parasite that can cause hallucinations. Today, we know barley water as a healthful, detoxifying drink popular in many cultures. Remember to place some as an offering at your altar or pour a little out on the earth to give thanks for another turn round the Wheel.

SERVES 2

¼ cup pearl barley

3 cups water

1 lemon, zested and juiced

1 packed tablespoon of fresh mint or lemon balm leaves, finely chopped, plus more for garnish

3 tablespoons honey

2 lemon slices for garnish

Rinse the barley and add to a small pot with the water, lemon zest, and mint. Simmer, with the lid on but slightly askew to release some steam, for 10 minutes. Strain and save the barley for another use. Stir in the honey and dissolve, and add the lemon juice to taste. Serve hot or chilled with mint and a lemon slice as garnish.

Pithivier

Fall is nut harvest season and if you're lucky enough to find fresh local nuts at the market, get them! Use whichever are available to you. If you wish to be wise, hazelnuts are the proper magic for you. If it's enhanced creativity you seek, almonds will do the trick. This pastry should be eaten the same day it's made. One cup of nut flour is equivalent to ¾ cup whole blanched nuts.

SERVES 8 TO 12

1 cup ground almonds, sometimes called almond flour

1 cup ground hazelnuts, sometimes called hazelnut flour

½ cup sugar

Zest of 1 medium orange

2 tablespoons spiced rum

1 teaspoon almond extract

½ cup butter

2 eggs

¼ teaspoon sea salt

1-pound package frozen puff pastry (approximately 16 ounces), thawed and ready to roll out

1 egg yolk for glazing

1 tablespoon confectioners' sugar for caramelizing

In the bowl of a food processor, mix the nuts, sugar, and orange zest until powdered. Add the rum, almond extract, butter, eggs, and salt and blend until very smooth, about 2 minutes. Scrape out into a bowl and place in the refrigerator for an hour.

Roll half of the puff pastry out to about ¼ to ⅛ inch thick. Use a 9-inch cake pan as a guide to cut a circle and remove the excess dough. Place on a piece of parchment paper on a baking sheet. Roll the remaining pastry out the same way, but cut your circle about a half inch wider in diameter. Place on parchment paper, stack this one on top of your other dough circle, and place in the fridge for at least 30 minutes to chill. You want it to be firm but still pliable and easy to handle.

Preheat the oven to 400°F. Whisk the egg yolk well. Brush the egg yolk in a thin line just inside the edge of the smaller circle of dough. Don't allow it to touch the edge or it will prevent your pastry from rising. Use a spatula to transfer the nut mixture to a piping bag fitted with a large round tip. Starting in the center of the dough, pipe the filling in a coil working toward the edge but stop just short of touching the egg wash. If you have extra, pipe another layer of filling on top so it makes a pleasing mound. Cut a small hole in the center of the second larger circle of dough, then drape it over the nut filling. Press the edges down along the egg wash to seal well.

Brush egg yolk wash over the entire surface of the pastry, then use a knife to lightly draw lines from the center to the edge, like rays of the sun. Take care to just scratch the surface, not puncture the dough. Place in the fridge for 15 minutes to dry out slightly. Bake for 30 minutes, then remove from the oven briefly and sift the confectioners' sugar over the entire surface. Place back in the oven until the sugar has caramelized and is no longer visible on the surface, about 5 minutes. Remove from the oven and cool. Do not cover. Puff pastry with moist fillings like this should not be sealed tightly in plastic. Simply cover any cut edges with a piece of foil.

Cassoulet with Homemade Duck Confit

Julia Child brilliantly captured the essence of this dish: "Cassoulet, that best of bean feasts, is everyday fare for a peasant but ambrosia for a gastronome, though its ideal consumer is a 300-pound blocking back who has been splitting firewood nonstop for the last 12 hours on a sub-zero day in Manitoba." This recipe calls for canned cannellini beans, which allows you to whip up a cassoulet in just over an hour. But you can use any dried large white bean. Simply soak them with herbs and an onion overnight and extend the cook time provided here (in France this is often a 3-day recipe). I keep canned cannellini beans on hand for the express purpose of making a quick cassoulet. Duck is both traditional and symbolic, invoking friendship, abundance, and good fortune. You could use store-bought duck confit, but the homemade version is quite easy. If you're going this route, the duck confit must be started at least a day before your cassoulet. This recipe for duck confit will make double what you need for one cassoulet recipe, and it freezes well.

SERVES 6 TO 8

HOMEMADE DUCK CONFIT

3 tablespoons salt, plus more if needed

4 duck legs with thighs

6 garlic cloves, smashed

1 shallot, peeled and sliced

2 tablespoons thyme leaves

6 crushed juniper berries

2 crushed coriander seeds

½ teaspoon coarsely ground black pepper

4 cups duck fat

CASSOULET

2 legs of duck confit

1 large Toulouse sausage or other garlicky pork sausage

4 ounces pancetta or smoked bacon, cut into lardons (strips ¼ inch thick and 1 inch long)

¼ cup butter

3 medium leeks, white and pale green parts only, well cleaned and chopped

4 medium carrots, cut into ¼-inch slices

3 celery ribs, cut into ¼-inch slices

6 garlic cloves, chopped

4 thyme sprigs

1 bay leaf

Salt and coarsely ground black pepper

3 (19-ounce) cans cannellini beans, drained, rinsed, and drained again

4 cups chicken broth

BREAD CRUMB TOPPING

1 cup coarse bread crumbs

2 tablespoons olive oil

1 tablespoon chopped garlic

Salt and coarsely ground black pepper

2 tablespoons chopped parsley for garnish

TO MAKE THE DUCK CONFIT

Sprinkle 1 tablespoon of the salt in the bottom of a large dish and place the duck pieces in a single layer. Toss the garlic and shallots around them. Blend the remaining salt, thyme, and spices, and rub into the duck legs. Add more salt if the legs aren't thoroughly covered—the excess will be brushed off later. Cover and refrigerate for 1 to 2 days.

 *continued*

Preheat the oven to 225°F. Melt the duck fat in an ovenproof saucepan or Dutch oven. Remove the duck from the fridge and brush off all the salt and seasonings. Snugly fit the duck pieces into the ovenproof pan while keeping at least 1 inch of headspace between the lip of the pan and the top of the melted fat. The duck must be entirely submerged in fat. Place in the oven and cook at a very slow simmer until the duck is tender and can be easily pulled from the bone, about 2 to 3 hours. Remove from the oven. Remove two legs of duck confit from the fat and allow to drain on a baking rack set over parchment paper until needed. Transfer the rest of the confit to a sealable container, cover with fat, cool to room temperature, then refrigerate up to 3 months.

TO MAKE THE CASSOULET

In a Dutch oven over medium heat, brown two legs of duck confit on both sides. Remove to a plate to cool before deboning. Prick the sausage with a fork, then brown on all sides in the duck fat for a total of 10 minutes. Set aside to cool before slicing into bite-sized pieces. Fry the pan-cetta until browned, then remove with a slotted spoon to drain on a paper towel. Drain off all but 2 tablespoons of fat from the pan. Add the butter and melt over medium heat, then add the leeks, carrots, and celery. Once the vegetables have begun to soften, about 5 minutes, add the garlic, thyme, and bay leaf. Season with salt and pepper, stirring occasionally until soft and golden, about 15 minutes. Stir in the beans and broth. Simmer, partially covered, until the carrots are just tender, about 7 minutes more.

Preheat the oven to 350°F. Discard the bay leaf and mash some of the beans in the pot with the back of a spoon if you'd like a thicker stew. Gently stir in the pancetta, sausage, and duck confit meat. Season to taste.

TO MAKE THE BREAD CRUMB TOPPING

Toss the bread crumbs with the olive oil, garlic, salt, and pepper in a bowl until well coated.

Sprinkle the bread crumbs evenly on top of the cassoulet. Place in the oven uncovered until the bread crumbs are golden. Sprinkle with parsley before serving.

Hand-Raised Pork Pies

Pork pies, though generally served at Christmastime in Britain, are so decidedly homey with their rustic charm that they are just too good to put off until winter. They're meant to be served at room temperature, making them ideal picnic fare for an apple-picking excursion. If you decide you'd like to serve them warm, skip the gelatin step. Traditionally, the molded pie form is quickly created from the bottom up. But if you wait for the dough to cool a bit and flip the operation upside down, draping the dough over a jar, the process is much easier. You'll need a clean empty jar for each pie.

MAKES EIGHT 2-INCH PIES, FOUR 3½-INCH PIES (PERFECT FOR 2 PEOPLE TO SHARE), OR ONE 9-INCH SPRINGFORM PAN TO SERVE 8

HOT WATER DOUGH

1 cup lard

1 cup water

½ teaspoon salt

4 cups flour

Olive oil for jar molds

PORK FILLING

1 pound ground pork

1 cup cured smoked pork such as bacon or smoked ham, cubed

1 tablespoon finely chopped fresh rosemary

1 tablespoon thyme leaves

1 tablespoon Dijon mustard

1 teaspoon finely chopped sage

1 teaspoon salt, plus more for the molded pies

½ teaspoon anchovy paste (optional)

A grate or two of fresh nutmeg

1 egg yolk whisked for egg wash

Freshly cracked black pepper

GELATIN

1 tablespoon unflavored gelatin powder or gelatin sheets, following the manufacturer's instructions

1 cup chicken stock

Mustard, chutney, and pickles for serving

TO MAKE THE DOUGH

In a large saucepan, bring the lard, water, and salt to a simmer, stirring to dissolve any chunks of lard. When it is smooth and simmering, remove the pan from the heat and stir in the flour with a wooden spoon, trying your best to break up all the lumps. Once your dough comes together to form a ball, let it rest until you can handle it without burning your hands, about an hour. Turn out onto a floured board and knead until your dough is smooth and well-integrated. Divide it into four equal portions if using half pint (8-ounce) jars as molds, or eight portions if using 125 ml (4-ounce) jars. Brush the exterior bottoms and sides of the jar mold with olive oil. Take one portion of dough and pinch off enough to roll a lid for your pie. Use a round piping tip to punch a hole in the center as a steam vent. Mold the remaining dough ball onto the bottom of your mason jar. It must be even thickness with no cracks so the gelatin doesn't leak out. Once you've molded all the pie bottoms and rolled the lids, place them on a parchment-lined baking sheet in the refrigerator while you mix the filling. If using a springform pan, oil the inside of the pan, line it with dough, and chill 30 minutes.

continued

TO MAKE THE FILLING

Preheat the oven to 350°F. Mix all the filling ingredients except the egg yolk and pepper in a bowl and stir briskly until the mixture becomes somewhat shaggy. Quickly fry a tablespoon of the filling in a pan to see if you like the flavor before continuing to the next step. The flavor should be salty and strong because it will mellow at room temperature.

To remove the pie dough from the molds, fill the mason jar with very hot water. Wait a few moments and the dough will easily pull off the jar. Brush the insides of the dough cups with egg wash to help seal any tiny cracks.

Quickly fill the molds with the meat mixture and top with the rolled pie lid. Brush the lid with egg wash, then fold down the walls of the dough cup onto the lid to create a seal. Brush the entire outside of the pie with egg wash. Sprinkle with salt and black pepper.

Place the pies on a parchment-lined baking sheet. Bake until the internal temperature in the center reaches 165°F, about 45 minutes for small pies, or up to 2 hours if you make one large pie. Remove the pies from the oven and cool completely, at least 2 hours.

TO MAKE THE GELATIN AND FINISH THE PIES

Follow the manufacturer instructions to thicken the chicken stock with your gelatin, using the hot or cold method. Pour the gelatin-stock into the holes of your cooled pork pies and place in the refrigerator overnight. Bring to room temperature for at least 30 minutes before serving. Serve with mustard, chutney, and pickles.

HARVEST HOME

Garlicky Kale with Roasted Lemons

Among the peasantry of the Scottish Highlands in the Victorian era, "kail" was commonly eaten with pron, *essentially oat chaff that we'd now consider chicken feed. In this recipe, kale is a nutritious way to convey butter to your mouth and, for me, another act of ancestral healing for a lineage that struggled at times to make ends meet.*

SERVES 2

2 fistfuls of kale leaves

2 tablespoons extra virgin olive oil

2 large garlic cloves, finely chopped

½ teaspoon fine sea salt

¼ teaspoon freshly ground black pepper

1 lemon, cut into wedges

2 to 3 tablespoons butter, melted

Preheat the oven to 400°F. Rinse the kale and thoroughly pat dry. Remove and discard thick ribs and roughly chop the leaves. Toss with the olive oil, garlic, salt, pepper, and lemon wedges in a large bowl. Spread in a thick layer on a parchment-lined baking sheet. Place in the oven and roast, stirring every 5 minutes so it doesn't dry out, until the leaves are tender and just beginning to crisp on the edges, about 15 minutes. Remove from the oven, toss with melted butter, and serve.

Honeyed Carrots with Wild Carrot Seeds

*Carrots are a token of love and prosperity. To harvest wild carrot seed, look for the dried "bird nests" on Queen Anne's lace (*Daucus carota*) plants in the fall where the umbels of the flowers have contracted (as seen in the photo, right, between the rose and the rowan berries). The flowers are also edible and can be sprinkled on this dish at the last minute as a pretty garnish. This plant has a dangerous look-alike: poison hemlock. Only forage if you have a very good guidebook. Alternatively, you can harvest from your homegrown carrots if you let them go to seed. This dish will still be delicious if you omit the seeds altogether.*

SERVES 4 TO 6

3 pounds carrots, well-scrubbed

3 tablespoons butter

1 tablespoon liquid honey

½ teaspoon salt, plus more to taste

2 teaspoons lemon juice

2 teaspoons lemon zest

2 teaspoons wild carrot seeds (see above)

Freshly ground black pepper

½ cup finely chopped carrot tops

Flowers for garnish

The carrots should be no more than ½ to ¾ inch thick. Slice them lengthwise if necessary. Melt the butter with the honey and salt over medium heat. Add the carrots and cover with a tightly fitting lid. Stir occasionally until the carrots are fork tender, about 10 minutes. Uncover, add the lemon juice, zest, and carrot seeds. Continue to cook until the carrots have softened. Add a splash of water if necessary. Season with salt and pepper, toss with the carrot tops, garnish with flowers, and serve.

Beet and Apple Slaw

Massaging the kale before assembling this salad helps break down the toughness of raw kale fibers for easier digestion. Nigella (Nigella sativa) seeds will easily fall out of dried seed pods if you grow them, but they can also be found in Indian and North African markets, sometimes under the name black cumin, black seed, or kalonji. Nigella strengthens friendship and loving bonds.

SERVES 6 TO 8

DRESSING

⅓ cup Greek yogurt

3 tablespoons white wine vinegar

1 tablespoon honey

½ teaspoon dried tarragon

SLAW

1 large bunch kale, thinly chopped then massaged

2 grated red apples such as Pink Lady or Gala

3 thinly sliced radishes

1 grated carrot

1 grated beet

½ cup raw unsalted pistachios

1 to 3 teaspoons nigella seeds, to taste

TO MAKE THE DRESSING
Whisk together all the ingredients and place in the fridge for a few hours or overnight to help the flavors mingle.

TO MAKE THE SLAW
Toss together the kale, apples, radishes, and carrots with the dressing until evenly distributed and thoroughly coated. Gently blend in the beets and pistachios, then top with the nigella seeds and serve.

Tarte aux Pommes

This classic tart reminds me of my first term at cooking school. Paris in September, the first dessert you're taught to make. . . . It's a staple of French cuisine, so fundamental it's practically a life skill, like changing a tire or learning to swim. Today when I serve this, I think of all my witch ancestors, known and unknown, whose kitchen magic nourished the bodies and spirits of their communities. I think of this kitchen magic as another life skill, one I'm proud to share, and teach, and pass on to future generations.

MAKES A 7- OR 8-INCH TART

PÂTE BRISÉE SUCRÉE

1½ cups flour

¾ cup cubed cold butter

2 tablespoons sugar

½ teaspoon vanilla extract or ½-inch
   vanilla bean pod, scraped

Pinch of salt

1 egg

1 to 2 tablespoons cold water

POMMES FILLING

6 small to medium tart apples

¼ cup butter, plus extra for topping

¼ cup sugar, plus extra for topping

Juice of 1 lemon

¼ cup water

GLAZE

¾ cup quince or apricot jelly

1 tablespoon rose water or brandy

Dried rose petals for garnish

TO MAKE THE PÂTE BRISÉE SUCRÉE

Preheat the oven to 350°F. Add all the ingredients except the egg and water to a food processor. Pulse until blended and the butter chunks range in size from small pea to kidney bean. Turn the machine on to low speed and add the egg, then a slow steady stream of cold water until the dough pulls together. Remove from the processor and shape into a flattened disc, wrap in plastic wrap, and rest in the refrigerator for 30 minutes. Remove and roll out on a lightly floured surface to about ¼ inch thick. Press the dough evenly into the pan. Line with parchment or foil and weigh down with rice, beans, or sugar. Blind bake 15 minutes, remove the lining and pie weights, then continue to bake another 5 minutes or so. Remove from the oven and cool.

TO MAKE THE POMMES FILLING

Peel and core 3 of the apples and chop roughly. Melt the butter in a large pan and sauté the chopped apples, sugar, lemon juice, and water. Stir frequently until golden brown and smoothly glazed, 20 to 30 minutes. Allow to cool while you process the remaining apples.

TO ASSEMBLE

Peel and core the remaining 3 apples. Cut in half and slice crosswise about ⅛ inch thick. Fill the tart crust with the cooled cooked apples. Layer the slices on top starting with the outer ring, working toward the middle. Melt a little butter—just till creamy and spreadable, not totally liquid—and brush over the top of the tart. Sprinkle it with sugar. Cover the edge of the pie crust with aluminum foil to prevent burning. Bake the tart until the tips of the sliced apples are tender and golden, about 25 minutes. About 5 minutes before your tart is done, melt the jelly over low-medium heat. Add the rose water, remove from heat, and stir to blend well. Glaze the tart as soon as you remove it from the oven and sprinkle it with dried rose petals.

Magical Correspondences

One could make the argument that tables of correspondence for magical practice are patriarchal hand-me-downs from secret societies that serve to create a class distinction between folk magic and "high magic." I think that would be fair. But one can also make the argument that they've evolved well beyond that.

Tables of correspondence have their roots in technical Hermetica, treatises written in Greek as far back as the 2nd or 3rd century BCE. They display Greek, Jewish, and Egyptian influences, were translated into Arabic, Latin, and Armenian, and widely copied throughout the Middle Ages. They blend astrology, alchemy, magic, medicine, and pharmacology. They strongly influenced several branches of spiritual thought and major figures including Aleister Crowley, Arthur Waite, and the Hermetic Order of the Golden Dawn. In other words, they're the stuff of ceremonial magic, not folk magic.

However, I believe that over time, the morphic resonance of a thing gets stronger as the collective imagination coalesces around it. Under the influence of time, fashion, economy, cultural exchange, generations of individual actors, and countless reinterpretations, the meanings and efficacies have shifted. As I've experimented with herbs, stones, animals, elements, and The More Than over time, I've come to feel that tables are a good starting place for devising rituals. Very often, the results match the description. When they don't, I regard that as valuable information: This ingredient and I have a different relationship than expected or described in the literature. That's great feedback that I note in my own grimoire for future reference. And this is how it's always been. Readers two thousand years ago likewise probably found the *Corpus Hermeticum* fairly hit-or-miss. Tables of correspondence attempt to pattern influences, not absolutes. In other words, they are not universal laws. Not everything in the correspondences I provide here will land as true for you. If it doesn't, that's good data for your own grimoire. Experiment with these ingredients, attune to them, allow them to work alongside and through you.

I've included not only edible ingredients here but also other components you may wish to include in your magical workings through images, figurines, or other representations. When ingesting materials as part of your magic, only ingest what you *absolutely know* to be edible and safe.

A NOTE ON

Appropriation

At times I've listed deities from cultures other than my own because I've learned something about them in my research that I thought would be useful for some readers. Their inclusion does not imply permission to lift a deity out of their cultural context for self-enrichment. Personally, I've found that they rarely perform their supposed functions that well outside of their context. Any relationship with a deity not of my own cultural heritage that actually does work with me collaboratively has only done so after many years of courtship—deep devotion and relational work—and the nature of our relationship is mostly private. Please exercise discernment, restraint, and respect here.

ABUNDANCE: Duck, chicken, cow, cornucopia, all grains, calendula, cinnamon, ginger, gold and all precious metals, green, vigorous live plants, Venus.

ACONITUM (AKA MONKSHOOD, WOLFSBANE): Invisibility, protection. Sacred to Hekate. Poisonous.

ACORN: Fertility, creativity, innovation, good timing.

AGATE: Banishment, protection, balance, centering, concentration, security. Different types of agate have different meanings.

AIR ELEMENT: Breath, ideas, perception, spirit, celestial realms, sound waves, pressure, thunder, whirlwinds, disorientation, space, perspective. Mediation between earth and sky. Associated with dawn, spring, intellect, birds, smoke wands, incense, agate, aventurine, benzoin, borage, clover, lemon verbena, mint, red apples, turquoise, Inanna, Persephone, Lilith, Hekate, Hathor, Hel, Ishtar, Isis, Medusa, Sekhmet, Tara, Baba Yaga, the Cailleach, Iris, Ereshkigal, Valkyries, Dakinis, Zephyrus.

ALDER: Balance, harmony, communion, the Crone.

ALMOND: Divine favor, clairvoyance, creativity. A yonic symbol of conjugal happiness. Represents source energy.

AMETHYST: Recovery, awareness, spiritual connection, clarity, gentle protection, healing. Balance of all the elements. Amplifier.

AMPLIFIERS: Amber, frankincense, gold, grape, hazel, mandrake, quartz, sun, vervain, copper, fennel, birch, amethyst, blue goldstone, cedar, dandelion, echinacea, geranium, gold, goldstone, hawthorn, heather, juniper, lavender, mint, Queen Anne's lace, tansy, yarrow.

APHRODISIACS: Garlic, ginger, jasmine, henbane, lovage, saffron, tomato, cardamom, vanilla.

APPLE: Love magic. Invokes witch ancestors. Tree of Immortality. Connected to Freya, Aphrodite, Merlin, and King Arthur.

AQUAMARINE: Heart strength, processing anger, support during grief and loss, clarity, courageous communication, stress release.

ARTICHOKES: Cooked in pairs brings good luck in love, but in odd numbers brings misfortune.

ASH TREE: World Tree, Yggdrasil, Great Mother Tree, cosmic consciousness, manifestation, prosperity. Associated with faerie. Winged seed pods are protective against hostile magic.

ASPEN: Expansion, increase, fuller self-expression, spreading your wings.

AVENTURINE: Love, healing, prosperity, creativity.

BACHELOR'S BUTTON: Independence, luck, worn over the heart to attract love.

BALANCE: Amethyst, agate, benzoin, duck, feathers, bee propolis resin and honey, gold, brown, hawthorn, peacock ore, clear quartz, moonstone, pears, alder, amethyst, lapis lazuli, lavender, turquoise, clear quartz, sapphire.

BANISHING: Anise, asafoetida, bay laurel, basil, devil's claw, wormwood, rue, rosemary, pine, nettles, mistletoe, holly, thistle, hellebore, garlic, vinegar, salt, black salt, smoky quartz, tourmaline, agate, benzoin, cedar, daffodil, fennel, mugwort, iron, juniper, mullein, onion, poppy, rowan, sage.

BARLEY: Fertility, healing, blessing, grounding, ancestral connection. Sacred to Demeter.

BASIL: Dispels fear and confusion, brings courage, purification.

BAY: Protection, triumph, divination, clairvoyance, cleansing, high status and honor, divinatory when used as smoke. Represents the sun and fire. Sacred to Apollo.

BEANS: Ancestors, resurrection, reincarnation, immortality, manifestation, long life.

BEAUTY: Aphrodite, Freya, rose, jasmine, honey, evening primrose, apple.

BEES: Collectivism, productivity, nurturance, reward, joy, nobility, blessings, bliss. Transformation of the sun into riches. Omens of good luck but also carry a sting for thieves and cheats, such as billionaires and wealth hoarders. Connected to the Great Mother Goddess archetype.

BELLADONNA: A baneful herb used in flying ointments and love spells. Poisonous.

BINDING: Indigo, ivy, bindweed, melted wax, cordage and twine, locks and keys.

BIRCH: Community, new beginnings, cleansing the past. Protects from evil eye, faerie, and bad luck. Associated with Brigid and Freya. Amplifier.

BLACK: Solemnity, strength, protection (sending away and keeping at bay), comfort in darkness, enshrouding, fertility, resurrection, initiation, creation, maturity, patience, consummation, transformation, self-understanding, turning inward, eternity.

BLESSING: Salt, sugar, orange blossom water, rose water, rose petals, chamomile, coriander, cumin, rice, barley, daffodil, dandelion, dill, fennel, frankincense, gold, mugwort, St. John's wort, salt, silver, sun, valerian, vervain, amethyst, bees, honey, calendula, chestnut, chrysocolla, clover, coffee, corn, fluorite, grapes, heather, juniper, lunaria, olive, yarrow, sodalite, sandalwood.

BLUE: Teaching, mental acuity, training and skill development, apprenticeship, wisdom, elderhood, written communication, luxury, celestial realms.

BLUEBERRY: Recovery, healing, optimism, confidence, eternity.

BLUE CALCITE: Creativity, bone healing, visionary gifts, ancestral connection, clear written communication, space clearing (especially the bedroom or office).

BONES: Ancestors, animal kin, shape-shifting, nature as family of origin, Earth element.

BORAGE: "I, Borage, grant courage." Confidence, support for depression, overcoming fear.

BOUNDARIES: Cats, thistle, blackberries, datura, rosemary, vervain, red, black, salt, vinegar, sage, cloves, Florida Water, No. 4711 Eau de Cologne, incense, or saining smoke.

BREAD: Physical and spiritual nourishment, sustenance, miraculous transformation, rebirth, fecundity, grace, generosity, procreation, prosperity.

BROWN: Grounding, stabilizing, steadfastness, connection to land, ancestors and the Underworld, balance, decomposition, fecundity, dormancy, support.

BUSINESS: Hazelnuts, aventurine, carnelian, citrine, gold, silver, goldstone, emerald, citrus, lentils, cedar, fennel, chestnut, oregano, rowan, sweet woodruff, frankincense.

BUTTER: Calmness, nourishment, spiritual reward. Sacred to Inanna, Agni, and Brigid.

CALENDULA: Steadfastness, blessing, consecrating sacred space, constancy in love, good dreams. Associated with Midsummer and fire. Sacred to Freya.

CARDAMOM: Love and romance magic, aphrodisiac, eloquence. Connected to Erzulie.

CARNELIAN: Revitalization, regeneration, protection, success, justice, strength, confidence. Represents fire.

CARROT: Fertility, prosperity, wealth, a love token.

CATTLE: Abundance, communion with the moon, nurturance, soothing, maternal care, community, family bonds, fertilization, generosity, wealth and security. Sacred to Brigid, Hathor, Nut, Isis, Shiva, Indra, Krishna, and Helios.

CAULDRON: Receptacle of magical power, agent of alchemy, and vessel for spellcraft. Represents the womb, abundance, transformation, divination, healing, and well-being. For the modern witch, a large pot or Dutch oven easily becomes a cauldron.

CEDAR: Protection, cleansing, resourcefulness, success, spiritual healing, purification after contact with the dead and funerary rites. Banishes hostile spirits. Amplifier.

CELESTITE: Mental clarity, prophecy, contacting guardian spirits, connection with the celestial realms, sweet dreams.

CHAMOMILE: Blessing, protection from bad luck and evil forces, relieves melancholy, dreamwork.

CHESTNUT: Blessing, fertility, abundance, longevity, justice, success.

CHICKEN: Abundance, fertility, nurturance, world creator, protectiveness, renewal, devotion, connection. Corresponds to the sun. Roosters are sacred to Muhammad, Amaterasu, and Apollo.

CHRYSOCOLLA: Water energies, truth, communication, calmness, blessing, clarity, wisdom.

CHRYSOPRASE: Attracts love, abundance, promotes healing from a broken heart, relieves depression.

CINNAMON: Love magic, protection, passion, expansion, fire.

CITRINE: Abundance, prosperity, confidence, empowerment, attracts wealth and richness.

CLARITY: Lavender, lemon, mint, dill, clary sage, rosemary, lovage, thyme, tea, water, glass, blues, white, chrysocolla, fluorite, emerald, tiger's eye, amazonite, quartz, selenite, light, candles, duck, birds, feathers, fir, Queen Anne's lace, yarrow, air, fire.

CLEANSING: Salt, cinnamon, lavender, eucalyptus, lemon, lemon balm, lemon verbena, mint, rosemary, rue, Florida Water, fir, cranberries, flax, juniper, pine, schungite, thistle.

CLOVER: Blessing, prosperity, protection of animals and assets.

COFFEE: Mysticism, creativity, conviviality, psychoactive transcendence, revelation, blessing, release, connected to fortune-telling.

COMFREY: Healing, stability, endurance, magic connected to real estate.

CONFIDENCE: Garnet, sodalite, black tourmaline, apatite, jade, quartz, pyrite, lion, tiger, bear, orange, gold, red, iron, sunstone, citrine, peridot, borage, carnelian.

COMMUNICATION: Blue, chrysocolla, blue lace agate, blue calcite, blue goldstone, apatite, aquamarine, lapis lazuli, celestite, amethyst, crow, raven, feathers, horse, lavender, sodalite.

COPPER: Beauty, attraction, love magic. Used in earth-honoring workings, conducts energy well. Connected to Venus and Aphrodite.

CORN: Wealth, prosperity, fertility, life-giving qualities, security, sustenance, generosity, sweetness.

COURAGE: Lion, wolf, bear, borage, thyme, ginger, pine, cedar, sandalwood, tiger's eye, pyrite, amazonite, carnelian, labradorite, citrine, amber, aquamarine, cranberries, raspberries, strawberries, hawthorn, jasper, lovage, poplar, yarrow, wolf, pine.

CRANBERRIES: Healing, cleansing, action, rejuvenation, energy.

CREAM AND MILK: Abundance, nurturance, eternal life, procreation, food of the gods, the Mother archetype.

CREATIVITY: Citrine, lapis lazuli, carnelian, blue lace agate, quartz, amethyst, ametrine, apatite, tiger's eye, fluorite, rainbow moonstone, labradorite, tangerine, lavender, jasmine, peppermint, bergamot, cypress, orange, coffee, salmon, egg yolks, blueberries, dahlias, pine, mushrooms, yellow, orange.

CUMIN: Protection, resisting conformity. Take care: This spice can amplify anger.

DAFFODIL: Protection and banishing, carries solar energies.

DAHLIA: Elegance, inner strength, creativity, dignity, kindness, grace, eternal love.

DAISY: Love divination, faerie plant, attracts positive attention from nature spirits.

DANDELION: Divination, visionary powers, protection. Connected to the sun and Jupiter. Sacred to Brigid. Amplifier.

DATURA (DEVIL'S TRUMPET): Enlightenment, insight, revelation of the mysteries and astronomy, prophecy, connected to the moon and the ocean. Poisonous.

DEATH AND REBIRTH DEITIES: Astarte, Inanna, Ishtar, Lilith, Persephone, Proserpina, Demeter, Hekate, Hathor, Hel, Isis, Osiris, Tammuz, Adonis, Attis, Dionysus, Medusa, Tara, Baba Yaga, the Cailleach, Bride.

DEAD, THE BELOVED: Narcissus, amaranth, hawthorn, mint, poppy, yew, sage, St. John's wort, tansy, datura, aconitum, violet, amethyst, cypress, Persephone, Hekate, Osiris, Hades, Nephthys, pomegranate, wheat.

DEER: Gentleness, sensitivity, swiftness, calm, caution, grace, athleticism, transformation, initiation, belonging, reverence, renewal, spiritual growth, patience, fertility, generosity. Connected to the sun, the Great Mother Goddess archetype, and the World Tree due to the stag's antlers resembling branches. Sacred to the Cailleach, Diana, and Artemis.

DILL: Blessing, protection, mental clarity.

DUCK: Clarity, family, connection, devotion, balance, intuition, flow, friendliness, monogamous love, honesty, resourcefulness, simplicity, flexibility.

EARTH ELEMENT: Associated with browns, greens, physical body, bear, rabbit, burrowing animals, amulets, talismans, medicine pouches and magical foods, flower essences and oils, acorn, agate, amethyst, blue goldstone, bone, copper, dandelion, fir, goldstone, hazel, jasper, malachite, mullein, plantain, prehnite, rose, rose hips, salt, smoky quartz, sour green apple, tiger's eye, yarrow, Gaia, Demeter, Ceres, Flora, Isis, Uma, Inanna, Cailleach Beara, Cernunnos, Green Man, Mother Earth, Pachamama, Artemis, Freya, Diana, Shekinah.

ECHINACEA: Health, resilience, endurance, protection from poverty and troubled times. Amplifier.

EGG: In many creation myths, the universe is hatched from the World Egg. Yolks represent the sun. Represents rebirth. Healing through incubation and being broken open.

ELDERFLOWER: Happiness, beauty, attracts love, connection, protection, healing. Associated with Midsummer. Sacred to Frau Holle.

ELM: Heightens dreamwork, attracts faerie contact.

ELOQUENCE: Hazelnut, fennel, chestnut, cardamom, agate, Hermes, Mercury, chrysocolla, blue lace agate, turquoise.

EMERALD: Visionary powers, memory, successful partnerships, protection from trickery, truth stone, divination, strong Earth connection. Connected to Venus.

FEATHERS: Vision, transcendence, inspiration, insight, communication with the divine, convey prayers, balance, joy, ascension, celestial knowledge, altered states, air and sky.

FENNEL: Blessing, fertility, virility, healing, and protection from malefic spirits. Amplifier when used for banishment but can also amplify anger and sorrow, so use with care.

FERTILITY AND VIRILITY: Acorns, lilies, almond, barley, grapes, cat, catnip, chicken, fennel, corn, tomato, apple, asparagus, birch, chestnut, hawthorn, heather, monarda, oak, olive, geranium, amber, copper, moonstone, rose quartz, figs, honey, peaches, pears, goat, deer, green, black, holly, hollyhock, rabbit, snake, sun. Connected to Brigid, Freya, Hekate, Isis, Shakti Shiva, Hera, Zeus, moon, sun.

FIR: Fortitude, immortality, cleansing, clarity, continuity, ancestry. Conveys messages to other realms. Amplifier.

FIRE ELEMENT: Self-discovery, illumination, shapeshifting. Life-giving or life-taking. Associated with south, noon, summer, red, spiritual essence, primal spark, candles, incense, burn bundles, wands, sun, stars. Connected to Brigid, Hestia, Vesta, Hina, Pele, Amaterasu, Set, Lugh, Kali, Sekhmet, antler, bay laurel, birch, blue goldstone, calendula, carnelian, cedar, chamomile, chestnut, echinacea, fennel, goldstone, hawthorn, hibiscus, hops, jasper, juniper, lemon balm, milk thistle, mugwort, nettle, orange, oregano, stag, fox, Queen Anne's lace, rosemary, rowan, tiger's eye, wormwood, colors on the red/pink spectrum as well as yellows, oranges, and golds.

FLAX (SEED AND OIL): Purification, cleansing, extraction, healing.

FLUORITE: Blessings, focus, heart healing, protection, watery energy.

FOXGLOVE: A baneful plant that can also be applied for soothing and comfort. Attracts contact with nature spirits and faeries.

FRANKINCENSE: Creativity, divine love, transcendence, higher consciousness, spiritual development, purification, wealth, abundance, blessings, success.

FRIENDSHIP: Yellow roses, pansies and violas, zinnias, interlocking hands or hearts, chrysanthemum, geranium, lovage, topaz, jade plants, green, pink, yellow, lemon, yellow topaz, rose quartz, lapis lazuli, amethyst, peridot, moss agate, ametrine, infinity symbol, dog, olive.

GARLIC: Strength, potency, masculine aphrodisiac, banishment, protection against all forms of malevolence. Connected to Mars.

GARNET: Grounding, digestion (physical and emotional), sexual healing, ambition, prosperity, abundance, love, commitment, strength of will, warmth in relationships, sensuality, trust.

GERANIUM: Blessing, happiness, well-being, vitality, ingenuity, friendship. Amplifier.

GINGER: Awakens and energizes the spirit, courage, prosperity, good luck, sensuality, love, health, aphrodisiac.

GOAT: Humor, fearlessness, lusty pleasure, rowdy fun, generosity. Sacred to Pan, Dionysus, Aphrodite, and Thor.

GOLD: Prosperity, blessing, balance, healing, good fortune, nobility, spiritual development, attainment of goals, perfect balance of all elemental qualities. Related to the sun. Amplifier.

GOLDENROD: Abundance, healing, encouragement, growth, fortune, happiness, wholeness, new beginnings, wealth on its way.

GRAPES: Love magic, transformation, abundance, blessing, prosperity, conducts other energies well. Sacred to Bacchus, Dionysus.

GREEN: Grounding, abundance, wealth and vitality, connection to animal essence and wildness, healing, fertility, love, connection, trust, friendship, creativity, luck.

GRIEF: Goldenrod, marjoram, aquamarine, calcite, agate, chrysocolla, malachite, tourmaline, moonstone, lepidolite, onyx, rose quartz, cedarwood oil, pine, spruce, fir, valerian, frankincense, ylang-ylang, water, lentils, Hekate, Demeter, Persephone, Brigid, Miseria.

GROUNDING: Smoky quartz, cedar, calcite, onyx, sapphire, black tourmaline, tiger's eye, peacock ore, jasper, garnet, greens, browns, snowflake obsidian, schungite, root vegetables, meats, barley.

HAPPINESS: Basil, almond, honey, geranium, orange, oregano, rose, pearl, bergamot, hawthorn, elderflower, dogwood, goldenrod, lemon, oats, peridot, potato, tourmaline, dog, yellows, topaz.

HAWTHORN: The May Tree, guardian to the Otherworld, courage, balance, strength of heart, love, courtship, heart medicine, connection with nature spirits. So holy that no malicious spirit can approach it. Offerings should always be left when gathering from it. Amplifier.

HAZEL AND HAZELNUTS: Wisdom, prophecy, eloquence, oration, clear communication, intuitive gifts. Used for dowsing, magic wands, and talismans.

Supports entrepreneurial pursuits, wealth, and good fortune. Conducts energy cleanly and effectively. Connected to Hermes.

HEALING: Brigid, Hekate, Mielikki, Asclepius, dog, allspice, amaranth, bay laurel, barley, blueberries, cinnamon, echinacea, maple, oak, rose, violet, amethyst, amber, aquamarine, aventurine, blue calcite, copper, lapis lazuli, quartz, turquoise, ruby, sapphire, pine, garlic, juniper, lemon, nutmeg, rosemary, rue, elderberry, lavender, mushrooms, nettle, oats, olive, onion, peacock ore, poplar, potato, rose quartz, sage, serpent, St. John's wort, schungite, silver, sun, swan, thistle tourmaline, yarrow.

HEATHER: Blessings for initiations, new beginnings, peacemaking, attracts friendly spirits, good luck, summons good faeries to the garden, soothes fatigue, dreamless sleep. Amplifier.

HELLEBORE: A toxic plant known for banishing, exorcism, and invisibility spells.

HENBANE: A baneful herb. Psychoactive, sedative, soporific properties. Used in flying ointments. Smoke was thought to be inhaled by the priestesses at Delphi. Male aphrodisiac. Invokes Underworld deities. Poisonous.

HIBISCUS: Love magic, sensuality, divination, clairvoyance, protection.

HOLLY: Protection, peace, goodwill, eternal life. A wand made of holly will subdue and direct invoked entities. Associated with Father Winter, the Holly King, Thor, Taranis.

HOLLYHOCK: Cycle of life. Used in ancient funerary as well as fertility rites.

HOME: Hestia, Brigid, Hekate, basil, betony, indigo, chamomile, mugwort, olive, geranium, tomato, apple, rose quartz, wolfsbane, duck, chicken, dog, cat, rowan, seashells, snail shells. All tutelary spirits including house brownies.

HONEY: Abundance, wisdom, pleasure, grace, prosperity, plenitude, immortality, luck, joy, unity, fertility, sensuality, desire, attractiveness. Traditional offering and ingredient in baked goods for faerie folk. Eaten for communion with the sun.

INDIGO: Integrity, devotion, sincerity, intuition, inner voice, wisdom, nobility, luxury, innovation, spiritual power, fairness.

IOLITE: Intuition, contacting spirit guides, inspiration and creative flow, speaking your truth.

IRON: Banishing, protection, strength, fortitude, resoluteness, tenacity, confidence. Sharp edges will cut through etheric energy. Connected to Vulcan, Aries, Mars.

IVY: Tenacity, fidelity, loyalty, steadfastness, binding, fortitude, everlasting life. Connected to the Mother archetype.

JADE: Victory, long life, healing, repels attacks.

JASMINE: Creativity, divine love, soul connection, sensuality, aphrodisiac, relationship harmony, mood lifter.

JASPER: Protection, courage, grounding, nurturance, can be used to invoke rain.

JUNIPER: Cleansing, blessing, protection, safe journeying (physical and spiritual worlds), recover stolen property, banishment, purification, welcoming new spirit allies and also to politely dismiss them at the end of a ritual. Sacred to Hekate. Amplifier.

JUSTICE: Carnelian, jasper, ruby, swords, scales, feather, blindfold, keys, Athena, Ma'at.

KALE: Money, faith, strength. Fortune-telling plant associated with Samhain.

KEYS: To lock in or out, binding, security, protection, revelation, initiation, self-discovery, opportunity, freedom, power, esoteric knowledge. Sacred to Hekate, Ishtar, and Cybele.

LAPIS LAZULI: Truth, wisdom, visionary thinking, balance of generative and receptive energies. Connected to Inanna.

LAVENDER: Harmony, clarity, healing, intuition, psychic and visionary trance work. Balances by both calming and energizing. Amplifier.

LEEK: Protects from lightning and electrical hazards.

LEMON: Friendship, clarity, cleansing, happiness, healing, hope, purpose, optimism, and action.

LEMON BALM: Love magic, sympathy, compassion. Relieves melancholy, revives vital spirits. Connected to honeybees, wellness, restful sleep, calmness, longevity, and the elixir of life.

LEMON VERBENA: Gentle releasement, clarity, cleansing, purification, restores vitality.

LENTILS: Eaten during mourning and grief in some traditions, but also a symbol of prosperity, good luck, expansion, and marriage in others.

LETTUCE: Fertility. Connected to the element of water.

LILAC: Flexibility, freedom, acceptance, new love, spiritual connection.

LILY: Beauty, love, sensuality. Useful when single-mindedness is necessary. Sacred to Diana.

LOVE: Aphrodite, Erzulie, Freya, Eros, Selene, Venus, almond, apple, basil, rose, cinnamon, garlic, goldenrod, hawthorn, juniper, lemon, nutmeg, poppy, rosemary, wormwood, vervain, yarrow, agate, copper, garnet, lapis lazuli, moonstone, pearl, morganite, honey, jasmine, violet, tomato, vanilla, lilac, lemon balm, iris, hibiscus, green, grapes, garnet, elderflower, duck, dog, daisy, chrysoprase, dahlia, belladonna, bachelor's button, charoite, calendula, artichoke.

LUNARIA (HONESTY, SILVER DOLLAR PLANT): Prosperity, wealth, increase, moon blessings.

MAGNETITE: Manifestation, attraction, amplification, Underworld journeying, stability, balance, absorbs positive energies and repels fear.

MALACHITE: Protection of children, abundance, prosperity, regeneration, balance, emotional release, beneficial to heart and throat.

MAPLE: Sustenance, joy, connection, family, nurturance, hope, practical magic.

MARIGOLD: Consecration, protection, blessings, tribute to the dead. Associated with the sun.

MARRIAGE: Rosemary, apple, birch, hawthorn, Hera, Frigg, Freyr, Brigid, marigold, rose, garnet, smoky quartz, diamond, moonstone, yarrow, anise, lentils.

MILK THISTLE: Will purify the user who is the target of envy, anger, or hatred. Banishment.

MINT: Consecration, cleansing, protection, blessing, release, divination, clarity. Amplifier.

MOON: Rhythm, mood, emotions, intuition, psyche, fluidity, ocean, dew, menstrual cycles, ebb and flow, increase and diminishment. Kinship, maternal nurturance, dependability. Connected to the west, lunar hare, frog, cattle, water, fish, lettuce, lily, nutmeg, opal, quartz, silver, moonflower, selenite, moonstone, lunaria, Artemis, Hekate, Selene, Thoth.

MOONSTONE: Calmness, gentleness, receptivity, new beginnings, abundant crops, inner strength, creativity, intuition, hope, sensuality, strength of the in-dwelling spirit.

MUGWORT: Prophetic dreams, divination, banishing, protection, consecration, vigil, endurance and energy. Sacred to Artemis. Coastal mugwort has similar qualities with the added potency of the Spirits of Place of the West Coast. Do not ingest mugwort if pregnant as it stimulates menstruation, and avoid if breastfeeding.

MULLEIN: Protection of household and property, banishment of hostile spirits.

MUSHROOMS: Long life, creativity, enchantment, expansion, alteration, inspiration, connection, collaboration, messengers, sacred communion, coming forth from nothingness into being. Associated with faerie rings, spirit houses, Little People of the Forest, gnomes and other tutelary spirits. Related to shamanistic experiences, trance journeying, and Otherworldly wisdom and healing.

NETTLE: Boundaries, nourishment, communal resilience, strength of will, banishment, blessing, healing. Do not ingest if pregnant or suffer from heart or kidney problems.

NIGELLA: Harmony, love, bonding, intuition, glamour magic, women's power. Connected to Venus, Hypatia, St. Catherine.

NUTMEG: Love magic, connected to the moon, intensifies dreams. Combination of lunar and solar energies representing balance.

OAK: Protector and spiritual gatekeeper, bearer of endless, life-giving generosity. Bury an amulet in the roots of an oak tree so your magical working will endure beyond your death. Sacred to Zeus, Jupiter, and Thor.

OATS: Healing, calmness, kindness, material increase, wealth, plenty, clear perception, happiness.

OLIVE (TREE, FRUIT, AND OIL): Tree of Life for ancient Muslims, Hebrews, Greeks, and Romans. Evokes resilience, life everlasting, intergenerational family and ancestors. Sacred anointing, healing, friendship, blessing, prosperity, abundance, well-being, rebirth, asylum, and peace. Connected to Hercules and Abrahamic religions. Sacred to Pax, Athena, Zeus, and Ra.

ONION: Banishing, healing, memories, warding off evil spirits, protection.

ORANGE: Blessing, abundance, prosperity, joy, self-knowledge, strength, courage, power, justice. Orange blossom water blesses marriage in particular. Represents the sun.

ORANGE AND/OR YELLOW CALCITE: Creativity, fire, sensuality, passion, abundance, confidence, wealth.

OREGANO: Love magic and long-term commitment, success, blessing. Sacred to Aphrodite.

PANSY AND/OR VIOLAS: Modesty, humility, flirtation and emerging love, fidelity, friendship, platonic love, admiration.

PARSLEY: Actually, a rather bad omen in the ancient past, closely associated with Satan. It was said the seed had to travel to hell and back seven times before it would sprout. However, can be a soothing helper when working with the dead, and an ally in principled resistance.

PEACH: A Tree of Life whose branches extended to the sky as a ladder for the gods to move between the worlds. Connected with divinity yet also with erotic sensuousness. Food of the gods and sacred to Shou Lao, the bearded old god of long life.

PEAR: Balance, comfort, inner peace. Because of the womb-like shape, love that survives separation such as mothers allowing their children to grow up. Sacred to Hera.

PERIDOT: Manifestation, increase, wealth and prosperity, abundance, rejuvenation, health in aging, confidence, happiness.

PIG: Curiosity, fruitfulness, sociability, pragmatism, fecundity, resourcefulness, immortality, intelligence, generativity. Represents the Earth itself as well as the Underworld. Sacred to Freya, Freyr, Demeter, Artemis, Persephone, Nut, and Isis.

PINE: Tree of Life archetype. Connected to stars, night sky, immortality, courage, constancy, creativity, regeneration, cleansing, strength, steadfastness, release, wisdom of old age. Sacred to Zeus, Artemis, Confucius, Dionysus, Poseidon, Attis, and Cybele.

PLANTAIN: Banishment for nightmares and nocturnal visitations. Abundance, security, family.

POMEGRANATE: Wisdom, everlasting life, the Underworld, related to blood mysteries and eternal renewal. Sacred to Persephone and Hades.

POPLAR: Courage, faith, support, heart healing, vision, transformation, victory.

POPPY: Water, the moon, offerings to the dead, dreamwork, Underworld journeys, divination, love spells, prosperity magic, banishing. Connected to Persephone.

POTATO: Adaptability, healing, happiness, utility, nourishment.

PROTECTION: Bay laurel, pepper, cinnamon, clove, fennel, garlic, onion, pine, rue, St. John's wort, thyme, witch hazel, onyx, amethyst, clear quartz, wormwood, cedar, sage, prehnite, monkshood, agate, amber, antler, apple, benzoin, betony, birch, black, black tourmaline, carnelian, cedar, chamomile, hyssop, malachite, keys, iron, jasper, juniper, mullein, nettle, mint, marigold, raspberry leaf, red, rosemary, rue, rowan, sapphire, sheep, schungite, snowflake obsidian, silver, smoky quartz, tansy, thistle, tiger's eye, white, wolf, yarrow.

PURPLE: Integrity, self-control and discipline, grandeur, honor, sacredness, mysticism, spiritual growth, attracting allies and connection to other deities.

QUARTZ (CLEAR): Balance of all elements, spiritual connection, protection, divination, healing, clarity. Helps any talisman hold its charge.

QUEEN ANNE'S LACE: Passion, love magic, grounding. Amplifier. Do not ingest if pregnant, stimulates menstruation.

RABBIT: Shape-shifting, cunning, sensitivity, speed, invisibility, fertility, immortality, renewal, thresholds, guide of initiates. Connected to the moon, the Cailleach, Aphrodite.

RAINBOW: Optimism, promise, coming through the storm, transcendence, evanescence, freedom, transition, good luck, blessing, link to the supernatural world. Connected to Iris, Noah.

RASPBERRY: Kindness, calmness, courage, women's mysteries, love spells, glamour magic. Connected to maternal love and caregiving. Sacred to Venus and Zeus.

RASPBERRY LEAF: Blessing, support, protection, patience, positive benefits for pregnant and lactating women. Carries watery energies.

RED: Creativity, power, passion, sexuality, sensuality, confidence, protection, strength, courage, rootedness.

RICE: Blessing, prosperity, fertility, good health and long life, spiritual nourishment, security. Connected to the Mother archetype.

ROSE: Wholeness, heart, love, protects couples and partnership, soothes the inner child, helps heal wounded sexuality, thwarts the evil eye. Associated with the Great Mother, Aphrodite, Eros, Venus, Flora, Mother Mary, and Isis. Rose hips are used as offerings to invite friendly spirits to take up residence.

ROSEMARY: Ancestral memory, blessing of unions, purification, remembrance, clarity, protection, lifts depression. Connected to both sun and moon.

ROSE QUARTZ: Unconditional love, joy, warmth, emotional healing, nurturance, secure attachment, blessing, protection, peace, calm, stress reduction.

ROWAN (MOUNTAIN ASH): Success, protector tree, particularly against poor harvest, illness, theft, and misfortune. Banishes disruptive forces including mean faeries.

RUBY: Strength, vigor, love, fairness, justice. Amplifies fire.

RUE: Love spells, fertility charms, protection magic, processing remorse, cleansing, dispels envy, identified with witches as a sign of mutual recognition. Sacred to Diana and Mars.

ST. JOHN'S WORT: Protection of animals, dispels supernatural interference, healing, protection, vitality, fullness, connected to Midsummer.

SAFFRON: Spiritual humility, holiness, abundance, nobility, wealth. Connected to Hercules and the sun. Sacred to Hekate.

SAGE (CULINARY): Longevity, clarity, soothing, healing, wisdom, immortality, spiritual sanctity. Connected to Jupiter. Intensifies the magic of rue if grown nearby.

SALMON: Determination, endurance, fertilization, self-sacrifice, change and cycles, interconnectedness, wisdom, abundance, prosperity, renewal, spiritual journeys.

SALT: Highly valued as a gift of hospitality and indication of worth and esteem (it's where the term *salary* comes from). Cleansing, purification, can represent the elements of fire, water, or earth. Absorbs negative magical energies and holds them in a fixed, inactive form. Banishing, blessing, purification, health, wealth, employment, career, fertility, security, stability, ancestors, supports gentle release of grief.

SANDALWOOD: Purification, blessing, visionary trancework, strongly connected to the air element.

SAPPHIRE: Hope, faith, spiritual insight, balance, protection, good fortune, wisdom, truth, heightens intuition. Amplifies the water element.

SEASHELLS: Sea magic, home. Many of the qualities of bones including ancestral connection; however, they are mostly used for connection to the water element or the moon.

SEEDS: All types of seeds and pods are associated with Imbolc, Ostara, and Beltane magic, new beginnings, and growth.

SELENITE: Calm, clarity, rejuvenation, honesty, truth, personal growth, connection to the angelic realms, the moon. Sacred to the moon goddess, Selene.

SEQUOIA: Ambition, dreams, attainment, endurance, strength, well-being and long life.

SERPENT AND SNAKE: Renewal, transformation, change, healing, primordial life force, creation, death and rebirth, immortality, sensitivity, endurance, guardian of secrets and all that is hidden, oracular faculties, unblinking attunement, unflinching courage, incredible feats, nobility, majesty, seduction, shifting sexuality, related to all genders, potency, fertility, initiation, revelation, visionary dreams. Sacred to Persephone, Hekate, Shakti, Isis, Kali, Shiva, Asclepius, and the Great Mother Goddess archetype.

SHEEP: Lambs and ewes represent tenderness, gentleness, sociability, companionship, renewal, innocence, sweetness, generosity, simplicity, frolicsome fun, newness, the moon. Rams represent nobility, fierce protection, skillful warriorship, competence, sovereignty, competition, victory. Connected to Indra, Thor, Zeus, Amun-Ra, Hermes, Psyche, fire, the sun.

SILVER: Receptivity, healing, related to water and the moon. Can bear high levels of energy. Good for working with helpful nature spirits and ancestors. Protection from werewolves.

SMOKY QUARTZ: Grounding, banishing. Calls in the protection of Dark Goddesses such as Hekate and Lilith. Amplifies the energies of other stones.

SPIRIT ELEMENT: Associated with center, now, eternity, the cosmic self, unlimited potential, pure energy, beingness. Connected to Supreme Beings such as the sun, moon, Shiva, Shakti, Kronos, Rhea, Zeus, Hera, Shekinah, the Cailleach, First Woman, Mother of Ten Thousand Things, Maât, Avalokita, Ishtar, Chaos, Gaia, Tiamat, Ymir. Associated with wind, air, serpents, black, white, iridescence, spiral, salamander, spider.

SPRUCE: Generosity, conviviality, pure intentions, expressing our gifts, peace, serenity.

STONE: Presence, patience, steadfastness, wisdom, eternity, spirit house for ancestors and Spirits of Place. In Norse mythology, some elves could turn into stone to hide themselves. Connected to Mithra, Mercury, Medusa, Rhea.

STRAWBERRY: Love, passion, sensuality, desire, courage. Connected to Venus.

STRENGTH: Oak, garlic, mint, parsley, pine, orange, red, black, moonstone, almond, aquamarine, carnelian, saffron, onyx, iron, dahlia, hawthorn, horse, lava, lovage, nettle, garnet, sequoia, ruby, diamond, vervain, walnut, zinnia, Medusa, Inanna, Anat, Taweret, Hercules, Kratos, Artemis, the Cailleach, Hel, Boudicca.

SUN: Represents center, sensuality, fertility, the sacred, creativity, healing, vitality, dynamism, majesty, wholeness, prophecy. Represented by lion, tiger, jaguar, horse, ram, eagle, hawk, marigold, calendula, St. John's wort, egg yolk, circles, fire, lightning, gold, yellow, orange, sunstone, amber, ash, chamomile, daffodil, daisy, frankincense, lovage, malachite, marigold, rosemary, rowan, bay laurel, bees, honey, chicken, dandelion, deer, saffron, sheep, goldenrod. Connected to Ra, Rudra, Prometheus, Icarus, Sol, Sunna, Horus, Lugh, Sun Woman, Amaterasu, Helios.

TANSY: Principled resistance, connection with the recently dead, can also be used as a declaration of war. Amplifier. Do not ingest if you are pregnant, breastfeeding, or allergic to the ragweed family of plants.

THISTLE: Discernment, boundaries, banishing, resilience, victory, longevity, self-care, self-protection, love that endures suffering. Sacred to Aphrodite and the Virgin Mary.

THYME: Clarity, purification, spiritual vision, prevention of nightmares, soothing of nerves, good luck in finance. Connected to faeries and honeybees. Sacred to Freya.

TIGER'S EYE: Prosperity, grounding, protection, increases flow.

TOMATO: Love, life, fertility, endurance, sensuality, aphrodisiac, vigor.

TOPAZ: Healing, insomnia support, friendship, fidelity, happiness.

TOURMALINE: Joy, happiness, heart healing, grounding, earth reconnection, empowerment, loving energy, relief from depression and heartbreak.

TURQUOISE: Speaking truth, intuition, balance, integrating lost parts of self, nobility, spiritual connection, protection from falls on horseback, divination, accuracy, healing, balance.

VANILLA: Love, lust, luxury, attractiveness, desire, passion, relaxation. An aphrodisiac connected to Venus.

VERVAIN: Strength, visionary trance work, manifestation, wealth, rekindles dying love, inspiration for poets and musicians. Connected with Midsummer. Sacred to druids, Isis, Cerridwen, Thor, and Persephone.

VINEGAR: Banishment, particularly in the case of hauntings in the home. Leave a small bowl out in the affected room and refresh every 3 days.

VIOLET: Inner sanctum, dreams, spiritual wisdom, mysticism, faith, humility, honesty, nobility, everlasting love. Sacred to Artemis and the Virgin Mary.

WALNUT: Wisdom, strategy, intellect, virility, courage, strength, endurance.

WATER ELEMENT: Associated with emotions and the etheric body, potions, baths, washes, and oils, the moon, cleansing, purification, new life, rebirth, the Otherworld, marine animals, seashells, chrysocolla, fluorite, heather, hibiscus, malachite, blues, silver, geranium, rose, rose hips, rose quartz, salt, silver, sodalite, tansy, turquoise. Connected to Aphrodite, Oshun, Yemaya, Ba'al, Poseidon, Lady of the Lake, Sedna, Sarasvati, Morgan le Fay.

WEALTH: Allspice, almond, basil, chamomile, cinnamon, cloves, coffee, grapes, hazelnut, olive and olive oil, walnut, lentils, wine, goldenrod, mandrake, nutmeg, oak, poppy, rice, smoky quartz, pyrite, gold, silver, green, seeds, blackberry, corn, wheat, rice, cattle.

WHEAT: Life, prosperity, abundance, rebirth, nurturance, perpetuity.

WHEEL: Totality, cycles, seasons, circle and center, rayed spokes measure time and space.

WHITE: Intuitive development, compassion, protection, peace, newness, beginnings, delicateness, incandescence, integration.

WILLOW: Eternity, steadfastness, flexibility. Linked to the moon, women's mysteries, used for water dowsing, making sacred sun wheels, crowns, and wands. Sacred to Inanna and Circe.

WIND: Spirit messenger, breath, dispersion, change of course, renewal, movement, velocity, grace, gentleness, weather divination, sends magical workings to distant targets. Exemplified by Zephyrus, Odin, Aura, and Maui.

WOODRUFF: Humility, endurance, upliftment, eases agitation, induces drowsiness. Connected to Venus, Mother Mary, Freya.

WORMWOOD: Banishing dark energies, prophecy, protector when journeying in new places, baneful herb in absinthe and flying ointments. If used in combination with mugwort, they help conjure the dead, especially witch ancestors. Connected to faeries. Sacred to Artemis.

YAM: Nurturance, sustenance, family, abundance, joy, harmony, strength, ancestral spirits of Africa.

YARROW: Protection, clear perception, divination, intuition, courage, healing, love, clarity, blessing of committed partnerships. Intensifies the work of other herbs. Amplifier. Sacred to Achilles, Chiron, Thor, and Freya. Do not ingest if you are pregnant, breastfeeding, or allergic to the ragweed family of plants.

YELLOW: Joy, happiness, learning, creativity, imagination, friendship, abundance, fertility.

YEW: Death and rebirth, resilience, supreme portal to the Underworld, building fruitfully upon past accomplishments (our own work or that of our ancestors). Sacred to Hekate.

ZINNIA: Friendship, affection, faith, steadfastness, capability, acclaim, remembrance of the dead, connected to hummingbirds.

References

Archive for Research in Archetypal Symbolism. *The Book of Symbols: Reflections on Archetypal Images* (Taschen, 2010).

Beith, Mary. *Healing Threads: Traditional Medicines of the Highlands and Islands* (Origin, 2018).

Bennett, Margaret. *Scottish Customs: From the Cradle to the Grave* (Birlinn Limited, 1992).

Blackwood, Danielle. *Twelve Faces of the Goddess: Transform Your Life with Astrology, Magic and the Sacred Feminine* (Llewellyn Publications, 2018).

Blake, Deborah. *Midsummer: Rituals, Recipes & Lore for Litha* (Llewellyn Publications, 2015).

Brannen, Cyndi. *Keeping Her Keys: An Introduction to Hekate's Modern Witchcraft* (Moon Books, 2019).

"Bride's Mound." Pilgrimage in Glastonbury. www.unitythroughdiversity.org/brides-mound.htm.

Bureau of Meteorology, Commonwealth of Australia. "Indigenous Weather Knowledge." www.bom.gov.au/iwk/climate_culture/Indig_seasons.shtml.

Campbell, J. G. and Black, R. *The Gaelic Otherworld: John Gregorson Campbell's Superstitions of the Highlands and Islands of Scotland and Witchcraft and Second Sight in the Highlands and Islands* (Edinburgh: Birlinn, 2005).

Carmichael, Alexander, *The Carmina Gadelica* (Floris Books, 1992).

Carney, Don. "The Meal and Ale: The 1940s Disco Night For Rural Aberdeenshire Folk." ScottishHeritage.co.uk. www.scottishheritage.co.uk/the-meal-and-ale-the-1940s-disco-night-for-rural-aberdeenshire-folk.

Catháin, Séamas Ó. "Hearth-Prayers and Other Traditions of Brigit: Celtic Goddess and Holy Woman." *The Journal of the Royal Society of Antiquaries of Ireland*, vol. 122, 1992, 12–34.

Collins, Derek. "The Myth and Ritual of Ezili Freda in Hurston's *Their Eyes Were Watching God*." *Western Folklore*, vol. 55, no. 2, 1996, 137–154.

Costello, Eugene. "Temporary Freedoms? Ethnoarchaeology of Female Herders at Seasonal Sites in Northern Europe." *World Archaeology*, 2018, vol. 50, no. 1, 165–184.

Dashù, Max. "Female Divinity in South America." SuppressedHistories.net www.suppressedhistories.net/goddess/fdivsa.html.

Federici, Silvia. *Caliban and the Witch: Women, the Body and Primitive Accumulation* (Autonomedia, 2004).

Foster, Steven, and Little, Meredith. *The Four Shields: The Initiatory Seasons of Human Nature* (Lost Borders Press, 1999).

Frankfurter, David. "'As I Twirl This Spindle, . . .': Ritualization and the Magical Efficacy of Household Tasks in Western Antiquity." *Preternature: Critical and Historical Studies on the Preternatural*, vol. 10, no. 1, 2021, 117–139.

Grant, I. F. *Highland Folkways* (Routledge & Kegan Paul, 1961).

Greer, John Michael. *Natural Magic: Potions and Powers from the Magical Garden* (Llewellyn Publications, 2000).

Jonsson, Ella. "The Eight Seasons: A Swedish Lapland Story." SwedishLapland.com. www.swedishlapland.com/stories/the-eight-seasons/.

Jordan, Michael. *Dictionary of Gods and Goddesses* (Facts on File, 2004).

Kapalo, James Alexander, Pócs, Eva, and Ryan, William Francis. *The Power of Words: Studies on Charms and Charming in Europe* (Central European University, 2012).

Keller, Mara Lynn. "The Ritual Path of Initiation into the Eleusinian Mysteries." *Rosicrucian Digest*, no. 2, 2009, 28–42 .

Krohn, Elise. "Stinging Nettle." WildFoodsAndMedicines.com. wildfoodsandmedicines.com/nettle-restorative-food-purifying-medicine-guardian.

Linebaugh, Peter. *The Incomplete, True, Authentic, and Wonderful History of May Day* (PM Press, 2016).

Loughlin, Annie. "Rowan and Red Threads." Tairis

.co.uk. www.tairis.co.uk/practices/rowan-and
-red-threads/.

Mackenzie, Donald. *Wonder Tales of Scottish Myth and Legend* (Blackie and Son, 1917).

MacLeod, Sharon Paice. "A Confluence of Wisdom: The Symbolism of Wells, Whirlpools, Waterfalls and Rivers in Early Celtic Sources." *Proceedings of the Harvard Celtic Colloquium*, 26/27, 2006, 337–355.

———. "Oenach Aimsire Na mBan: Early Irish Seasonal Celebrations, Gender Roles and Mythological Cycles." *Proceedings of the Harvard Celtic Colloquium*, vol. 23, 2003, 257–283.

McDonough, Christopher Michael. "Carna, Proca and the Strix on the Kalends of June." *Transactions of the American Philological Association (1974–2014)*, vol. 127, 1997, 315–344.

McNeill, F. Marian. *The Scots Kitchen: Its Lore and Recipes* (Blackie and Son, 1964).

———. *The Silver Bough, Volume 1: Scottish Folklore and Folk-Belief* (William Maclellan, 1959).

———. *The Silver Bough, Volume 2: A Calendar of Scottish National Festivals—Candlemas to Harvest Home* (William Maclellan, 1959).

———. *The Silver Bough, Volume 3: A Calendar of Scottish National Festivals—Hallowe'en to Yule* (William Maclellan, 1959).

———. *The Silver Bough, Volume 4: The Local Festivals of Scotland* (William Maclellan, 1959).

Mirga-Kruszelnicka, Anna, and Dunajeva, Jekatyerina. *Re-thinking Roma Resistance throughout History: Recounting Stories of Strength and Bravery* (The European Roma Institute for Arts and Culture, 2020).

Müller-Ebeling, Claudia, Rätsch, Christian, Storl, Wolf-Dieter. *Witchcraft Medicine: Healing Arts, Shamanic Practices, and Forbidden Plants* (Inner Traditions, 2003).

Nagy, Gregory. "Homeric Hymn to Demeter." chs.harvard.edu. chs.harvard.edu/primary-source/homeric-hymn-to-demeter-sb.

Newton, Michael. *A Handbook of the Scottish Gaelic World* (Four Courts Press, 2000).

Owens-Celli, Morgyn Geoffrey. *The Book of Wheat Weaving and Straw Craft* (Sterling, 1998).

Paradise Fibres. "Basket Weaving Resources, Techniques, and More". Paradis eFibres.com. www.paradisefibers.com/pages/basket-weaving-resources.

Patterson, Nerys Thomas. *Cattle Lords and Clansmen: The Social Structure of Early Ireland* (University of Notre Dame Press, 1994).

———. "Woman as Vassal: Gender Symmetry in Medieval Wales." *Proceedings of the Harvard Celtic Colloquium*, vol. 8, 1988, 31–45.

Pearson, Nicholas. *Crystal Basics: The Energetic, Healing & Spiritual Power of 200 Gemstones* (Destiny Books, 2020).

Ross, Anne. *The Pagan Celts* (John Jones Publishing Ltd, 1970).

Ryan, W. F. *The Bathhouse at Midnight: An Historical Survey of Magic and Divination in Russia* (Penn State University Press, 1999).

Spretnak, Charlene. *Lost Goddesses of Early Greece: A Collection of Pre-Hellenic Myths* (Beacon Press, 1992).

Snodgrass, Mary Ellen. *Encyclopedia of Kitchen History* (Routledge, 2004).

Strange, Thomasin. "An Exploration of Jar, Bottle, and Container Spells." Crowsbone.com, www.crowsbone.com/blog-index/the-long-history-of-jar-bottle-amp-container-spells.

Tippett, Krista. *Becoming Wise: An Inquiry into the Mystery and Art of Living* (Penguin Books, 2017).

Towrie, Sigurd. "Orcadian Customs and Traditions." OrkneyJar.com. www.orkneyjar.com/tradition/index.html.

Washinsky, John. "Pysanky Preparation." AllThings Ukrainian.com. www.allthingsukrainian.com/Class/Beginner/Pysanky_Preparation.htm.

"Whiskey: Is It Good For You?" WebMD.com. www.webmd.com/diet/whiskey-good-for-you#2.

Whitman-Salkin, Sarah. "Cranberries, a Thanksgiving Staple, Were a Native American Superfood." NationalGeographic.com. www.nationalgeographic.com/science/article/131127-cranberries-thanksgiving-native-americans-indians-food-history.

Winick, Stephen. "Ostara and the Hare: Not Ancient, but Not as Modern as Some Skeptics Might Think." Library of Congress. blogs.loc.gov/folklife/2016/04/ostara-and-the-hare.

Acknowledgments

I acknowledge with deep gratitude and respect that this book was written on the lands of the Songhees and Esquimalt First Nations. I'd like to thank my aunties, Deb Croteau and Karen Mannix, who help me remember the resilience and honorable character of my lineage. I'm grateful to Trish Pontious for early and memorable experiences of cooking as creativity, discovery, self-confidence, and secure attachment. I still have the blue Dutch oven you gave me 30 years ago. I want to thank Barb Housser for teaching me the two most important skills in the kitchen: anticipate and multitask. My gratitude to both you and Bruce for modeling the elegance and dignity of hospitality. My deep admiration and thanks to Tamara Bailey for showing me that meal planning is love, and dining together is spiritual communion. Special thanks to Farm + Field for impeccable service and products, and to Bill Milliken for foraging support.

I'm so lucky to have landed at Countryman Press with such an impressive team, including my wonderful editor, Isabel McCarthy. All thanks to my agent, Sharon Bowers. Thank you for seeing something promising in me and taking a chance.

To all the Numini, students, and workshop guests who've cheerleaded me and helped me hone my craft—you initiated me. Thank you. To my recipe testers, especially Christi and Kate Jarland: Your input was so, so valuable and appreciated. To Lauren Bacon for early support and to Sophie Macklin for a patient first read: Thank you for holding me with grace and care. Deep thanks to friends who always have my back and champion my work: Ande Down, Thérèse Cator, D Smith, Breeda McKibbin, Jennie Biltek, Aurelie Richards, and my Quest fam.

Eternal thanks and undying love to my dear collaborator and creative soulmate, Stephanie Rae Hull, for sharing your impressive talent so generously to bring my vision to life. This would not have been half as good without you: from the first shoot to the finished result, your style, meticulousness, professionalism, care, and talent carried us through. I can't thank you enough, my friend.

To my Committee of Care, Patricia Petersen, Holly Truhlar, and Jane Rioseco: How can I even begin to express my love and gratitude? You mopped me off the floor so many times. You are the best quality friends imaginable. I'm so lucky to have you as my people. Thank you for being my chosen family.

To my radiantly beautiful cosmic miracle: I love you, kiddo. I hope you crack the covers of this book someday and actually find it useful. It's what I want you to know when one day I'm not here to tell you. I hope you feel my heart reaching for you from the pages.

Finally, this book, this whole life path, is made possible by my helpmate, my sous chef, my husband rock, Ruben. You are the most loving, devoted person I've ever met. It's a noble struggle to match your ability to love so completely; the way you love me teaches me every day what sacred devotion really means. I love you like the moon loves the night, utterly at home. Thank you for solving so many problems for me and for taking on my dreams as your own. Being your partner is such a privilege and honor. Our marriage is good food.

Index